Mergers, Acquisitions, and Other R(
By Donald DePamphilis

CW00402762

This highly-recommended text
to improve student exposure to the industry. It presents topics
according to the context in which they occur during the M&A
process, enhancing the teaching and learning experiences without
deemphasizing the importance of mathematics and theory.

To learn more, visit www.elsevierdirect.com/9780123748782 where
you'll find access to case studies, ordering information, and more.

To request an instructor review copy please visit
http://textbooks.elsevier.com.

MERGERS AND ACQUISITIONS BASICS

Negotiation and Deal Structuring

Donald DePamphilis

Amsterdam • Boston • Heidelberg • London
New York • Oxford • Paris • San Diego
San Francisco • Singapore • Sydney • Tokyo

Academic Press is an imprint of Elsevier

Academic Press is an imprint of Elsevier
30 Corporate Drive, Suite 400, Burlington, MA 01803, USA
Elsevier, The Boulevard, Langford Lane, Kidlington, Oxford, OX5 1GB, UK

Notices
Knowledge and best practice in this field are constantly changing. As new research and experience
broaden our understanding, changes in research methods, professional practices, or medical treatment
may become necessary.

Practitioners and researchers must always rely on their own experience and knowledge in
evaluating and using any information, methods, compounds, or experiments described herein.
In using such information or methods they should be mindful of their own safety and the safety of
others, including parties for whom they have a professional responsibility.

To the fullest extent of the law, neither the Publisher nor the authors, contributors, or editors, assume
any liability for any injury and/or damage to persons or property as a matter of products liability,
negligence or otherwise, or from any use or operation of any methods, products, instructions, or ideas
contained in the material herein.

Library of Congress Cataloging-in-Publication Data
DePamphilis, Donald M.
   Mergers and acquisitions basics: negotiation and deal structuring/Donald DePamphilis.
      p. cm.
   Includes bibliographical references and index.
   ISBN 978-0-12-374949-9
   1. Negotiation. 2. Deals. 3. Consolidation and merger of corporations—United States—
   Management. 4. Negotiation in business—United States. 5. Organizational change—United
   States—Management. 6. Corporate reorganizations—United States—Management.   I. Title.
   HG4028.M4D474 2011
   658.1'620973—dc22   2010023984

British Library Cataloguing-in-Publication Data
A catalogue record for this book is available from the British Library.

For information on all Academic Press publications
visit our website at www.elsevierdirect.com

Printed in The United States of America

10 11 12 13   9 8 7 6 5 4 3 2 1

TABLE OF CONTENTS

VIEWING NEGOTIATIONS AS A TEAM EFFORT

Negotiating, in essence, is a process in which two or more parties representing different interests attempt to achieve consensus on a particular issue. Although much has been written about alternative negotiating strategies, the process of negotiating mergers and acquisitions (M&A) and structuring M&A deals tends to be described from a somewhat narrow point of view—often that of the investment banker, attorney, accountant, or business manager.

Investment bankers provide strategic and tactical advice to clients; screen potential buyers and sellers; often make the initial contact; arrange financing; and provide negotiation support, valuation, and deal-structuring guidance. Typically, attorneys are intimately involved in structuring the deal, performing due diligence, evaluating risk, negotiating many of the terms and conditions, drafting important documents, and coordinating the timing and sequence of events to complete the transaction. Accountants provide input into M&A negotiating and deal structuring on tax and financial structures and on performing financial due diligence; they also prepare financial statements. The key role of business managers in the negotiation process is to provide the strategic and tactical justification for the proposed business combination, offering their "real-world" operating experience to help everyone understand the practical implications of what is being proposed. Their input is crucial because they are ultimately responsible for executing the acquirer's business strategy and integrating the target and acquiring businesses to achieve business plan objectives.

The problem with describing the M&A negotiation process by conveying only the specific points of view of these participants is, obviously, that it does not convey the full picture of what is involved.

The Book's Objective

The overarching objective of this book is to help the reader see M&A negotiations and deal structuring in a way that integrates the perspective of these players. By presenting a "macro" approach, the book demonstrates that the process is a team effort in which the skills of the various participants are combined to achieve consensus among the parties to the negotiation.

Negotiation is a series of highly interactive steps (some of which run in parallel) that involve decisions about what is being acquired (stock or assets), the appropriate form of payment (cash, stock, or some combination), and the appropriate choice of legal structures best suited for acquiring the business and operating the acquired business following closing. The process also entails developing appropriate tax and accounting strategies. Negotiating is a dynamic process; it evolves as new information becomes available. Changes made in one area of a negotiation often will have significant implications for other parts of the negotiation. The failure to understand these feedback effects inevitably leads to inadequate risk assessment and often makes it impossible to complete the transaction.

The Book's Unique Features

This book achieves a middle ground between those that provide intensive coverage of every aspect of negotiation and deal structuring—often involving abstruse discussions of the legal and tax implications of the deal—and those that "dumb down" the subject matter. These latter texts often provide, at best, a superficial overview of the subject and, at worst, an inaccurate or misleading explanation of a multifaceted topic. Although the book does not require that the reader have significant knowledge of finance, economics, business law, and accounting, a passing acquaintance with these disciplines is helpful.

While reader-friendly, the text also draws on academic studies to substantiate key observations and conclusions that are empirically based. Details of these studies are often found in chapter footnotes.

Each chapter concludes with a section called "A Case in Point" that illustrates the chapter material with a real-world example. These sections include thought-provoking questions that encourage you, the reader, to apply the concepts explored in the chapter.

Who Should Read This Book

This book is intended for anyone interested in understanding how all aspects of M&A negotiations and deal structuring fit together. Buyers and sellers of businesses, as well as business brokers, finders, and investment bankers, should have an interest in this text. Others include individuals directly involved in negotiating transactions, such as accountants, tax experts, and attorneys. CEOs, board members, senior managers, financial analysts, chief financial officers, auditors, lenders, and investors will all benefit from this overview of the process.

In addition, this book may be used as a companion or supplemental text for undergraduate and graduate students in courses on mergers and acquisitions, corporate restructuring, business strategy, management, governance, and entrepreneurship. Supplemented with newspaper and magazine articles, the book could serve as a primary text. Other courses in which this book could be useful include finance, tax, management, negotiation, and governance, and it should be particularly applicable in Executive MBA courses, especially those that are highly focused and less than a semester in duration.

For a more rigorous and detailed discussion on mergers and acquisitions and other forms of corporate restructuring, the reader may wish to see the author's textbook on the subject, *Mergers, Acquisitions, and Other Restructuring Activities*. The 5th edition (2010) is published by Academic Press. The reader also may be interested in the author's *Mergers and Acquisitions Basics: All You Need to Know*, also published by Academic Press in 2010.

ACKNOWLEDGMENTS

I would like to express my sincere appreciation for the many resources of Academic Press/Butterworth-Heinemann/Elsevier in general and for the ongoing support provided by Karen Maloney, Managing Editor, and J. Scott Bentley, Executive Editor, as well as Scott M. Cooper, who helped streamline this manuscript for its primary audience. Finally, I would like to thank Alan Cherry, Ross Bengel, Patricia Douglas, Jim Healy, Charles Higgins, Michael Lovelady, John Mellen, Jon Saxon, David Offenberg, Chris Manning, and Maria Quijada, as well as a number of anonymous reviewers, for their many constructive comments.

CHAPTER 1

Introduction to Negotiating Mergers and Acquisitions

Pfizer, the pharmaceutical industry behemoth, was growing increasingly uneasy in early 2008. It had few blockbuster drugs in the pipeline, and several of its major revenue-generating drugs were about to lose patent protection. Pfizer had made several major acquisitions earlier in the decade and now looked to acquire another drug company to offset potential revenue losses. CEO Jeffrey Kindler placed a call to Wyeth Pharmaceutical's chief executive that spring.

Talks heated up in the summer months but appeared to collapse when the global banking system went into a meltdown that September. Each in a series of what appeared to be restarts over the next several months faltered on Wyeth's concerns that Pfizer could not finance the deal. Only in late January 2009, when a consortium of banks signed a loan commitment, was an agreement reached.

Pfizer, like many firms that have engaged in mergers and acquisitions (M&As) over the years, followed a pattern: management determined that an acquisition was the best way to implement the firm's business strategy; a target was selected that fit with the strategy; and a preliminary financial analysis yielded satisfactory results. It was then time to approach the target and initiate negotiations, a process that generally begins with the buyer establishing what it believes to be a reasonable initial offer price range based on preliminary information. Although a potential buyer may wish to avoid being too specific at first contact, it may be unavoidable. The seller may demand some indication of price before proceeding to release any additional information to the buyer. A wise buyer intent upon proceeding will provide a tentative purchase price or indication of value for the target firm subject to performing adequate due diligence.

Here, negotiation is considered a process that begins when the prospective buyer makes its initial contact with the potential target firm, and the target expresses interest in exploring the possibility of being acquired. You will learn about common negotiating strategies and the complexities of deal structuring. Also here, negotiation in the M&A context is viewed

Mergers and Acquisitions Basics
ISBN: 978-0-12-374949-9, DOI: 10.1016/B978-0-12-374949-9.00001-4

from a comprehensive, or macro, perspective, not the narrow viewpoint of negotiation often held by one or another of the key participants whose close collaboration is required for success, whether they are lawyers, accountants, investment bankers, or business managers.

Words in **bold italics** are the ones most important for you to understand fully; they are all included in a glossary at the end of the book.

Throughout this book, a firm that attempts to acquire or merge with another company is called an ***acquiring company***, ***acquirer***, or ***bidder***. The ***target company*** or ***target*** is the firm being solicited by the acquiring company. ***Takeovers*** or ***buyouts*** are generic terms for a change in the controlling ownership interest of a corporation.[1]

KEY PARTICIPANTS IN NEGOTIATING MERGERS AND ACQUISITIONS

Many individuals contribute to a successfully completed negotiation. Four groups play pivotal roles: senior or operating management, investment bankers, lawyers, and accountants.

Senior/Operating Management

Ultimately, senior management is responsible for the business strategy adopted by the firm and the firm's decision to use an acquisition to implement this strategy in order to achieve the firm's vision and objectives rather than "going it alone" or partnering with another firm. When the decision to acquire is made, senior management must assemble a team to find suitable target firms, approach the targets, and negotiate and complete an acquisition.

Senior management is responsible for communicating its preferences about how the acquisition process should be managed, a timetable for completing the acquisition, and who will be the "deal owner"—the individual responsible for making it all happen. Management preferences provide guidance by stipulating selection criteria for potential acquisition targets, and may include the industry or market segment to be targeted; the approximate size of the firm or maximum purchase price; financial characteristics of a desirable target including profitability and growth rate; and nonfinancial attributes such as intellectual property, manufacturing, or distribution capabilities. Management may also express a willingness to engage in a hostile takeover. Preferences could also indicate management's choice of the form

---

[1] For a more detailed discussion of this material, see DePamphilis (2009).

of payment (stock, cash, or debt), willingness to accept temporary earnings per share dilution, preference for a stock or asset purchase, desire for partial or full ownership, and limitations on contacting competitors.

The "deal owner"—frequently a high-performing manager—leads the acquisition effort and the negotiation, and should be appointed by senior management very early in the process. It could be a full- or part-time position for someone in the firm's business development unit or an individual expected to manage the operation once acquired. Some deal owners are members of the firm's business development team with substantial deal-making experience. Depending on circumstances, it may make sense to appoint two deal owners: the individual who will be responsible for eventual operation and integration of the target and an experienced dealmaker in a supporting role.

It is the deal owner's responsibility to oversee the negotiation process and ensure that the final agreement of purchase and sale satisfies the acquiring firm's key objectives. In an asset purchase, the contract should entitle the acquirer to rights to specific products; patents; copyrights or brand names; and all needed proprietary technologies, processes, and skills. The deal owner (in consultation with senior management) will have to choose which liabilities to assume. With a purchase of target stock all known and unknown assets and liabilities transfer to the buyer, and the deal owner ultimately is responsible for ensuring that a thorough due diligence has taken place so that the extent of the risk assumed by the buyer is well understood.

Investment Bankers

Amid the turmoil of the 2008 credit crisis, the traditional model of the mega-independent *investment bank* as a highly leveraged, largely unregulated, innovative securities underwriter and M&A advisor floundered. Lehman Brothers was liquidated, and Bear Stearns and Merrill Lynch were acquired by commercial banks JPMorgan Chase and Bank of America, respectively. In an effort to attract retail deposits and to borrow from the U.S. Federal Reserve System (the "Fed"), Goldman Sachs and Morgan Stanley converted to commercial bank holding companies subject to Fed regulation.

Although the era of the thriving independent investment banking behemoth may be over, the financial markets will continue to require investment banking services. Traditional investment banking activities will continue to be in demand. They include providing strategic and tactical advice and acquisition opportunities; screening potential buyers and sellers; making initial contact with a seller or buyer; and providing negotiation support, valuation, and deal-structuring guidance. Along with these traditional investment banking functions, the large "universal banks" (e.g., Bank of America/Merrill Lynch) will maintain substantial broker-dealer operations, serving wholesale and retail clients in brokerage and advisory capacities to assist with the complexity and often huge financing requirements of the mega-transactions. Investment banks also often provide large databases of recent transactions, which are critical in valuing potential target companies.

Lawyers

Lawyers play a pervasive role in most M&A transactions. They are intimately involved in structuring the deal, evaluating risk, negotiating many of the tax and financial terms and conditions (based on input received from accountants; see following section), arranging financing, and coordinating the timing and sequence of events to complete the transaction. Specific tasks include drafting and reviewing the agreement of purchase and sale and other transaction-related documentation, providing opinion of counsel letters to the lender, and defining due diligence activities.

The legal framework surrounding a typical large transaction has become so complex that no one individual can have sufficient expertise to address all the issues. For these complicated transactions, legal teams can consist of more than a dozen attorneys, each bringing specialized expertise in a given aspect of the law such as M&As, corporate, tax, employee benefits, real estate, antitrust, securities, environmental, and intellectual property. In a hostile transaction, the team may grow to include litigation experts. In relatively small private transactions, lawyers play an active role in preacquisition planning, including estate planning for individuals or family-owned firms, tax planning, and working with management and other company advisors to help better position a client for a sale.

Accountants

Accountants advise on the most appropriate tax and financial structures and on performing financial due diligence. The accountant's input will affect not only how the transaction is structured, but ultimately the after-tax amount each party will pay or receive in the deal.

A transaction can be structured in many ways, each structure having different tax implications for the parties involved. Because there is often a conflict in the tax advantages associated with the sales agreement from the buyer's and seller's perspective, the accountant must understand both points of view and find a mechanism whereby both parties benefit. Income tax, capital gains, sales tax, and sometimes gift and estate taxes are all at play in negotiating a merger or acquisition.

Accountants also prepare financial statements and perform audits. Many agreements require that the books and records of the acquired entity be prepared in accordance with Generally Accepted Accounting Principles (GAAP), so the accountant must be intimately familiar with those principles to assure that they have been applied appropriately. The accountant must recognize where GAAP has not been followed. In performing due diligence, accountants also perform the role of auditors by reviewing the target's financial statements and operations through a series of onsite visits and interviews with senior and middle-level managers.

The roles of the lawyer and accountant may blur depending on the size and complexity of the transaction. Sophisticated law firms with experience in mergers and acquisitions usually have the capacity to assist with the tax analysis. Furthermore, lawyers are often required to review financial statements for compliance with prevailing securities laws. It is helpful, especially when there can be an overlap of responsibilities, to define clearly which professional will be responsible for which tasks.

PRENEGOTIATION: PROFILING THE TARGET MARKET AND FIRM

Profiling requires collecting information on the target market and firm, which is then used to develop an initial valuation of the firm as well as a baseline notion of the initial terms and conditions (e.g., an all-cash or all-stock offer) that might make an acquisition proposal attractive to a target firm.

Profiling the Market/Industry

Selecting a target firm begins with identifying a target market or industry (i.e., a collection of markets) in terms of those factors that determine how firms compete and make money. Michael Porter's "Five Forces" framework—which characterizes a firm's market or industry environment in terms of such competitive dynamics as the firm's customers, suppliers, current competitors, potential competitors, and product or service substitutes—is a convenient way to group the information required to evaluate a firm's attractiveness.[2] Exhibit 1-1 illustrates a modified Porter framework.[3]

---

[2] Porter (1985).
[3] For a more detailed discussion of market and firm profiling, see DePamphilis (2009), 5th edition, Chapter 4.

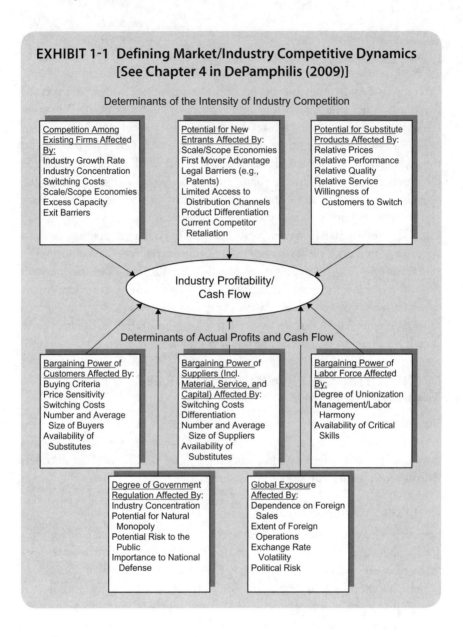

EXHIBIT 1-1 Defining Market/Industry Competitive Dynamics [See Chapter 4 in DePamphilis (2009)]

Determinants of the Intensity of Industry Competition

Competition Among Existing Firms Affected By:
Industry Growth Rate
Industry Concentration
Switching Costs
Scale/Scope Economies
Excess Capacity
Exit Barriers

Potential for New Entrants Affected By:
Scale/Scope Economies
First Mover Advantage
Legal Barriers (e.g., Patents)
Limited Access to Distribution Channels
Product Differentiation
Current Competitor Retaliation

Potential for Substitute Products Affected By:
Relative Prices
Relative Performance
Relative Quality
Relative Service
Willingness of Customers to Switch

Industry Profitability/ Cash Flow

Determinants of Actual Profits and Cash Flow

Bargaining Power of Customers Affected By:
Buying Criteria
Price Sensitivity
Switching Costs
Number and Average Size of Buyers
Availability of Substitutes

Bargaining Power of Suppliers (Incl. Material, Service, and Capital) Affected By:
Switching Costs
Differentiation
Number and Average Size of Suppliers
Availability of Substitutes

Bargaining Power of Labor Force Affected By:
Degree of Unionization
Management/Labor Harmony
Availability of Critical Skills

Degree of Government Regulation Affected By:
Industry Concentration
Potential for Natural Monopoly
Potential Risk to the Public
Importance to National Defense

Global Exposure Affected By:
Dependence on Foreign Sales
Extent of Foreign Operations
Exchange Rate Volatility
Political Risk

The three potential determinants of the intensity of competition in an industry include competition among existing firms, the threat of entry of new firms, and the threat of substitute products or services. Although the degree of competition determines whether there is potential to earn abnormal profits (i.e., those in excess of what would be expected for the degree of assumed risk), the actual profits or cash flow are influenced by the relative bargaining power of the industry's customers and suppliers.[4] A wide variety of data is required to analyze industry competitive dynamics: types of products and services; market share in terms of dollars and units; pricing; selling and distribution channels and associated costs; type, location, and age of production facilities; product quality; customer service; compensation by major labor category; research and development (R&D) expenditures; supplier performance metrics; and financial performance in terms of growth and profitability. These data must be collected on all significant competitors in the firm's chosen markets.

This framework may be modified to include other factors that determine actual industry profitability and cash flow, such as the severity of government regulation or the impact of global influences such as fluctuating exchange rates. Labor costs may also be included. Although they represent a relatively small percentage of total expenses in many areas of manufacturing, they frequently constitute the largest expense in the nonmanufacturing sector. With the manufacturing sector in most industrialized nations continuing its long-term decline as a percentage of the total economy, the analysis should also include factors affecting the bargaining power of labor.

Profiling the Firm

Within the targeted market, a potential target firm should be identified based on selection criteria such as size, market share, reputation, growth, and so on. The potential buyer should then attempt to profile that firm. For publicly traded firms, obtaining the necessary information is relatively easy. Publicly traded firms must submit audited financial statements to the Securities and Exchange Commission (SEC), often are monitored by securities analysts, may be topics of discussion in the popular press, and have executives who talk publicly about the firm. Obtaining information on privately owned firms is much more challenging, requiring excellent detective work. Where possible, it may involve talking to the firm's customers, suppliers, and current or former employees and reviewing trade press articles and speeches by the firm's management.

Often, potential acquirers pay business brokers or investment bankers to value private firms based on what was paid in recent transactions

---

[4] Walmart provides an extreme example of relative bargaining power. Given the ubiquity of the chain's stores, most suppliers of retail products would like to have their products displayed on Walmart's store shelves nationwide. The ability of Walmart to attract millions of customers each week gives the firm a huge advantage in negotiating the prices it pays its suppliers.

involving similar businesses. Although such estimates are useful, the information for many businesses simply is not available. Consequently, the potential buyer must piece together available data to reconstruct the firm's financial statements to the degree possible. The financial statements of similar publicly traded firms may be a useful starting point; while these "proxy" public firms are often much larger than the target private firm, the relationships among various financial variables may be similar. For example, the analyst can compute the ratio to sales of cost of sales; sales, general, and administrative expenses; assets; capital spending; accounts receivable; inventory; and so on. Such ratios may be applied to estimates of revenue for the target firm to approximate its financial statements. However, the analyst should adjust for possible differences in operating efficiency, recognizing that the larger proxy firm may be more efficient than the smaller firm.[5] Revenue or some measure of size such as unit sales of the target firm often can be obtained from newspaper accounts, speeches, or interviews. The target's estimated revenue can be multiplied by the financial ratios for the proxy firm.[6]

There are many possible sources of information. They include computerized databases and directory services such as Standard & Poor's *Corporate Register,* the *Thomas Register*, and Dun & Bradstreet's *Million Dollar Directory*, which can be used to identify qualified candidates. Potential acquirers may also query their law, banking, and accounting firms to identify candidates. Investment banks, brokers, and private equity firms can be fertile sources of candidates, although they are likely to require an advisory or finder's fee. The Internet makes research much easier than in the past, putting considerable information at the analyst's fingertips. Services such as Google Finance, Yahoo! Finance, Hoover's, or EDGAR Online enable researchers to gather data quickly about competitors and customers, and provide easy access to a variety of public documents filed with the SEC. Exhibit 1-2 provides a listing of commonly used sources of information that can be highly useful in conducting a search for prospective acquisition candidates as well as for performing due diligence.

---

[5] Consequently, the proxy firm's cost of sales as a percent of sales ratio should be increased before it is multiplied by the smaller target firm's revenue to reflect its potentially lower operating efficiency.

[6] Therefore, if the proxy firm's cost of sales and assets as a percent of sales are 60 percent and 40 percent, respectively, multiplying these ratios by the target's estimated annual sales of $40 million results in estimates of the target firm's cost of sales and assets of $24 million and $16 million, respectively.

EXHIBIT 1-2 Information Sources on Individual Companies
SEC Filings (Public Companies Only)

10-K: Provides detailed information on a company's annual operations, business conditions, competitors, market conditions, legal proceedings, risk factors in holding the stock, and other related information.

10-Q: Updates investors about the company's operations each quarter.

S-1: Filed when a company wants to register new stock. Can contain information about the company's operating history and business risks.

S-2: Filed when a company is completing a material transaction such as a merger or acquisition. Provides substantial detail underlying the terms and conditions of the transaction, the events surrounding the transaction, and justification for the merger or acquisition.

8-K: Filed when a company faces a "material event" such as a merger.

Schedule 14A: A proxy statement. Gives details about the annual meeting and biographies of company officials and directors including stock ownership and pay.

Websites
www.capitaliq.com
www.factset.com
www.sec.gov
www.edgar-online.com
www.freeedgar.com
www.quicken.com
www.hooversonline.com
www.aol.com
finance.yahoo.com
www.bizbuysell.com
www.dialog.com
www.lexisnexis.com
www.mergernetwork.com
www.mergers.net
www.washingtonresearchers.com
www.twst.com
www.worldm-anetwork.com
www.onesource.com
google.com/finance

Organizations
Value Line Investment Survey: Information on public companies
Directory of Corporate Affiliations: Corporate affiliations

(*Continued*)

EXHIBIT 1-2 (Continued)

Lexis/Nexis: Database of general business and legal information

Thomas Register: Organizes firms by products and services

Frost & Sullivan: Industry research

Findex.com: Financial information

Competitive Intelligence Professionals: Information about industries

Dialog Corporation: Industry databases

Ward's Business Directory of U.S. Private and Public Companies

Predicasts: Provides databases through libraries

Business Periodicals Index: Business and technical article index

Dun & Bradstreet Directories: Information about private and public companies

Dun & Bradstreet *Million Dollar Directory*: Specific data on large U.S. corporations

Experian: Information about private and public companies

Nelson's Directory of Investment Research: Wall Street research reports

Standard & Poor's Publications: Industry surveys and corporate records

Harris Infosource: Information about manufacturing companies

Hoover's *Handbook of Private Companies*: Information on large private firms

Washington Researchers: Information on public and private firms, markets, and industries

The *Wall Street Journal* Transcripts: Wall Street research reports

Directory of Corporate Affiliations (Published by Lexis-Nexis Group)

Estimating the Price Range of an Initial Offer

Prior to making contact with the target firm, you should have an idea of what that the firm may be worth. Again, the seller may refuse to provide the necessary proprietary information without some indication of value from the buyer. How can a range of values be determined?

Transactions in Which Synergy Is Believed to Exist

For transactions in which there is potential synergy between the acquirer and target firms, the initial offer price for the target firm lies between the minimum and maximum offer prices. In a purchase of stock transaction, the minimum offer price may be defined as the target's standalone or present value (PV_T) or its current market value (MV_T) (i.e., the target's current stock price times its shares outstanding). Present value is the current value of a firm based on its expected future cash flows, the risk associated with those cash flows, and financial rates of return on alternative investments exhibiting similar risk. The standalone value is the price a business would command if

---

**EXHIBIT 1-3 Determining the Initial Offer Price (PV_{IOP})—
                 Purchase of Stock**

a. $PV_{MIN} = PV_T$ or MV_T, whichever is greater. MV_T is the target firm's current share price times the number of shares outstanding.

b. $PV_{MAX} = PV_{MIN} + PV_{NS}$, where $PV_{NS} = $ PV (sources of value) – PV (destroyers of value).

c. $PV_{IOP} = PV_{MIN} + \alpha\,PV_{NS}$, where $0 \le \alpha \le 1$.

d. Offer price range for the target firm $= (PV_T$ or $MV_T) < PV_{IOP} < (PV_T$ or $MV_T) + PV_{NS}$.

---

its projected cash flows reflected fully all revenues and costs at market values. The maximum price is the sum of the minimum price plus the present value of net synergy (PV_{NS}). PV_{NS} is the difference between the present value of those factors adding to cash flow (e.g., cost savings) less those factors reducing cash flows (e.g., the assumption of certain target liabilities) as a result of combining the acquirer and target firms. The initial offer price (PV_{IOP}) is the sum of both the minimum purchase price and some percentage between 0 and 1 of the PV of net synergy (see Exhibit 1-3).

The standalone value is applicable for privately held firms. In a market in which both the buyer and seller have access to the same information, the standalone value would be the price the rational seller expects to receive. In practice, markets for small, privately owned businesses are often inefficient; that is, either the buyer or seller does not have access to all relevant information about the economic value of the target firm, perhaps due to the absence of recent comparable transactions. If the seller is uninformed, you, as the buyer, may be able to purchase the target firm at a discount from what you believe to be the actual economic or fair market value.

In an asset purchase, the target's equity would have to be adjusted to reflect the fair market value of the target assets and liabilities that are to be excluded from the transaction. The minimum price would be the liquidation value of the target firm's assets less the book value of the liabilities assumed by the buyer. The maximum price would be the minimum price plus the present value of net synergy. The initial offer price would lie somewhere between the minimum and maximum prices.

Determining Distribution of Synergy between Acquirer and Target

In determining the initial offer price, the acquiring company must decide how much of the anticipated synergy it is willing to share with the target firm's shareholders. This is often determined by the portion of anticipated synergy contributed by the target firm. For example, if the results of due diligence suggest that the target would contribute 30 percent of the synergy resulting from combining the acquirer and target firms, the acquirer may choose to share up to 30 percent of the estimated net synergy with the target firm's shareholders.

There are at least three reasons behind the logic that the offer price should fall between the minimum and maximum prices. One, it is unlikely that the target company can be purchased at the minimum price because the acquiring company typically must pay a premium to the current market value to induce target shareholders to transfer control to another firm. In an asset purchase, the rational seller would not sell at a price below the liquidation value of the net assets being acquired. Two, at the maximum end of the range, the acquiring company would be ceding to the target company's shareholders all of the net synergy value created by the combination of the two companies. Three, it is prudent to pay significantly less than the maximum price because the amount of synergy actually realized often tends to be less than the anticipated amount.

Transactions Involving a Control Premium

For many transactions, the purchase price premium—the amount a buyer pays the seller in excess of the seller's current share price—includes both a premium for anticipated synergy and a premium for control. The value of control is distinctly different from the value of synergy. The value of synergy represents revenue increases and cost savings that result from combining two firms, usually in the same line of business. In contrast, the value of control provides the right to direct the activities of the target firm on an ongoing basis.

Control can include the ability to select management, determine compensation, set policy and change the course of the business, acquire and liquidate assets, award contracts, make acquisitions, sell or recapitalize the company, and register the company's stock for a public offering. Control also involves the ability to declare and pay dividends, change the articles of incorporation or bylaws, or block any of the aforementioned actions. Owners of controlling blocks of voting stock may use this influence to extract special privileges or benefits not available to other shareholders, such as directing the firm to sell to companies owned by the controlling shareholder at a discount to the market price and to buy from suppliers owned by the controlling shareholder at premium prices. Furthermore, controlling shareholders may agree to pay unusually high salaries to selected senior managers who may be family members. For these reasons, the more control a block investor has, the less influence a minority investor will have and the less valuable its stock will be. Therefore, a **control premium** is the amount an investor is willing to pay to direct the activities of the firm.

Purchase price premiums may reflect only control premiums when a buyer acquires a target firm and manages it as a largely independent operating subsidiary. The **pure control premium** is the value the acquirer believes can be created by replacing incompetent management, changing the strategic direction of the firm, gaining a foothold in a market not currently served, or achieving unrelated diversification.[7] Other examples of pure control premiums include premiums paid for firms going private through a leveraged buyout (LBO) in which the target firm generally is merged into a shell corporation without any synergy being created and managed for cash after having been recapitalized—that is, after a change in the composition of the target's pre-LBO capital (i.e., equity and debt) structure to one comprising substantially more debt. Although the firm's management team may remain intact, the board of directors consists usually of representatives of the financial sponsor (i.e., equity or block investor) and selected LBO managers.[8]

PRENEGOTIATION: FIRST CONTACT

Assuming the target firm is willing to consider the buyer's preliminary proposal for acquisition, the two parties usually proceed to negotiate certain preliminary legal documents. They include a confidentiality agreement

---

[7] As a practical matter, business appraisers hired by buyers and sellers to estimate the values of businesses frequently rely on the *Control Premium Study*, published annually by Mergerstat. Another source is Duff & Phelps. Mergerstat estimates median control premiums and control premiums by industry by comparing the per share total consideration paid to the target to the "unaffected" price. The "unaffected" price is determined by examining the target price and volume statistics for the year preceding the takeover announcement. The use of these data is problematic because the control premium estimates provided by Mergerstat include the estimated value of synergy as well as the amount being paid to replace current management or change the firm's strategy.

[8] Although empirical studies generally confirm the existence of a pure control premium, there is considerable disagreement over its size. Country comparison studies indicate a huge variation in median control premiums from as little as 2 to 5 percent in countries such as the United States and the United Kingdom, where corporate ownership often is widely dispersed and investor protections are relatively effective, to as much as 60 to 65 percent in countries where ownership tends to be concentrated and governance practices are relatively poor, such as Brazil and the Czech Republic. Median estimates across countries are 10 to 12 percent. (See Barclary and Holderman, 1989; Dyck and Zingales, 2004; Massari, Monge, and Zanetti, 2006; Nenova, 2003.)

and either a term sheet or letter of intent. Sometimes, the buyer and seller will agree to bypass the letter of intent and proceed directly to negotiating an agreement of purchase and sale.

Confidentiality Agreement

All parties to the deal are likely to want a *confidentiality agreement* (also called a nondisclosure agreement), which is generally mutually binding; that is, it covers all parties to the transaction. In negotiating the confidentiality agreement, the buyer requests as much audited historical data and supplemental information as the seller is willing to provide. The prudent seller requests similar information about the buyer to assess the buyer's financial credibility. It is important for the seller to determine the buyer's credibility early in the process so as not to waste time with a potential buyer incapable of raising the financing to complete the transaction. The agreement should cover only information that is not publicly available and should have a reasonable expiration date.

Note that the confidentiality agreement can be negotiated independently or as part of the term sheet or letter of intent.

Term Sheet

A *term sheet* outlines the primary terms with the seller and is often used as the basis for a more detailed letter of intent. Involving lawyers and accountants at this stage may not be necessary. It is the last point before the parties to the potential transaction start incurring significant legal, accounting, and consulting expenses.

A standard term sheet is typically two- to four-pages long and stipulates the total consideration or purchase price (often as a range), what is being acquired (i.e., assets or stock), limitations on the use of proprietary data, a *no-shop agreement* preventing the seller from sharing the terms of the buyer's proposal with other potential buyers with the hope of instigating an auction environment, and a termination date. Many transactions skip the term sheet and go directly to negotiating a letter of intent.

Letter of Intent

A *letter of intent* (LOI) can be useful in identifying, early in the process, areas of agreement and disagreement. However, because it takes time to negotiate, an LOI may delay the signing of a definitive agreement of purchase and sale. For public companies, compliance with securities laws may necessitate a public announcement if the agreement is likely to have a "material" impact on the buyer or seller.

The LOI formally stipulates the reason for the agreement and major terms and conditions. It also indicates the responsibilities of both parties while the agreement is in force, a reasonable expiration date, how all fees associated with the transaction will be paid, and a purchase price, which may be expressed as a specific dollar figure, range, or formula (e.g., a multiple of some measure of value such as operating earnings or cash flow). The LOI also specifies the types of data to be exchanged and the duration and extent of the initial due diligence.

Price or other provisions are generally subject to *closing conditions*, which could include the buyer having full access to all of the seller's books and records; having completed due diligence; obtaining financing; and having received approval from boards of directors, stockholders, and regulatory bodies. Other standard conditions include the requirement for signed employment contracts for key target firm executives and the completion of all necessary M&A documents. Failure to satisfy any of these conditions will invalidate the agreement.

In recent years, some letters of intent have included a *go-shop agreement* that allows the seller to continue to solicit higher bids for several months. However, if the seller accepts another bid, the seller would have to pay a *breakup fee* to the bidder with whom it has a signed agreement. This fee often equals 3 to 5 percent of the purchase price. The less-common *reverse breakup fee* is paid to the seller by a buyer that wishes to break a signed contract, and compensates the seller for damages if the buyer cannot obtain adequate financing.[9]

NEGOTIATION

Unlike the prenegotiation activities just described, the negotiation phase is an interactive, iterative process, as shown in Exhibit 1-4. It formally begins after initial contact and the target's expression of interest in exploring the possibility of being acquired. Many activities are conducted concurrently by various members of the acquisition team. The actual purchase price paid for the acquired business is determined during negotiation and often is considerably different from the initial valuation of the target company, which was based on limited publicly available information.

---

[9] Reverse breakup fees became much more common in 2008 and 2009 due to the extreme difficulty in buyers obtaining financing.

EXHIBIT 1-4 Viewing Negotiation as a Process

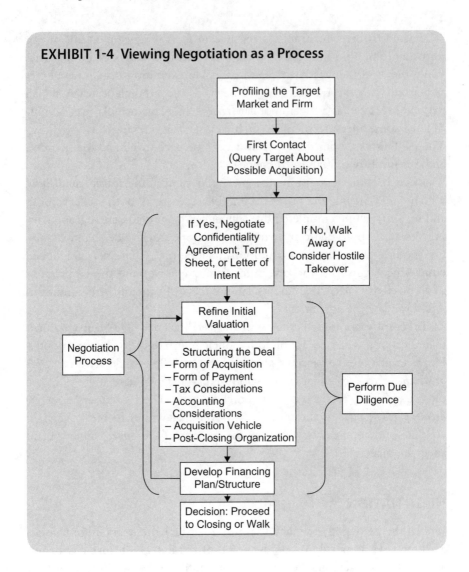

Developing a Negotiating Strategy

Negotiating is essentially a process in which two or more parties, representing different interests, attempt to achieve a consensus on a particular issue. It is useful to start a negotiation by determining any areas of disagreement, which can be done by having all parties review the facts pertaining to the deal at the beginning. Generally, parties reach agreement on most facts relatively easily. From there, it is easy to identify areas in dispute. Each party then determines whether there are any issues that could be a *deal breaker*— something that a party to the negotiation cannot concede without making the deal unacceptable.

Good negotiators make concessions on issues not considered deal breakers, but only if they receive something in return. By the time only a few remain, all parties to the negotiation have invested a great deal of money, time, and emotional commitment to the process and will be looking forward to resolving any remaining issues quickly. All positions should be explained logically. Unreasonable demands at this point in the negotiation are likely to evoke frustration by the other party and encourage someone to end discussions. If the parties can reach a point where one side is at least willing to state a price range, final agreement is in sight.

Sound planning is the key to successful negotiation. Prior to negotiating, each party should determine its own goals (i.e., highest priority needs) and prioritize those goals. Is money the major issue, or is it more about gaining control? Each party should also make an effort to identify the other party's goals and priorities based on public statements and actions, as well as information uncovered during due diligence. With clearly identified goals, each party can develop strategies for achieving those goals. Each party needs to recognize that allowances must be made so other parties can achieve—or at least *believe* they have achieved—their primary goals.

All moves in a negotiation should be supported by the most objective rationale possible; a well-reasoned and well-structured proposal is difficult to counter. The first move of any negotiation can set the tone for the entire process. A reasonable offer is more likely to appeal to the other side and more likely to elicit a reasonable counteroffer. Skilled negotiators often employ a series of techniques to reach consensus. For example, negotiators may try to determine the minimum outcome the other party will accept and then adjust their demands accordingly, without giving up their highest priority objectives.

Traditional negotiating has been referred to as the "win-lose" approach, based on the assumption that one's gain is necessarily another's loss. This is true when only one issue is at stake. For example, if a seller accepts a lower cash purchase price, and if cash is a high-priority concern to the buyer and the seller, the buyer gains at the seller's expense. "Win-win" negotiations, in contrast, presume there are outcomes in which both parties to a negotiation gain; these negotiations involve multiple related issues. In a win-win negotiation, one party can concede what it believes to be a relatively low-priority item in exchange for the other party's acceptance of something else that is highly important.

When it comes to issues of money, it can be important to reach agreement first on a formula or framework for determining what both parties believe is a fair value. This may require intense discussion. A formula might be that the purchase price will be some multiple of earnings or cash flow; a framework might comprise a series of steps, such as the extent of due diligence to be allowed, before a purchase price is proposed. The formula or framework can help avoid the thorny issue of how much to offer at the outset and enables negotiators to proceed to the data collection or due diligence stage.

Concurrent Activities

The negotiation phase comprises four iterative activities that may begin at different times but tend to overlap. One activity is refining the preliminary valuation, which provides the starting point for negotiating the agreement of purchase and sale. This is based on new information uncovered as part of due diligence, another of the four activities, which provides additional information to enable the buyer to understand better the nature of the liabilities that may be assumed and to confirm perceived sources of value. Deal structuring involves meeting the needs of both parties by addressing issues of risk and reward by constructing an appropriate set of compensation, legal, tax, and accounting structures. The fourth of these activities is developing a financing plan, which provides a reality check for the buyer by defining the maximum amount the buyer can reasonably expect to finance and, in turn, pay for the target company.

Refining Valuation

The starting point for negotiation is to update the preliminary target company valuation, based on new information. A buyer requests and reviews at least three to five years' worth of historical financial data. Although it is highly desirable to examine data that have been audited in accordance with GAAP, such data may not be available for small, privately owned companies. In fact, small companies rarely hire outside accounting firms to conduct expensive audits unless they are required to do so as part of a loan agreement.

The historical data should be normalized, or adjusted for nonrecurring gains, losses, or expenses. Nonrecurring gains or losses can result from the sale of land, equipment, product lines, patents, software, or copyrights.

Nonrecurring expenses include severance payments, employee signing bonuses, and settlements of litigation. These adjustments allow the buyer to smooth out irregularities in the historical information and better understand the underlying dynamics of the business. After the data have been normalized, each major expense category should be expressed as a percentage of revenue. By observing year-to-year changes in these ratios, sustainable trends in the data are more discernable.

Deal Structuring

Fundamentally, the **deal-structuring process** is about satisfying as many of the primary objectives (or needs) of the parties involved as necessary and determining how risk will be shared. Common examples of high-priority buyer objectives include paying a "reasonable" purchase price, using stock in lieu of cash (if the acquirer's stock is believed to be overvalued), and having the seller finance a portion of the purchase price by carrying a seller's note. Buyers may also want to put a portion of the purchase price in an escrow account, defer a portion of the price, or make a certain percentage of the purchase price contingent upon realizing some future event to minimize risk. Common closing conditions desired by buyers include obtaining employee retention agreements and noncompete agreements. Sellers that are also publicly traded companies are typically driven to maximize purchase price. However, their desire to maximize price may be tempered by other considerations such as the perceived ease of doing the deal or a desire to obtain a tax-free transaction—those in which the seller receives primarily buyer stock for its stock. The transaction is tax free for the selling firm's shareholders until they actually sell the buyer's stock. Private or family-owned firms may be less motivated by price than by other factors such as protecting the firm's future reputation and current employees, as well as obtaining rights to license patents or to utilize other valuable assets.

Risk sharing refers to the extent to which the acquirer assumes all, some, or none of the liabilities, disclosed or otherwise, of the target. The appropriate deal structure is that which satisfies, subject to an acceptable level of risk, as many of the primary objectives of the parties involved as necessary to reach overall agreement. The process may be highly complex in large transactions involving multiple parties, approvals, forms of payment, and sources of financing. Decisions made in one area inevitably affect other areas of the overall deal structure. Containing risk associated with a complex deal is analogous to catching a water balloon. Squeezing one end of the balloon simply forces the contents to shift elsewhere.

Key Components of the Deal-Structuring Process

Exhibit 1-5 summarizes the deal-structuring process, which begins with addressing a set of key questions that help define initial negotiating positions, potential risks, options for managing risk, levels of tolerance for risk, and conditions under which the buyer or seller will "walk away" from the negotiations. These questions are listed on the left side of Exhibit 1-5 and grouped according to the part of the deal-structuring process to which they apply.

The various components of the deal-structuring process denoted in Exhibit 1-5 are defined next. The *form of payment* or total consideration may consist of cash, common stock, debt, or a combination of all three. The payment may be fixed at a moment in time, contingent on future performance of the acquired unit, or payable over time. The form of payment influences the selection of the appropriate form of acquisition and post-closing organization. The *form of acquisition* reflects what is being acquired (stock or assets) and, as such, tax considerations. The form of acquisition also defines how the ownership of assets will be conveyed from the seller to the buyer, either by rule of law as in a merger or through transfer and assignment as in a purchase of assets. *Tax considerations* entail tax structures and strategies that determine whether a transaction is taxable or nontaxable to the seller's shareholders and influence the choice of postclosing organization, which affects the potential for double taxation and the allocation of losses to owners. Transactions in which the form of payment is primarily acquirer stock generally are tax free to the selling firm's shareholders. *Accounting considerations* refer to the potential impact of financial reporting requirements on the earnings volatility of business combinations due to the need to periodically revalue acquired assets to their fair market value as new information becomes available. The *legal form of the selling entity* (i.e., whether it is a C or S chapter corporation, LLC, or partnership) also has tax implications.

The *acquisition vehicle* refers to the legal structure created to acquire the target company. The *postclosing organization* or structure is the organizational and legal framework used to manage the combined businesses following the consummation of the transaction. Commonly used structures for both the acquisition vehicle and postclosing organization include the corporate or divisional, holding company, joint venture (JV), partnership, limited liability company (LLC), and employee stock ownership plan (ESOP) structures. The choice of acquisition vehicle and postclosing organization has liability, tax, and financing implications that are discussed in more detail later in this book.

EXHIBIT 1-5 Mergers and Acquisitions Deal-Structuring Process

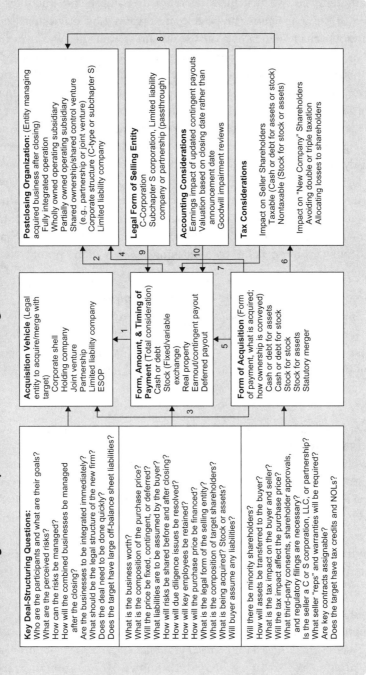

Key Deal-Structuring Questions:
Who are the participants and what are their goals?
What are the perceived risks?
How can the risks be managed?
How will the combined businesses be managed after the closing?
Are the businesses to be integrated immediately?
What should be the legal structure of the new firm?
Does the deal need to be done quickly?
Does the target have large off-balance sheet liabilities?

What is the business worth?
What is the composition of the purchase price?
Will the price be fixed, contingent, or deferred?
What liabilities are to be assumed by the buyer?
How will risks be shared before and after closing?
How will due diligence issues be resolved?
How will key employees be retained?
How will the purchase price be financed?
What is the legal form of the selling entity?
What is the composition of target shareholders?
What is being acquired? Stock or assets?
Will buyer assume any liabilities?

Will there be minority shareholders?
How will assets be transferred to the buyer?
What is the tax impact on the buyer and seller?
Will the tax impact affect the purchase price?
What third-party consents, shareholder approvals, and regulatory filings are necessary?
Is the seller a C or S corporation, LLC, or partnership?
What seller "reps" and warranties will be required?
Are key contracts assignable?
Does the target have tax credits and NOLs?

Acquisition Vehicle (Legal entity to acquire/merge with target)
Corporate shell
Holding company
Joint venture
Partnership
Limited liability company
ESOP

Form, Amount, & Timing of Payment (Total consideration)
Cash or debt
Stock (Fixed/variable exchange)
Real property
Earnout/contingent payout
Deferred payout

Form of Acquisition (Form of payment, what is acquired; how ownership is conveyed)
Cash or debt for assets
Cash or debt for stock
Stock for stock
Stock for assets
Statutory merger

Postclosing Organization: (Entity managing acquired business after closing)
Fully integrated operation
Wholly owned operating subsidiary
Partially owned operating subsidiary
Shared ownership/shared control venture (e.g., partnership or joint venture)
Corporate structure (C-type or subchapter S)
Limited liability company

Legal Form of Selling Entity
C-Corporation
Subchapter S corporation, Limited liability company or partnership (passthrough)

Accounting Considerations
Earnings impact of updated contingent payouts
Valuation based on closing date rather than announcement date
Goodwill impairment reviews

Tax Considerations
Impact on Seller Shareholders
Taxable (Cash or debt for assets or stock)
Nontaxable (Stock for stock or assets)
Impact on "New Company" Shareholders
Avoiding double or triple taxation
Allocating losses to shareholders

Although the two structures are often the same before and after completion of the transaction, the postclosing organization may differ from the acquisition vehicle depending on the acquirer's strategic objectives for the combined firms. An acquirer may choose a corporate or divisional structure to purchase the target firm and to rapidly integrate the acquired business to realize synergies. Alternatively, the acquirer may opt to undertake the transaction using a JV or partnership vehicle to share risk. When the operation of the acquired entity is better understood, the acquirer may choose to buy out its partners and to operate within a corporate or divisional structure. Similarly, the acquirer may complete the transaction using a holding company legal structure. The acquirer may operate the acquired firm as a wholly owned subsidiary to preserve the attractive characteristics of its culture for an extended time period and later move to a more traditional corporate or divisional framework. All of these terms in bold type will be explained in considerably greater detail in the remaining chapters of this book.

Common Linkages within the Deal-Structuring Process

For simplicity, many of the linkages or interactions that reflect how decisions made in one area affect other aspects of the deal are not shown in Exhibit 1-5. Common linkages or interactions among various components of the deal structure are illustrated through examples described next and are explained in more detail later in this book.

Form of Payment Influences Choice of Acquisition Vehicle and Postclosing Organization (Exhibit 1-5: Arrows 1–2)

If the buyer and seller agree on a price, the buyer may offer a purchase price that is contingent on the future performance of the target. The buyer may choose to acquire and operate the acquired company as a wholly owned subsidiary within a holding company during the term of the "deal-structuring process," which facilitates monitoring the operation's performance and minimizes the potential for litigation following the deal-structuring process initiated by deal-structuring process participants.

Form of Acquisition (Exhibit 1-5: Arrows 3–6) Affects Numerous Components of the Deal Structure

- *Choice of Acquisition Vehicle and Postclosing Organization:* If the form of acquisition is a statutory merger, all known and unknown or contingent liabilities are transferred to the buyer. Under these circumstances, the buyer may choose to change the type of acquisition vehicle to one better able to protect the buyer from the liabilities of the target, such as a holding company arrangement. Acquisition vehicles and postclosing organizations that facilitate a sharing of potential risk or of the purchase price include JV or partnership arrangements.

- *Form, Timing, and Amount of Payment:* The assumption of all seller liabilities through a merger also may induce the buyer to change the form of payment by deferring some portion of the purchase price to decrease the present value of the cost of the transaction. The buyer also may attempt to negotiate a lower overall purchase price.
- *Tax Considerations:* The transaction may be tax free to the seller if the acquirer uses its stock to acquire substantially all of the seller's assets or stock in a stock for stock or stock for assets purchase.

Tax Considerations (Exhibit 1-5: Arrows 7–8) Affect Purchase Price and Selection of Postclosing Organization

- *Amount, Timing, and Composition of the Purchase Price:* If the transaction is taxable to the target's shareholders, it is likely that the purchase price will be increased to compensate the target's shareholders for their tax liability. The increase in the purchase price may affect the form of payment. The acquirer may maintain the present value of the total cost of the acquisition by deferring some portion of the purchase price by altering the terms to include more debt or installment payments.
- *Selection of the Postclosing Organization:* The decision as to what constitutes the appropriate organizational structure of the combined businesses is affected by the desire to minimize taxes and passthrough losses to owners. The S corporation, LLC, and partnership eliminate problems of double taxation. Moreover, current operating losses, loss carry forwards or carry backs, or tax credits generated by the combined businesses can be passed through to the owners if the postclosing organization is a partnership or a LLC.

Legal Form of Selling Entity Affects Form of Payment (Exhibit 1-5: Arrow 9)

Because of the potential for deferring shareholder tax liabilities, target firms that qualify as C corporations often prefer to exchange their stock or assets for acquirer shares. In contrast, owners of S corporations, LLCs, and partnerships are largely indifferent as to whether the transaction is taxable or nontaxable because 100 percent of the proceeds of the sale are taxed at the shareholders' ordinary tax rate.

Accounting Considerations Impact Form, Amount, and Timing of Payment (Exhibit 1-5: Arrow 10)

Earnouts and other forms of contingent considerations are recorded at fair value on the acquisition date under changes in financial reporting guidelines (i.e., SFAS 141R and SFAS 157) that became effective in December 2009 and are subsequently adjusted to fair value as new information becomes available. Such changes can increase or decrease reported earnings. Because earnouts must be recorded at fair value on the acquisition date and subsequently adjusted, the potential for increased earnings volatility may make performance-related payouts less attractive as a form of payment. Furthermore, the use of equity securities to pay for target firms may be less attractive due to recent changes in financial reporting requirements. The value of the transaction will not be known until the closing because the value of the transaction will be measured at the close of the deal rather than at the announcement date. If the length of time between announcement and closing is substantial due to the need to obtain regulatory approval, the value of the deal may change significantly. Finally, the requirement to review periodically the book or carrying value of such assets as goodwill for impairment (e.g., fair market value is less than book value) may discourage acquirers from overpaying for a target firm due to the potential for future asset write downs. Exhibit 1-6 provides a summary of these common linkages.

Conducting Due Diligence

Although some degree of protection is achieved through a well-written contract, legal documents should never be viewed as a substitute for conducting formal due diligence. While most often performed by the buyer on the seller, the seller also may be well advised to perform due diligence on both itself and the buyer. Finally, lenders also are likely to perform due diligence on the target company if that firm's assets are going to be used to collateralize loans made to the acquirer.

Note that Exhibit 1-4 implies that the due diligence activity spans the entire negotiation period. In practice, this may not always be the case. The length, timing, and extent of due diligence is negotiated early in the process, usually in the letter of intent, and is largely determined by the relative leverage of the buyer and seller. In some cases, due diligence may precede formal negotiations and may be very limited or in rare instances nonexistent.

Buyer Due Diligence

Buyers use due diligence to validate assumptions underlying valuation. The primary objectives of buyer's due diligence are to identify and confirm

EXHIBIT 1-6 Summary of Common Linkages within the Deal-Structuring Process

Component of Deal-Structuring Process	Influences Choice Of
Form, Amount, and Timing of Payment	Acquisition vehicle Postclosing organization Accounting considerations
Form of Acquisition	Acquisition vehicle Postclosing organization Form, amount, and timing of payment Tax structure (taxable or nontaxable)
Tax Considerations	Form, amount, and timing of payment Postclosing organization
Legal Form of Selling Entity	Tax structure (taxable or nontaxable)

sources of value or synergy and mitigate real or potential liability by looking for fatal flaws that reduce value. Exhibit 1-7 identifies potential sources of value and how they may affect a firm's financial performance.

Due diligence involves three primary reviews: (1) a strategic/operational/marketing review conducted by senior operations and marketing management; (2) a financial review directed by financial and accounting personnel; and (3) a legal review conducted by the buyer's legal counsel. A rigorous due diligence requires the creation of comprehensive checklists. The strategic and operational review questions focus on the seller's management team, operations, and sales and marketing strategies. The financial review questions focus on the accuracy, timeliness, and completeness of the seller's financial statements. Finally, legal questions deal with corporate records, financial matters, management and employee issues, tangible and intangible assets of the seller, and material contracts and obligations of the seller such as litigation and claims. The interview process provides invaluable sources of information. By asking the same questions of a number of key managers, the acquirer is able to validate the accuracy of their conclusions.

An expensive and exhausting process, due diligence is, by its nature, highly intrusive and places considerable demands on managers' time and attention. Frequently, the buyer wants as much time as necessary to complete due diligence, whereas the seller will want to limit the length and scope as much as possible.

EXHIBIT 1-7 Identifying Potential Sources of Value

Potential Source of Value	Examples	Potential Impact
Operating Synergy:		
• Eliminating functional overlap	• Reduce duplicate overhead positions	• Improved margins
• Productivity improvement	• Increased output per employee	• Same
• Purchasing discounts	• Volume discounts on material purchases	• Same
• Working capital management	• Reduced days in receivables due to improved collection of accounts receivable	• Improved return on total assets
	• Fewer days in inventory due to improved inventory turns	• Same
• Facilities management		
– Economies of scale	• Increased production in underutilized facilities	• Improved return on total assets
– Economies of scope	• Data centers, R&D functions, call centers, etc., support multiple product lines/operations	• Same
• Organizational realignment	• Reducing the number of layers of management	• Improved communication
		• Reduced bureaucratic inertia
Financial Synergy:		
• Increased borrowing capacity	• Target has little debt and many unencumbered assets	• Increased access to financing
• Increased leverage	• Access to lower-cost source of funds	• Lower cost of capital
Marketing/Product Synergy:		
• Access to new distribution channels	• Increased sales opportunities	• Increased revenue
• Cross-selling opportunities	• Selling acquirer products to target customers and vice versa	• Same
• Research & development	• Cross-fertilization of ideas	• More innovation
• Product development	• Increased advertising budget	• Improved market share
Control:		
• Opportunity identification	• Acquirer sees opportunities not seen by target's management	• New growth opportunities
• More proactive management style	• More decisive decision-making	• Improved financial returns

Due diligence rarely works to the advantage of the seller because a long and detailed due diligence is likely to uncover items the buyer will use as an excuse to lower the purchase price. Consequently, the seller may seek to terminate due diligence before the buyer feels it is appropriate.

In some instances, buyers and sellers may agree to an abbreviated due diligence period on the theory that the buyer can be protected in a well-written agreement of purchase and sale in which the seller is required to make certain representations and warrant that they are true. These could include the seller's acknowledgement that it owns all assets listed in the agreement "free and clear" of any liens, with a mechanism for compensating the buyer for any material loss (defined in the contract) should the representation be breached (i.e., found not to be true).

One way sellers try to limit due diligence is to sequester the acquirer's team in a *data room*. Typically, this is a conference room filled with file cabinets and boxes of documents requested by the buyer's due diligence team. Formal presentations by the seller's key managers are given in the often cramped conditions of the data room. In other instances, the potential buyer may have limited access to information on a password-protected website. Not surprisingly, the data room is a poor substitute for a tour of the seller's facilities. Virtual data rooms are becoming more commonplace, with potential buyers allowed to access a password-protected website containing financial and other data relevant to the seller.

Seller Due Diligence

Although the bulk of due diligence is performed by the buyer on the seller, the prudent seller should also perform due diligence on the buyer. In doing so, the seller can determine whether the buyer has the financial wherewithal to finance the purchase. Frequently, as part of its own due diligence, a seller will require its managers to sign affidavits attesting (to the "best of their knowledge") to the truthfulness of what is being represented in the contract that pertains to their areas of responsibility.

Prudent sellers also conduct internal due diligence. Through an investigation of its own operations, the seller hopes to mitigate liability stemming from inaccuracies in the seller's representations and warranties made in the definitive agreement of purchase and sale.

Lender Due Diligence

If the acquirer is borrowing to buy a target firm, the lender or lenders will want to perform their own due diligence independent of the buyer's effort. Multiple lender due diligences, often performed concurrently, can be quite burdensome to the target firm's management and employees, and the seller should agree to these disruptive activities only if confident that the transaction will be consummated within a reasonable period.

Developing the Financing Plan or Strategy: The Reality Check

The final activity of the negotiation phase is to develop balance sheet, income, and cash-flow statements for the combined firms. Unlike the financial projections of cash flow made to value the target, these statements should include the expected cost of financing the transaction. Developing the financing plan is a key input in determining the purchase price because it places a limitation on the amount the buyer can offer the seller.

The financing plan is appended to the acquirer's business and acquisition plans and is used to obtain financing for the transaction. No matter the size the transaction, lenders and investors will want to see a coherent analysis of why the proposed transaction is a good investment opportunity. It largely is used as a marketing or sales document to negotiate the best possible terms for financing the proposed transaction.

★ ★ ★

Of the various activities involved in the negotiating process, deal structuring is the most challenging. It involves satisfying as many of the primary objectives as necessary of the parties involved and determines how risk will be shared. After a set of key questions has been answered, the parties to the negotiation can define their initial negotiating positions, potential risks, options for managing risk, levels of tolerance for risk, and conditions under which one or the other will "walk away" from the negotiation. Then the deal structuring may begin, addressing the form of the acquisition vehicle, the postclosing organization, the form of payment, the form of acquisition, the legal form of the selling entity, and accounting and tax considerations.

A Case in Point: Pfizer Acquires Wyeth in an Attempt to Kick-Start Growth

On January 26, 2009, Pfizer Inc. announced it had reached an acquisition agreement with Wyeth Pharmaceuticals in a cash and stock deal valued at $66.8 billion ($68 billion including the value of Wyeth stock options exercised at closing). The purchase price was a 12.6 percent premium over Wyeth's closing share price the day before the announcement and a 29 percent premium over its closing price the same day one month earlier. The premium represented a combination of anticipated synergy created in combining the two businesses and the amount paid to gain control of Wyeth. At about $52 billion in 2008, Pfizer's annual revenues were about double those of Wyeth. Wyeth's shares rose 12.6 percent and Pfizer's 1.4 percent on the news.[10]

Pfizer's record in making mega transactions is spotty. The firm acquired Warner-Lambert for $90 billion in 2000 and Pharmacia for $60 billion in 2003. Although substantial cost reductions were achieved in both instances, neither acquisition appears to have contributed to improved operating performance for Pfizer. In fact, at the time of the Wyeth announcement, Pfizer's stock had dropped by 50 percent since it completed the Warner-Lambert deal.

The Wyeth acquisition represents a departure from the general trend in recent years to avoid big horizontal mergers (i.e., those among competitors) and to focus on vertical mergers in which a big pharmaceutical firm acquires a smaller company. As is true of other large pharmaceutical companies, Pfizer faces serious revenue erosion as its patents expire on a number of major drugs; for example, patent rights on Lipitor, the cholesterol-lowering drug that accounted for 25 percent of Pfizer's 2008 revenue, expire in 2011, and 14 other patents expire through 2014 on drugs expected to generate $35 billion during that period. Pfizer is not alone in suffering from patent expirations. Diversification is one of Pfizer's tactics for offsetting this revenue erosion. In addition to its existing products, Wyeth brings to Pfizer a significant capability in biologics, which—unlike traditional chemical-based drugs such as tablets and capsules—are developed with live processes.

Pfizer's strategy was to acquire Wyeth—an attractive-looking acquisition because there is little overlap between the two firms' drug offerings, and hence few regulatory issues—when transaction prices were depressed because of the recession and tight credit markets. Pfizer projected $4 billion in annual savings from the combination through job eliminations and some plant closures, phased in over three years. The biggest issue Pfizer faced was how to achieve and maintain an innovative culture in the new firm and retain good people.

The negotiations were contentious, not because of differences over price or strategy but rather the circumstances in which Pfizer could back out of the deal. Many transactions announced during 2008 were never closed because buyers were unable to arrange financing due to the upheaval in the global capital markets. This deal established that Pfizer would be liable to pay Wyeth $4.5 billion if its credit rating dropped prior to closing and it could not finance the transaction. That made for a breakup fee around 6.6 percent—about twice the norm for similar transactions. Pfizer also agreed to pay $50.19 per Wyeth share: $33 in cash and the

---

[10] Although the expectation was that the deal would dilute earnings per share during the first full year following closing, because the increase in earnings of the combined firms would be less than the increase in Pfizer shares issued to buy Wyeth, Pfizer forecast that the deal would add to consolidated earnings per share by the second full year after closing.

remainder in 0.985 shares of Pfizer stock valued at $17.19 per share exchanged for each Wyeth share outstanding. Wyeth's management would be terminated.

Pfizer came to the negotiation with a $22.5 billion bridge financing commitment letter from Goldman Sachs, JPMorgan Chase, Citigroup, Bank of America, and Barclays, along with $26 billion in cash and marketable securities. The buyer cut its quarterly dividend in half to help finance the transaction.

The Pfizer-Wyeth deal allowed limited circumstances in which a financing failure could be claimed in limited circumstances. Specifically, Pfizer could renege only if its lenders refused to finance the transaction because of a credit downgrade of the company. If the condition was not satisfied and the lenders refused to finance primarily for this reason, Wyeth was permitted either to demand that Pfizer attempt to find alternative financing or terminate the agreement—creating an obligation that Pfizer pay Wyeth $4.5 billion.

Things to Think About:

1. What were the primary reasons Pfizer wanted to acquire Wyeth? Why do you think Wyeth found the deal attractive, despite the depressed state of transaction prices at that time? Be specific.

2. What do you believe is the risk associated with this deal for the Pfizer shareholders? For the Wyeth shareholders? Be specific.

3. Goldman Sachs was both an advisor and a lender on this deal. What is your opinion of the dual role played by Goldman? Be specific.

4. In view of the reaction of both firm's share prices immediately following the announcement of the deal, what do you think investors are assuming about the deal?

5. The reverse breakup fee represents 6.6 percent of purchase price. How would you as a negotiator for Wyeth justify such a large fee?

Answers can be found at:
www.elsevierdirect.com/companion.jsp?ISBN=9780123749499

CHAPTER 2

Selecting the Form of Acquisition Vehicle and Postclosing Organization

Present in all transactions, the *acquisition vehicle* is the legal or business structure employed to acquire a target firm, and the *postclosing organization* is that used to operate the new company following closing. There are various options, as the following examples illustrate, and making the right choices for both is integral to the negotiation process.[1]

On July 9, 2000, in a share-for-share exchange valued at $41 billion, the boards of JDS Uniphase (a fiberoptic components manufacturer) and SDL (a pump laser producer) unanimously approved an agreement to merge SDL with a newly formed entity—K2 Acquisition, Inc., a wholly owned subsidiary of JDS Uniphase created as a shell corporation to be the acquisition vehicle to complete the merger. K2 Acquisition, Inc. was merged into SDL, with SDL as the surviving entity. The postclosing organization consisted of SDL as a wholly owned subsidiary of JDS Uniphase.

In another deal, Rupert Murdoch's News Corp.—a holding company (the acquisition vehicle)—acquired a controlling interest in Hughes Electronics Corporation (a subsidiary of General Motors Corporation and owner of DirecTV) on April 10, 2003. News Corp. subsequently transferred its stake in Hughes to its Fox Entertainment Group subsidiary (the postclosing organization), in which it owned an 81 percent interest at the time, to strengthen Fox's competitive position while retaining control over DirecTV.

More recently, the Tribune Company (Tribune) announced on April 2, 2007, that the firm's publicly traded shares would be acquired in a multistage transaction valued at $8.2 billion. The acquisition vehicle was an

---

[1] References to business structures throughout the chapter refer to such arrangements as joint ventures and strategic business alliances (which may or may not involve legal entities). For example, the joint venture (JV) routinely is used to describe a collaboration among partners. The JV can be a corporation, partnership, or some other form of legal entity; or, the JV can be an informal, nonlegally binding agreement involving multiple parties collaborating in an effort to achieve specific business objectives.

Mergers and Acquisitions Basics
ISBN: 978-0-12-374949-9, DOI: 10.1016/B978-0-12-374949-9.00002-6

employee stock ownership plan (ESOP), and the postclosing organization was a subchapter S corporation. Converting Tribune into a subchapter S corporation eliminated the firm's current annual tax liability of $348 million. Such entities pay no corporate income tax but must pay all profit directly to shareholders, who then pay taxes on these distributions. Because the ESOP is the sole shareholder, the restructured Tribune would be largely tax exempt, since ESOPs are not taxed.

In a cross-border transaction, the biggest banking deal on record was announced on October 9, 2007, resulting in the dismemberment of one of Europe's largest and oldest financial services firms, ABN Amro (ABN)— then the largest bank in the Netherlands. The acquisition vehicle was a buyer partnership comprising The Royal Bank of Scotland, Spain's Banco Santander, and Belgium's Fortis Bank, which won control of ABN in a buyout valued at $101 billion. The acquisition partners agreed in advance who would retain which ABN assets, and these were merged into the respective buyers' corporate subsidiaries (the postclosing organizations).

Finally, Cablevision Systems Corporation (CVC) acquired Newsday Media Group from Tribune Company in early 2008 by creating a partnership (the acquisition vehicle) in which CVC has a 97 percent and Tribune a 3 percent interest. Tribune contributed the Newsday assets, and CVC contributed newly issued parent company bonds with a fair market value of $650 million of senior debt maturing in 10 years. The CVC debt is equivalent to contributing a deferred cash payment, with the cash actually paid to the partnership when the bonds mature. The partnership will borrow $650 million for 10 years from Bank of America, guaranteed by Tribune, and the proceeds will be distributed to Tribune—which will not have to pay capital gains taxes on the $650 million, despite having earned a profit on the "deferred sale" of Newsday. CVC, with its controlling interest in the partnership (the postclosing organization), has effective control over Newsday.

This chapter focuses on the alternative forms of legal and organizational structures that can serve as acquisition vehicles and postclosing organizations, as in the preceding examples, and discusses the implications of each for risk management, financing flexibility, tax optimization, and management control. Here, you will find the information needed to answer this question: Which legal entities or business structures should I use to achieve my objectives as an acquirer?[2]

---

[2] For more information on this topic, see DePamphilis (2009), Chapter 11.

ALTERNATIVE ACQUISITION VEHICLE AND POSTCLOSING ORGANIZATIONAL STRUCTURES

Determining the legal form or business structure of an acquisition vehicle or postclosing organization should follow the creation of a coherent business strategy. The choice of legal structure should be made only after the acquirer is comfortable with the venture's objectives, potential synergy, and preliminary financial analysis of projected returns and risk. As Exhibit 2-1 summarizes, each has its own advantages and disadvantages with respect to taxation, control by the owners, ability to trade ownership positions, limitations on liability, duration, and ease of raising capital.

Corporate Structure

A *corporation* is a legal entity created under a particular business statute. The entity may be owned by one or more shareholders who, in turn, may be actual persons or other legal entities. From a legal perspective, a corporation is regarded as having an existence entirely separate from that of its owners. As such, shareholders generally are not liable for corporate obligations. This distinctive aspect of the corporation as being legally independent from the people who created it enables shareholders to claim limited liability, according to which shareholders (i.e., owners) normally lose only their investment if the corporation fails. Despite not being actual persons, corporations are recognized by law to have rights like actual people; consequently, they can be sued and sue others.

Limited liability also means that creditors cannot seize the personal assets of the owners. However, owners of corporations can be held personally liable if they directly injure someone or personally guarantee a bank loan or a business debt on which the corporation defaults. Other exceptions to personal liability include the failure to deposit taxes withheld from employees' wages, or the commission of intentional fraud that causes harm to the corporation or to someone else. Finally, owners may be liable if they fail to follow certain formal procedures in the formation and operation of a corporation, including failure to capitalize the corporation adequately, holding regular directors and shareholders meetings, or keeping business records and transactions from the owners. Note as in the case of a holding company, which holds investments in multiple firms, the shareholder can be the parent firm.

In addition to having limited shareholder financial liability, a corporation is a legal entity created under state law in the United States with an unending life. Corporate legal structures include a generalized corporate

EXHIBIT 2-1   Alternative Legal Forms/Business Structures of Acquisition Vehicles and Postclosing Organizations

Legal Form/Business Structure	Advantages	Disadvantages
Corporate Structures:		
– C Corporation	Continuity of ownership Limited liability Provides operational autonomy Provides for flexible financing Facilitates tax-free merger	Double taxation Inability to pass losses on to shareholders Relatively high set-up costs including charter and bylaws
– Subchapter S	Avoids double taxation Limited liability	Maximum of 100 shareholders Excludes corporate shareholders Must distribute all earnings Allows only one class of stock Lacks continuity of C corporate structure Difficult to raise large sums of money
Limited Liability Company (LLC)	Limited liability Owners can be managers without losing limited liability Avoids double taxation Allows an unlimited number of members or owners Allows corporate shareholders Can own more than 80 percent of another company Allows flexibility in allocating investment, profits, losses, and operational responsibilities among members Life set by owners Can sell shares to "members" without SEC registration Allows foreign corporations as investors	Owners also must be active participants in the firm Lacks continuity of a corporate structure State laws governing LLC formation differ making it difficult for LLCs doing business in multiple states Member shares often illiquid because consent of members required to transfer ownership

Partnership Structures:		
– General Partnerships	Avoids double taxation Allows flexibility in allocating investment, profits, losses, and operational responsibilities Life set by general partner	Partners have unlimited liability Lacks continuity of corporate structure Partnership interests illiquid Partners jointly and severally liable Each partner has authority to bind the partnership to contracts
– Limited Liability Partnerships	Limits partner liability (except for general partner) Avoids double taxation State laws consistent (covered under the Uniform Limited Partnership Act)	Partnership interests illiquid Partnership dissolved if a partner leaves Private partnerships limited to 35 partners
Equity Partnerships/ Minority Investments	Facilitates close working relationship Potential prelude to merger May preempt competition	Limited tactical and strategic control
ESOP	Investment earnings are tax-free Offers alternative to a divestiture Contributions are tax deductible for sponsor	Size of potential transaction limited by size of ESOP assets and ability to borrow May limit realization of synergy if done within a holding company structure
Holding Company[1]	Achieve control at relatively low cost May facilitate financing Offers diversification	Creates management challenges Minority shareholders Potentially subject to triple taxation

[1] Note a holding company can take many legal forms such as a C corporation or limited liability company. It is best viewed as a legal framework for holding or owning multiple investments in other businesses.

form (also called C-type corporations) and the subchapter S (S-type) corporations. The latter has certain tax advantages intended to facilitate the formation of small businesses, which are perceived to be major contributors to job growth.[3]

Corporations are created when their owners obtain a certificate of incorporation and disappear when they become insolvent—that is, when the fair market values of the firm's assets are less than the book values of its liabilities. Consequently, when the corporation is liquidated, some liabilities are unpaid and shareholders' equity is wiped out. In the modern corporation, shareholders delegate control to a board of directors. Finally, shares are transferable, usually on a listed stock exchange such as the New York Stock Exchange.

As previously noted, joint ventures—formal or informal alliances among participants—are business structures commonly used to achieve specific objectives. A JV's purpose is to pool resources and share risk associated with specific investments. The JV may be formal in that it assumes a specific legal structure such as a corporation or a partnership (described later in this chapter); it may be informal, based on a handshake agreement or a memorandum of understanding (MOU) that outlines the objectives of the JV and the responsibilities of the parties in terms of their contributions (of operating assets, money, management, etc.) to the ongoing operation of the organization. Partners in JVs often choose a corporate legal structure for reasons outlined in the following text.

Setting up a corporate legal structure may be more time consuming and costly than other legal forms because of legal expenses incurred in drafting a corporate charter and bylaws. Although the corporate legal structure does have adverse tax consequences and may be more costly to establish, it does offer a number of important advantages over other legal forms.

A corporate legal structure may be warranted if a JV's goals are long term and if the parties choose to contribute cash directly to the JV, in return for which the JV partners receive stock in the new company. If the initial strategic reasons for the JV change and it no longer benefits one of the partners, the stock in the JV can be sold. Alternatively, the partner/shareholder can withdraw from active participation in the JV corporation but can remain a passive shareholder in anticipation of potential future appreciation of the stock. In addition, the corporate structure facilitates a tax-free merger in which the stock of the acquiring firm can be exchanged for the stock or assets of another firm. In practice, the transferability

---

[3] For an excellent discussion of the corporation, see Truitt (2006).

of ownership interests is strictly limited by the stipulations of a shareholder agreement created when the corporation is formed.

Ownership can be easily transferred under a corporate structure, which facilitates raising money. Because a corporate structure is viewed as independent of those who created it, corporate shareholders can more readily trade their shares with others as compared with partnerships or limited liability companies in which participants are viewed as an integral part of the organization (and often must petition other partners, or members, if they wish to sell their interests). Shareholders' interests in a corporation are evidenced by share certificates, which are generally freely transferable. The corporation permits the greatest flexibility in the transfer of ownership interests. However, as is the case with limited partnerships, securities laws may otherwise restrict the transferability of shares.

A corporate structure also may be justified for a joint venture if it is expected to have substantial future financing requirements. A corporate structure provides a broader array of financing options than other legal forms. They include the ability to sell interests in the form of shares and the issuance of corporate debentures and mortgage bonds. The capacity to sell new shares enables the corporation to raise funds to expand while still retaining control if less than 50.1 percent of the corporation's shares are sold. This capacity to offer a wide variety of financial instruments such as various forms of equity and debt gives corporations the ability to appeal to a wider range of investors and lenders with different needs and objectives, and thus makes it easier and relatively inexpensive for the corporation to raise capital in the debt and equity markets.

A corporation files its own tax return. A disadvantage to the corporate form is that "double taxation" may occur because income received by the corporation will be taxed at the corporate level and, if distributed to its shareholders as dividends, will be taxed again at their personal income tax rates. Increasing salaries to officers, obtaining loans from shareholders, and adopting a subchapter S election (meaning that the corporation elects not to be taxed at the corporate level but rather to have its income channeled through directly to its shareholders) are all methods that can be employed to minimize the impact of double taxation.

C-Type Corporation

A C-type corporate structure has four primary characteristics: managerial autonomy, continuity of ownership or life, ease of transferring ownership and raising money, and limited liability. In the context of a joint venture, managerial autonomy most often is used when the JV is large or complex enough to require a separate or centralized professional management organization. The corporate structure works best when the JV requires a certain amount of operational autonomy to be effective. The parent companies would continue to set strategy, but the JV's management would manage day-to-day operations. The parent firms retain control largely by approving annual budgets, five-year budgets, and major investments.

Unlike other legal forms, the C-type corporation (or simply, C corporation) has an indefinite life because it does not have to be dissolved as a result of the death of the owners or if one of the owners wishes to liquidate his or her ownership position. The corporation is the most suitable form of business if continuity is desired. The Articles of Incorporation can provide for perpetual existence and, as a result, the corporation can continue without interruption upon the death or withdrawal of any of its shareholders, officers, or directors.

Subchapter S Corporation

A firm having 100 or fewer shareholders may qualify as a subchapter S (S-type) corporation[4] and may elect to be taxed as if it were a partnership, thus avoiding double taxation. Members of a single family—for instance, a husband and wife (and their estates)—may be considered a single shareholder.[5] Moreover, an ESOP maintained by a subchapter S corporation is not in violation of the maximum number of shareholders' requirement because the subchapter S corporation contributes stock to the ESOP.

The major disadvantages to an S-type corporation are the exclusion of any corporate shareholders, the requirement to issue only one class of stock, the necessity of distributing all earnings to the shareholders each year, and that no more than 25 percent of the corporation's gross income may be derived from passive income.

C corporations may convert to subchapter S corporations to eliminate double taxation on dividends. Asset sales within 10 years of the conversion from a C to a subchapter S corporation are subject to taxes on capital gains at the prevailing corporate income tax rate. However, after 10 years such gains are tax free to the subchapter S corporation but are taxable when distributed to shareholders at their personal tax rates. Sales of assets acquired by a subchapter S corporation or after a 10-year period following conversion from one form of legal entity to

---

[4] To be treated as an S-type corporation, all shareholders must simply sign and file IRS Form 2553.

[5] Members of a family refer to individuals with a common ancestor, lineal descendants of the common ancestor, and the spouses (or former spouses) of such lineal descendants or common ancestor.

a subchapter S corporation are taxed at the capital gains tax rate, which is generally more favorable than the corporate income tax rate. The 10-year "built-in-gains" period is designed by the Internal Revenue Service to discourage C corporations from converting to subchapter S corporations to take advantage of the more favorable capital gains tax rates on gains realized by selling corporate assets. Gains on the sale of assets by C corporations are taxed at the prevailing corporate tax rate rather than a more favorable capital gains tax rate.

The overall popularity of S-type corporations has declined with the proliferation of limited liability companies, which offer owners the significant advantage of greater flexibility in allocating profits and losses and are not subject to the many restrictions of the subchapter S corporation.

Limited Liability Company

A limited liability company (LLC) must be set for a limited time, typically 30 years. Each state has different laws about LLC formation and governance, so an LLC that does business in several states may not meet the requirements in every state. LLCs are formed when two or more "persons" (i.e., individuals, LLPs, corporations, etc.) agree to file Articles of Organization with the secretary of state's office. The most common types of firms to form LLCs are family-owned businesses, professional services firms such as lawyers, and companies with foreign investors.

Managing a limited liability company is significantly easier than running a corporation. Like a corporation, the LLC limits the liability of its owners (called members) to the extent of their investment. Like a limited partnership, the LLC passes through all the entity's profits and losses to its owners without itself being taxed.

For the LLC to obtain this favorable tax status, the IRS generally requires that it adopt an organization agreement that eliminates management autonomy, continuity of ownership or life, and free transferability of shares—characteristics of a C corporation. Management autonomy is limited by expressly placing decisions about major issues pertaining to the management of the LLC (e.g., mergers or asset sales) in the hands of all its members. LLC organization agreements require that they be dissolved in case of the death, retirement, or resignation of any member, thereby eliminating continuity of ownership or life. Free transferability is limited by making a transfer of ownership subject to the approval of all members. Unlike in a corporation, the individuals who create and own the LLC are not viewed as separate from the legal entity.

Unlike S-type corporations, LLCs can own more than 80 percent of another corporation and have an unlimited number of members. Also,

LLC shares can be owned by other corporations as well as by non-U.S. residents. Equity capital is obtained through offerings to owners or members. Capital is sometimes referred to as *interests* rather than *shares* because the latter denotes something that may be freely traded.

The LLC can sell shares or interests to members without completing the costly and time-consuming process of registering them with the Securities and Exchange Commission (SEC), as required for corporations that sell their securities to the public. LLC shares are not traded on public exchanges—an arrangement that works well for corporate JVs or projects developed through a subsidiary or affiliate. The parent corporation can separate a JV's risk from its other businesses while getting favorable tax treatment and greater flexibility in the allocation of revenues and losses among owners. LLCs can incorporate tax free before an initial public offering. This is necessary because they must register such issues with the SEC. The life of the LLC is determined by the owners and is generally set for a fixed number of years, in contrast to the typical unlimited life for a corporation.

Although a limited liability company must have members or owners, its management structure may be determined in whatever manner the members choose. Members may manage the LLC directly or provide for the election of a manager, an officer, or a board to conduct the LLC's activities. Members hold final authority in the LLC, with the right to approve—through meetings, written consent, or conference calls—extraordinary actions such as mergers or asset sales. Managers may represent the LLC in dealings with third parties.

The LLC's drawbacks are evident if one owner decides to leave: all other owners must formally agree to continue the firm. Also, all of the LLC's owners must take active roles in managing the firm. LLC interests are often illiquid, as transfer of ownership is subject to the approval of other members.

Partnership Structures

Partnership structures, both general and limited, are often used as an alternative to a corporation. Although the owners of a partnership are not legally required to have a **partnership agreement**, it usually makes sense to have one that spells out how business decisions are to be made and how profits and losses will be shared.[6]

---

[6] With the exception of Louisiana, every U.S. state has adopted either the Uniform Limited Partnership Act (ULPA) or the Revised Uniform Limited Partnership Act (RULPA), which constitute the body of law governing partnerships in the United States.

General Partnership

A *general partnership* is created by agreement, either oral or written, and the relations of the partners are governed by that understanding. Partners typically agree to share in the profits, losses, and assets of the partnership. Apart from the agreed-upon duties and liabilities of the partners, a fiduciary relationship also exists between the partners. Each partner is personally liable for the debts of the partnership—a feature that makes this business form undesirable to many entrepreneurs.

The death or withdrawal of a general partner, or the expiration of the term, will dissolve the partnership. Continuation of the partnership following such events may be dealt with, however, in the partnership agreement. Because a partnership is generally a "voluntary" association, any general partner who no longer desires to be associated with the partnership may withdraw and force dissolution. Dissolution of a partnership, as a general rule, requires winding up its affairs and liquidation of the partnership's assets.

Under the general partnership legal structure, investment, profits, losses, and operational responsibilities are allocated to the partners, but the arrangement has no effect on the autonomy of the partners. Because profits and losses are allocated to the partners, the partnership is not subject to tax. The partnership structure also offers substantial flexibility in how profits and losses are allocated. Typically, a corporate partner will form a special-purpose subsidiary to hold its interest, which not only limits liability but also may facilitate disposition of the JV interest in the future. The partnership structure is preferable to the other options when the business alliance is expected to have short (three to five years) duration and if high levels of commitment and management interaction are necessary for short time periods.

The ownership interest of a general partner receives different treatment. A general partner's interest in the partnership is an intangible interest that includes his or her proportionate share of assets and liabilities. This intangible interest may be assigned or transferred freely. Although a general partnership pays no federal income tax, all general partners are required to declare their share of partnership income or loss on their individual tax returns.

The primary disadvantage of the general partnership is that all the partners have unlimited liability and may have to cover the debts of less financially sound partners. Each partner is said to be *jointly and severally liable* for the partnership's debts. For example, if one partner negotiates a contract resulting in a substantial loss, each partner must pay for a portion of the loss, based on a previously determined agreement on the distribution of profits and losses. Because each partner has unlimited liability for all the firm's debts, creditors of the partnership may claim assets from one or more of the partners if the remaining partners are unable to cover their share of the loss. Another disadvantage is that any partner can bind the entire business to a contract or other business deal. Consequently, if one partner purchases inventory at a price the partnership cannot afford, the partnership is still obligated to pay.

Partnerships also lack continuity: they must be dissolved if a partner dies or withdraws, unless a new partnership agreement can be drafted. To avoid this possibility, a partnership agreement should include a buy-sell condition or right of first refusal allowing the partners to buy out a departing partner's interest so the business can continue. Partnership interests may be difficult to sell because of the lack of a public market, thus making it a challenge to liquidate the partnership or transfer partnership interests.

General partnerships often have difficulty in financing new investment opportunities. The partners' contributions of cash or property constitute the initial capital investment. The general partnership also is limited in its ability to borrow because partners typically must pledge their personal assets as collateral.

Forming a partnership generally requires applying for a local business license or tax registration certificate. If the business name does not contain all of the partners' last names, the partnership must register a fictitious or assumed business name in the county in which it is established.

Limited Partnerships

A limited liability partnership is a business form in which, by complying with certain statutory requirements, one or more of the partners has only limited liability for partnership debts and obligations. One or more of the partners can be designated as having limited liability as long as at least one partner has unlimited liability. The price for this liability protection is a limitation on participation in management.

Typical limited partnerships are in real estate, oil and gas, and equipment leasing, but they also are used to finance movies, R&D, and other projects. Limited liability partnerships are also very popular for accountants, physicians, attorneys, and consultants. Public limited partnerships are sold through brokerage firms, financial planners, and other registered securities representatives. Public partnerships may have an unlimited number of investors, and their partnership plans must be filed with the SEC. Private limited partnerships are constructed with fewer than 35 limited partners who each invest more than $20,000; their plans do not have to be filed with the SEC.

This type of partnership is similar to a general partnership in certain respects and to a corporation in others. A limited partnership is governed by state law and, unless the partnership strictly conforms to state restrictions, is regarded as a general partnership. Limited partners usually cannot lose more than their capital contribution. Those who are responsible for the day-to-day operations of the partnership's activities, whose individual acts are binding on the other partners, and who are personally liable for the partnership's total liabilities are called *general partners*. Those who contribute only money and who are not involved in management decisions are called *limited partners*. Usually, limited partners receive income, capital gains, and tax benefits, whereas general partners collect fees and a percentage of the capital gains and income.

The relationship between the general partner and limited partner in a limited partnership is different from that of a general partnership. If there is at least one general partner, the death or withdrawal of another general partner in a limited partnership will not result in a termination of the partnership. Moreover, a limited partner, as a passive investor, is like a shareholder of a corporation, and his or her withdrawal or death will not affect the continuity of the partnership.

For the most part, limited partnerships are treated like general partnerships for tax purposes, with tax events proportionately passing through to general and limited partners. This is one reason limited partnerships are a favored form of enterprise to conduct certain types of tax-sensitive business activities.

Unless otherwise provided in the partnership agreement, the ownership interest in a limited partnership held by a limited partner is freely transferable. Depending on the circumstances under which a limited partnership interest was obtained, securities laws may limit the otherwise free transferability of this ownership interest.

The sources of equity capital for limited partnerships are the funds supplied by the general and limited partners. The total amount of equity funds needed by a limited partnership is typically committed when the partnership is formed. Therefore, ventures that are expected to grow are not usually set up as limited partnerships. The capital infusion mechanism of a limited partnership is analogous to that of a corporation: they often obtain capital from the contributions of the partners. A pledge of partnership assets may be sufficient for borrowings, although general partner guarantees are not uncommon.

Equity Partnership or Minority Investment

An equity partnership involves a company's purchase of stock in another company (resulting in a less-than-controlling interest) or a two-way exchange of stock by the two companies. These partnerships commonly are used in purchaser-supplier relationships, technology development alliances, marketing alliances, and when a larger firm makes an investment in a smaller firm to ensure its continued financial viability or demonstrate its commitment to the relationship. In exchange for an equity investment, a firm typically receives a seat on the board of directors and possibly an option to buy a controlling interest in the company.

The equity partnership may be desired when there is a need to have a long-term or close strategic relationship, a need to preempt a competitor from making an alliance or acquisition, or as a prelude to an acquisition or merger. Often, the form of the investment is made in preferred rather than common equity because preferred stock is senior if the firm is liquidated.

Equity partnerships often are referred to as *minority investments*. They have the advantage of generally not requiring a substantial commitment of management time and may be highly liquid if the investment is in a publicly traded company. Investing companies may choose to assist small or startup companies in developing products or technologies useful to the investing company. Such investments may also be opportunistic in that passive investors take a long-term position in a firm believed to have significant appreciation potential. For example, Berkshire Hathaway, Warren Buffett's investment company, invested $5 billion in investment bank Goldman Sachs in 2008 by acquiring convertible preferred stock paying a 10 percent dividend. Such preferred stock may be convertible to common equity at some future date, with the conversion privilege likely to be exercised when the firm's common share price rises significantly above the preferred stock's conversion price. Berkshire Hathaway also received warrants (i.e., long-term options to buy common shares) to purchase $5 billion of Goldman Sachs' common stock at $115 per share. This exercise price is less than one-half of the firm's year-earlier share prices.

Employee Stock Ownership Plans

An *employee stock ownership plan* (ESOP) is a trust fund that invests in the securities of the firm sponsoring the plan. Such plans are defined contribution employee benefit pension plans that invest at least 50 percent of the plan's assets in the common shares of the firm sponsoring the ESOP. The plans may receive the employer's stock or cash, which is used to buy the sponsoring employer's stock. The sponsoring corporation can make tax-deductible contributions of cash, stock, or other assets into the trust. The plan's trustee holds title to the assets for the benefit of the employees (i.e., beneficiaries) and is charged with investing the trust assets productively. Unless specifically limited, the trustee also can sell, mortgage, or lease the assets.[7]

Stock acquired by the ESOP is allocated to accounts for individual employees based on some formula, and vest over time.[8] When employees leave the company, they receive their vested shares, which the company or the ESOP buys back at an appraised fair market value. ESOP participants must be allowed to vote their allocated shares at least on major issues such as selling the company, but there is no requirement that they be allowed to vote on other issues such as choosing the board of directors.

The ESOP's assets are allocated to employees and are not taxed until withdrawn by employees. Cash contributions made by the sponsoring firm to pay both interest and principal payments on bank loans to ESOPs are tax deductible by the firm. Dividends paid on stock contributed to ESOPs also are deductible if they are used to repay ESOP debt. The sponsoring firm could use tax credits equal to 0.5 percent of payroll, if contributions in that amount were made to the ESOP. Finally, lenders must pay taxes on only one-half of the interest received on loans made to ESOPs owning more than 50 percent of the sponsoring firm's stock.

ESOPs may also be used by employees in leveraged or management buyouts to purchase the shares of owners of privately held firms. This is particularly common where the owners have most of their net worth tied up in their firms. As such, an ESOP can be viewed by the owners of a firm as an alternative to a divestiture. If a subsidiary cannot be sold at what the parent firm believes to be a reasonable price, and liquidating the subsidiary would be disruptive to customers, the parent may sell directly to employees through a *shell corporation*—one that is incorporated but has no significant assets or liabilities. The shell sets up the ESOP, which borrows the money to buy the subsidiary. The parent guarantees the loan. The shell operates the subsidiary, whereas the ESOP holds the stock. As income is generated from the subsidiary, tax-deductible contributions are made by

---

[7] According to the National Center for Employee Ownership, there were about 10,000 ESOPs in existence nationwide in 2007, with most formed by privately owned firms. These plans covered about 11 million workers and had assets totaling about $1 trillion.

[8] Six years is a typical vestment period.

the shell to the ESOP to service the debt, and as the loan is repaid, the shares are allocated to employees who eventually own the firm.

ESOPs can be an attractive way to acquire other firms or an interest in other firms. If a passthrough entity is acquired, such as a partnership or LLC, income earned by the acquired entity is taxed only once at the owner's ordinary tax rate because such entities are required to pay out 100 percent of their earnings. Because ESOPs are not subject to tax, the earnings distributed to ESOPs are tax free. A major disadvantage of using an ESOP as an acquisition vehicle is that the size of the acquisition is limited by the ESOP's assets and any restrictions on its ability to borrow. The fiduciary responsibility of the ESOP's trustee may limit the integration of businesses owned by the ESOP with other businesses held in a holding company structure. Consequently, using an ESOP as an acquisition vehicle may limit the realization of potential synergies resulting from combining businesses.

Holding Company

A *holding company* is a legal entity with a controlling interest in one or more companies. Its primary function is to own stock in other corporations. In general, the parent firm has no wholly owned operating units. The segments owned by the holding company are separate legal entities, which in practice are controlled by the holding company. The key advantage of the holding company structure is the leverage achieved by gaining effective control of other companies' assets at a lower overall cost than if the firm were to acquire 100 percent of the target's outstanding shares.

Effective control sometimes can be achieved by owning as little as 30 percent of the voting stock of another company when the firm's bylaws require approval of major decisions by a majority of votes cast rather than a majority of the voting shares outstanding. This is particularly true when the target company's ownership is highly fragmented, with few shareholders owning large blocks of stock. Effective control in such cases typically is achieved by acquiring less than 100 percent, but usually more than 50 percent, of the firm's equity. One firm is said to have *effective control* when control has been achieved by buying voting stock, it is not likely to be temporary, there are no legal restrictions on control (such as from a bankruptcy court), and there are no powerful minority shareholders.

The holding company structure can create significant management challenges. Because it can gain effective control with less than 100 percent ownership, the minority shareholders who remain may not always agree with the strategic direction of the company. Consequently, implementing holding company strategies may become very contentious. Furthermore, in highly diversified holding companies, managers may also have difficulty making optimal investment decisions because of their limited understanding of the different competitive dynamics of each business.

The holding company structure can create significant tax problems for its shareholders. Subsidiaries of holding companies pay taxes on their operating profits. The holding company then pays taxes on dividends it receives from its subsidiaries. Finally, holding company shareholders pay taxes on dividends they receive from the holding company. This is equivalent to triple taxation of the subsidiary's operating earnings.

Holding companies may be organized as corporations, limited liability partnerships, or limited liability companies. For instance, the limited liability statute in Delaware—a particularly attractive state in which to do business, and representative of many other states—allows for high flexibility and simplicity in operating LLCs in a holding company structure. It allows for the establishment of different classes of interests, including voting and nonvoting interests, and for the creation of a single LLC to house multiple separate entities. As such, the holding company and its classes of ownership interests can be formed within a single LLC.

CHOOSING THE APPROPRIATE ACQUISITION VEHICLE

The decision about which legal entity to use as an acquisition vehicle requires consideration of a host of practical, financial, legal, and tax issues, which could include the cost and formality of organization, ease of transferability of ownership interests, continuity of existence, management, control, ease of financing, method of distribution of profits, extent of personal liability, and taxation. Each form of legal entity has markedly different risk, financing, tax, and control implications for the acquirer. The selection of the appropriate entity can help to mitigate risk associated with the target firm, maximize financing flexibility, and minimize the net cost of the acquisition to the acquiring firm. Exhibit 2-2 relates common acquirer objectives with the legal forms best able to achieve the objectives.

The corporate structure or some variation is the most commonly used acquisition vehicle. This legal form tends to offer most of the features acquirers desire, including limited liability, financing flexibility, continuity of ownership, and deal flexibility (e.g., an option to engage in a tax-free deal). Moreover, the corporate structure enables the acquirer to retain control over

EXHIBIT 2-2 Selecting the Appropriate Acquisition Vehicle

Acquirer Objective	Appropriate Acquisition Vehicle
Limited Liability	C Corporation
	Subchapter S Corporation
	Limited Liability Company
	Limited Liability Partnership
Minimizing Taxes	Subchapter S Corporation
	General and Limited Partnership
	Limited Liability Company
	Employee Stock Ownership Plan
Minimizing Risk from the Target's Known and Unknown Liabilities	Holding Company
Maintaining Continuity of Existence	C Corporation
Achieving Financing Flexibility	C Corporation
Achieving Ease of Transferring Ownership	C Corporation
Sharing Risk and Resources	Partnership
	Limited Liability Company
Achieving a Tax-Free Merger	C Corporation
Short Duration of Existence*	Partnership

* In some instances, the partners may wish to achieve short-term objectives (e.g., the ABN Amro acquisition described in the outset of this chapter). Consequently, the partnership agreement is established with a stipulated dissolution date.

the implementation of the business plan and the acquisition process, something that may not be possible under partnership arrangements. When using a corporate structure as the acquisition vehicle, the target company typically is integrated into an existing operating division or product line within the corporation.

The corporate structure may also be appropriate for those situations in which there is a desire to share the risk of acquiring the target or because the partner has skills and attributes viewed as valuable in operating the target after closing. Used as an acquisition vehicle, the JV corporation or partnership offers a lower level of risk than a direct acquisition of the target firm by one of the JV corporate owners or individual partners. By acquiring the target firm through the JV, the corporate investor limits the potential liability to the extent of its investment in the joint venture. The joint venture arrangement also enables the inclusion of partners with a particular skill, proprietary knowledge, intellectual property, manufacturing facility, or distribution channel that offers potential synergy with the target firm.

There are many common motivations for using other legal forms. For small, privately owned firms, an employee stock ownership plan structure may be a convenient vehicle for transferring the owner's interest in the business to the employees, while offering significant tax advantages. Non-U.S. buyers intending to make additional acquisitions may prefer a holding company structure. The advantages of this structure over a corporate merger for both foreign and domestic firms are the ability to control other companies by owning only a small portion of the company's voting stock and to gain this control without getting shareholder approval.

If the form of acquisition is a statutory merger, all known and unknown or contingent liabilities are transferred to the buyer. Under these circumstances, the buyer may choose to change the type of acquisition vehicle to one that offers better protection from the target's liabilities, such as a holding company arrangement. By merging the target firm into a subsidiary of the holding company, the acquirer may better insulate itself from the target's liabilities. Again, though, this risk could be shared under a joint venture or partnership arrangement.

If the buyer and seller cannot agree on a price, the buyer may offer a purchase price that is contingent on the future performance of the target. The buyer may choose to acquire and to operate the acquired company as a wholly owned subsidiary within a holding company during the term of the "earnout." The *earnout* is an arrangement in which the target firm's owners receive additional payments if they are able to achieve certain goals negotiated in the agreement of purchase and sale. The holding company framework facilitates monitoring the target's performance during the earnout period and minimizes the potential for postearnout litigation initiated by earnout participants. Any attempt by the acquirer to realize certain cost savings by merging acquirer and target departments or functions can provide the target firm with a pretext for filing a lawsuit in which the participants argue that they were prevented from achieving the earnout goals as a result of actions taken by the parent firm.

CHOOSING THE APPROPRIATE POSTCLOSING ORGANIZATION

The postclosing organization refers to the legal or organizational framework used to operate the acquired firm following closing, and so can be the same as that chosen for the acquisition vehicle: corporate, general partnership, limited partnership, and limited liability company. Common organizational business structures include divisional and holding company arrangements. The choice will depend on the objectives of the acquirer. Exhibit 2-3 summarizes the legal and organizational forms most appropriate for achieving specific acquirer objectives.

A division generally is not a separate legal entity but rather an organizational unit, whereas a holding company can take on many alternative legal forms. An operating division is distinguishable from a legal subsidiary in that it typically will not have its own stock or board of directors that meet on a regular basis. However, divisions as organizational units may have managers with some of the titles normally associated with separate legal entities, such as a president or chief operating officer. Because a division is not a separate legal entity, its liabilities are the responsibility of the parent firm.

The postclosing organization needs to be discussed during negotiations to ensure that all parties are in agreement. In a friendly transaction in which the target's board and management support the takeover, the

EXHIBIT 2-3 Selecting the Appropriate Postclosing Organization

Acquirer Objective	Appropriate Postclosing Organization
Facilitating Postclosing Integration	C Corporation
	Divisional Structure
Preserving Unique Target Attributes (e.g., culture)	Holding Company
Maintaining Target Independence During Duration of an Earnout	Holding Company
Maintaining Continuity of Existence	C Corporation
Maintaining Financing Flexibility	C Corporation
Achieving Ease of Transferring Ownership	C Corporation
Allocation of Profits and Losses Among Members	Limited Liability Corporation
	Partnership
Tax Minimization	Subchapter S Corporation
	Limited Liability Company
	Partnership
	ESOP
Preserving Tax-Free Status of the Deal	Corporation
	Corporate Holding Company

acquirer generally will attempt to reach consensus during the negotiation process on how the acquired firm will be operated after closing.

The acquiring firm may have a variety of objectives for operating the target firm after closing, including facilitating postclosing integration, minimizing risk to owners from the target's known and unknown liabilities, minimizing taxes, passing through losses to shelter the owners' tax liabilities, preserving unique target attributes, maintaining target independence during the duration of an earnout, and preserving the tax-free status of the deal. If the acquirer is interested in integrating the target business immediately following closing, the corporate or divisional structure may be most desirable because it may make it possible for the acquirer to gain the greatest control. In other structures, such as JVs and partnerships, the dispersed ownership may render decision making slower or more contentious because it is more likely to depend on close cooperation and consensus building that may slow efforts at rapid integration of the acquired company.

In contrast, a holding company structure in which the acquired company is managed as a wholly owned subsidiary may be preferable when the target has significant known or unknown liabilities, an earnout is involved, the target is a foreign firm, or the acquirer is a financial investor. By maintaining the target as a subsidiary, the parent firm may be able to isolate significant liabilities within the subsidiary. Moreover, if necessary, the subsidiary could be placed under the protection of the U.S. Bankruptcy Court without jeopardizing the existence of the parent.

In an earnout agreement, the acquired firm must be operated largely independently from other operations of the acquiring firm to minimize the potential for lawsuits. If the acquired firm fails to achieve the goals required to receive the earnout payment, the acquirer may be sued for allegedly taking actions that prevented the acquired firm from reaching the necessary goals. When the target is a foreign firm, it is often appropriate to operate the target separately from the rest of the acquirer's operations because of the potential disruption from significant cultural differences. Prevailing laws in the foreign country may also affect the form of the organization. Finally, a financial buyer may use a holding company structure because it has no interest in operating the target firm for any length of time.

A partnership or JV structure may be appropriate if the risk associated with the target firm is believed to be high. Consequently, partners or JV owners can limit their financial exposure to the amount they have invested. The acquired firm may benefit from being owned by a partnership or JV because of the expertise that the different partners or owners might provide. The availability of such expertise may actually reduce the overall risk of managing the business.

A partnership or LLC may be most appropriate for eliminating double taxation and passing through current operating losses, tax credits, and loss carry forwards and carry backs to the owners. Cerberus Capital Management's conversion of its purchase of General Motors Acceptance Corporation (GMAC) from General Motors in 2006 from a C corporation to a limited liability company at closing reflected its desire to eliminate double taxation of income while continuing to limit shareholder liability. Similarly, when legendary investor Sam Zell masterminded a leveraged buyout of media conglomerate Tribune Company in 2007, he used an ESOP as the acquisition vehicle and a subchapter S corporation as the postclosing organization. The change in legal structure enabled the firm to save an estimated $348 million in taxes because S corporation profits are not taxed if distributed to shareholders—which in this case included the tax-exempt ESOP as the primary shareholder. It should be noted, however, that the deal's excessive leverage rendered it unable to withstand the meltdown of the credit markets in 2008, when it was forced to seek bankruptcy protection.

Finally, it is important to maintain the existence of the target firm to preserve the tax-free status of the transaction. Preserving the tax-free status of a deal results from satisfying conditions such as maintaining continuity of ownership, which requires previous target firm shareholders to receive a significant percentage of the purchase price in acquirer stock, and continuity of business enterprise, which requires that the acquirer retains a significant share of the target's assets after closing. These concepts are detailed in Chapter 5.

★ ★ ★

Which legal entity or business structure to use as an acquisition vehicle or postclosing organization—corporation, partnership, holding company, ESOP, or minority investment—requires careful consideration. There are various practical, financial, legal, and tax issues to address, and each form of legal entity has markedly different risk, financing, tax, and control implications for the acquirer.

A Case in Point: Vivendi Universal and GE Combine Entertainment Assets to Form NBC Universal

Ending a four-month auction process, Vivendi Universal SA agreed on October 5, 2003, to sell its Vivendi Universal Entertainment (VUE) businesses—film and television assets—to General Electric Corporation's wholly owned NBC subsidiary. Vivendi received a combination of GE stock and stock in the combined company valued at approximately $14 billion. The plan was that Vivendi would combine the Universal Pictures movie studio, its television production group, three cable networks, and the Universal theme parks with NBC, creating a new company with annual revenues of $13 billion based on 2003 pro forma statements.

This transaction was among many made by Vivendi in its effort to restore the firm's financial viability. Having started as a highly profitable distributor of bottled water, the French company undertook a diversification spree in the 1990s, which pushed the firm into many unrelated enterprises and left it highly in debt. With its stock plummeting, Vivendi had been under considerable pressure to reduce its leverage and refocus its investments.

Applying a multiple of 14 times estimated 2003 earnings before interest, tax, depreciation, and amortization (EBITDA) of $3 billion, the combined company had an estimated value of approximately $42 billion. This multiple is well within the range of comparable transactions and is consistent with the share price multiples of television media companies at the time. Of the $3 billion in 2003 EBITDA, GE provided $2 billion and Vivendi $1 billion. This valued GE's assets at $28 billion and Vivendi's at $14 billion, for a total of $42 billion in assets for NBC Universal.

Vivendi chose to receive a $4 billion cash infusion of liquidity at closing by selling its right to receive $4 billion in GE stock, as well as the transfer of $1.6 billion in debt carried by VUE's businesses to NBC Universal—a total of $5.6 billion in liquidity at closing. Vivendi also retained an ongoing ownership of approximately 20 percent in the new company, valued at $8.4 billion, with the option to sell that interest beginning in 2006 at fair market value, to which GE had the right of first refusal.

GE anticipated that its 80 percent ownership position in the combined company would be accretive (i.e., add to earnings) for GE shareholders beginning in the second full year of operation, with a neutral impact in the first year. In late 2009, GE and Comcast announced an agreement to form a joint venture corporation in which GE would contribute NBC Universal and Comcast selected TV network assets.

Things to Think About:

1. From a legal standpoint, identify the acquirer and the target firms.
2. What is the form of acquisition? Why might the parties involved in the transaction have agreed to this form?
3. What is the form of acquisition vehicle and the postclosing organization? Why do you think the legal entities you have identified were selected?
4. What is the form of payment or total consideration? Why do you believe the parties to this transaction agreed to this form of payment?
5. Based on a total valuation of $42 billion, Vivendi's assets contributed one-third and GE's two-thirds of the total value of NBC Universal. However, after the closing, Vivendi would own only a 20 percent equity position in the combined business. Why?

Answers can be found at:
www.elsevierdirect.com/companion.jsp?ISBN=9780123749499

CHAPTER 3

Selecting the Form of Payment

In November 2006, real estate investment trust Equity Office Products (EOP) signed a definitive agreement to be acquired by the Blackstone Group, a private equity investor, for $48.50 per share in cash. Publicly traded Vornado Realty countered with a $52.00 per share bid—60 percent in cash and the remainder in Vornado stock. But EOP favored the lower Blackstone offer because the value was more certain. It could take Vornado three or four months to get shareholder approval. What if the value of Vornado's stock declined or shareholders nixed the deal?

Vornado agreed to increase the cash portion of its offer and pay EOP shareholders the cash more quickly. However, Vornado made no offer to pay EOP shareholders a fee if its shareholders failed to approve the deal. The next day, Blackstone increased its bid to $55.25 and, eventually, to the winning bid of $55.50 per share.

The EOP board had carefully weighed the greater certainty of Blackstone's all-cash offer against the greater value of the combined cash and stock offer proposed by Vornado in making its decision. The form of payment was a key part of the board's considerations.

The form of payment refers to the composition of the purchase price for a target firm and can be structured in many different ways. That makes it a potent tool during negotiation to persuade the target to agree on terms acceptable to both the buyer and seller. In this chapter, you will learn about the alternative structures that can be used as payment in negotiating with a target firm's board and management and how these various forms of payment can be used to bridge differences between the seller's asking price and the price the acquirer is willing to pay. You will also learn about noncash and nonequity methods of payment, as well as ways to preserve shareholder value using various forms of collar arrangements.[1]

FORM OF PAYMENT OR TOTAL CONSIDERATION

Determining the proper form of payment can be complicated. Each form of payment can have significantly different implications for the parties

---

[1] For more information on this topic, see DePamphilis (2009), Chapter 11.

Mergers and Acquisitions Basics
ISBN: 978-0-12-374949-9, DOI: 10.1016/B978-0-12-374949-9.00003-8
55

involved in the transaction. Cash and noncash forms have advantages and disadvantages, depending on the specific circumstances of the transaction. Between 1980 and 2006, on average, cash accounted for 45 percent, stock for 30 percent, and cash/stock combinations for 25 percent of total transactions.[2]

Cash Payment

Cash is the simplest and most commonly used means of payment for acquiring shares or assets. Although cash payments generally result in an immediate tax liability for the target company's shareholders, there is no ambiguity about the value of the transaction as long as no portion of the payment is deferred. Whether cash is used as the predominant form of payment depends on a variety of factors, including the acquirer's current leverage, potential near-term earnings per share dilution, the seller's preference for cash or acquirer stock, and the extent to which the acquirer wishes to maintain control.

A highly leveraged acquirer may be unable to raise sufficient funds at an affordable rate of interest to make a cash purchase practical. Issuing new shares may result in significant erosion of the combined firm's earnings per share immediately following closing, which may prove to be unacceptable to current investors. The seller's preference for stock or cash will reflect the potential capital gains and the attractiveness of the acquirer's shares, as well as the desire for a tax-free transaction. Finally, a bidder may choose to use cash rather than issue voting shares if the voting control of its dominant shareholder is threatened as a result of the issuance of voting stock to acquire the target firm.[3] Issuing new voting shares would dilute the amount of control held by the dominant shareholder.

The preference for using cash appears to be much higher in Western European countries, where ownership tends to be more heavily concentrated in publicly traded firms, than in the United States. In Europe, 63 percent of publicly traded firms have a single shareholder who directly or indirectly controls 20 percent or more of the voting shares; the U.S. figure is 28 percent.[4]

Noncash Payment

The use of common equity may involve certain tax advantages for the parties involved—especially shareholders of the selling company. However, using shares is much more complicated than cash because it requires compliance

---

[2] Various issues of *Mergerstat Review* (2008).
[3] Faccio and Marsulis (2005).
[4] Faccio and Lang (2002).

with the prevailing security laws. Moreover, the acquirer's share price may suffer if investors believe the newly issued shares will result in a long-term dilution in earnings per share (EPS), that is, a reduction in an individual shareholder's claim on future earnings and the assets that produce those earnings.

Using convertible preferred stock or debt can be attractive to both buyers and sellers. These securities offer holders the right (but not the obligation) to convert to common stock at a predetermined "conversion" price. The conversion generally takes place after the firm's common share price exceeds the conversion price. Convertible preferred stock provides some downside protection to sellers in the form of continuing dividends, while providing upside potential if the acquirer's common stock price increases above the conversion point. Acquirers often find convertible debt attractive because of the tax deductibility of interest payments.

The major disadvantage in using securities of any type is that the seller may find them unattractive because of the perceived high risk of default or bankruptcy associated with the issuer. When offered common equity, shareholders of the selling company may feel the growth prospects of the acquirer's stock may be limited or that the historical volatility of the stock makes it unacceptably risky. Debt or equity securities may also be illiquid because of the small size of the resale market for such securities. Consequently, those wanting to sell such securities may do so only at a significant discount from their face value.

Acquirer stock may be a particularly useful form of payment when valuing the target firm is difficult, such as when the target firm has hard-to-value intangible assets, new product entries whose outcome is uncertain, or large research and development outlays. In accepting acquirer stock, a seller may have less incentive to negotiate an overvalued purchase price if it wishes to participate in any appreciation of the stock it receives. A seller could attempt to negotiate the highest price possible for its business and immediately sell its stock following closing.[5]

Other forms of noncash payment include real property, rights to intellectual property, royalties, earnouts, and contingent payments. Real property consists of things such as a parcel of real estate. So-called like-kind exchanges or swaps may have favorable tax consequences, such as the ability to defer

---

[5] In a sample of 735 acquisitions of privately held firms between 1995 and 2004, Officer (2007) found that acquirer stock was used as the form of payment about 80 percent of the time. The unusually high (for acquirers) 3.8 percent abnormal rate of return earned by acquirers in this sample around the announcement suggests that sellers willing to accept acquirer stock were more likely to see significant synergies in merging with the acquiring firm. Abnormal rates of returns are those earned by shareholders of acquirers or target firms in excess of returns that would normally be expected for investing in the shares of firms exhibiting a specific level of risk.

payment of capital gains taxes. Real property exchanges are most common in commercial real estate transactions. Granting the seller access to valuable licenses or franchises lessens the need to use cash or securities at the time of closing; however, it does raise the possibility that the seller could become a future competitor. It may require that the seller sign an agreement not to compete with the buyer for a certain period in selected markets. Using debt or other types of deferred payments reduces the overall present value of the purchase price to the buyer by shifting some portion of the purchase price into the future. By paying less at closing, the buyer is able to earn interest on money that would have been paid to the seller at that time.

Cash and Stock in Combination

Bidders may use a combination of cash and noncash forms of payment as part of their bidding strategies to broaden the appeal to target shareholders. The combination of cash and stock should appeal to sellers who value cash but who also want to participate in any appreciation in the acquirer's stock.

The bidding strategy of offering target firm shareholders multiple payment options increases the likelihood that more target firm shareholders will participate in a tender offer. It is a bidding strategy common in "auction" environments or when the bidder is unable to borrow the amount necessary to support an all-cash offer or unwilling to absorb the potential earnings per share dilution in an all-stock offer. The multiple option bidding strategy does, however, introduce a certain level of uncertainty in determining the amount of cash the acquirer ultimately will have to pay out to target firm shareholders because the number of shareholders choosing the all-cash or cash–and–stock option is not known prior to completion of the tender offer.

Acquirers resolve this issue by including a **proration clause** in tender offers and merger agreements that allows them to fix—at the time the tender offer is initiated—the total amount of cash they will ultimately have to pay out. For example, assume that the total cost of an acquisition is $100 million, the acquirer wishes to limit the amount of cash paid to target firm shareholders to one-half of that amount, and the acquirer offers the target firm's shareholders a choice of stock or cash. If the number of target shareholders choosing cash exceeds $50 million, the proration clause enables the acquirer to pay all target firm shareholders tendering their shares one-half of the purchase price in cash and the remainder in stock.

The highly politicized battle over nearly four months between Chevron and Chinese oil producer China National Offshore Oil Corporation (CNOOC) for ownership of Unocal illustrates some of the form of payment issues. Chevron, the second-largest U.S. oil producer, made a cash-and-stock bid in April 2005 valued at $61 per share, which the Unocal board accepted when it appeared CNOOC would not counterbid. Soon, though, CNOOC did make a counteroffer: an all-cash bid of $67 per share. Chevron amended the merger agreement with a new cash-and-stock bid valued at $63 per share in late July. Despite the significant difference in the value of the two bids, the Unocal board recommended its shareholders accept the amended Chevron bid. Why? There were growing doubts that U.S. regulatory authorities would approve a takeover by CNOOC.

In its strategy to win Unocal shareholder approval, Chevron offered Unocal shareholders three options for each of their shares: $69 in cash, 1.03 Chevron shares, or 0.618 Chevron shares plus $27.60 in cash. Unocal shareholders not electing any specific option would receive the combination option. The all-cash and all-stock offers were subject to proration to preserve an overall per share mix for all of the 272 million outstanding shares of Unocal common stock. This mix of cash and stock provided a "blended" value of about $63 per share of Unocal common stock on the day Unocal and Chevron entered into the amendment to the merger agreement on July 22, 2005—calculated by multiplying 0.618 by the $57.28 value of Chevron stock on that day, plus $27.60 in cash. This resulted in a targeted purchase price that was about 56 percent Chevron stock and 44 percent cash.

MANAGING RISK AND CLOSING THE GAP ON PRICE

In an all-cash transaction, the risks accrue entirely to the buyer. Even exhaustive due diligence can provide no assurance that the buyer will have uncovered all the risks associated with the target.

During the negotiation phase, the buyer and seller maneuver to share the perceived risk and apportion the potential returns. In doing so, substantial differences arise between what the buyer is willing to pay and what the seller believes its business is worth. Postclosing balance sheet adjustments and escrow accounts, earnouts and other contingent payments, contingent value rights, distributed or staged payouts, rights to intellectual property, licensing fees, and consulting agreements are all typically used to consummate the deal when the buyer and seller cannot reach agreement on purchase price.

Postclosing Price Adjustments

Postclosing price adjustment mechanisms include escrow or holdback accounts and adjustments to the target's balance sheet. Both mechanisms, most often used in cash rather than stock-for-stock purchases (particularly when the number of target shareholders is large), rely on an audit of the target firm to determine its "true" value, and generally are applicable only when what is being acquired is clearly identifiable, such as in a purchase of tangible assets. The buyer and seller typically share the cost of the audit.

Attempting to recover a portion of the shares paid to target shareholders may trigger litigation. For instance, Google's share-for-share purchase of YouTube involved a holdback of a portion of the purchase price because of the potential for copyright infringement litigation. Also, retaining a portion of the shares paid to target shareholders may signal a suspicion that there are problems with the target and trigger a sale by target shareholders of acquirer shares.

With *escrow accounts*, the buyer retains a portion of the purchase price until completion of a postclosing audit. *Balance sheet adjustments* are used most often in purchases of assets when there is a lengthy time between the agreement on price and the actual closing date. This may result from the need to obtain regulatory or shareholder approvals, or from ongoing due diligence. During this period, balance sheet items may change significantly—particularly those related to working capital—and so the purchase price is adjusted up or down. Balance sheet adjustments can be employed broadly to guarantee the value of the target firm's shareholder equity, or more narrowly to guarantee the value of working capital (i.e., the difference between current operating assets and operating liabilities) to ensure the acquirer will have sufficient liquidity to manage the target firm following closing.

With a shareholder equity guarantee, both parties agree to an estimated equity value as of the closing date. Target equity value is often calculated by taking the book value of equity on the balance sheet of the target firm at a given point and then increasing (or decreasing) it by the amount of net profit earned (or lost) between that date and closing. The purchase price is then increased or decreased to reflect any change in the book value of equity. A guarantee of this sort protects the buyer from risks such as any distribution of company profits by the seller after the signing date, or unusually large salary payments or severance benefits between the contract signing and closing dates. Although attractive to the buyer, the equity guarantee can be unattractive to the seller because of the difficulty in forecasting revenue during the period between signing and closing at the signing date. Consequently, sellers often will demand a higher purchase price to compensate them for this increase in risk.

Both parties may more easily reach an agreement with a working capital guarantee, which insures against fluctuations in the company's current operating assets. It is critical, though, to define clearly what constitutes working capital and equity in the agreement of purchase and sale because—similar to equity—what constitutes working capital is ambiguous.

As Exhibit 3-1 indicates, the buyer—to protect the buyer or seller—reduces the total purchase price by an amount equal to the decrease in net working capital or shareholders' equity of the target and increases the purchase price by any increase in these measures during this period.

Earnouts and Other Contingent Payments

Earnouts and warrants frequently are used whenever the buyer and seller cannot agree on the probable performance of the seller's business over some future period or when the parties involved wish to participate in the upside potential of the business. Earnout agreements may also be used to retain and motivate key target firm managers. An **earnout agreement** is a financial contract whereby a portion of the purchase price of a company is to be paid in the future, contingent on realizing future earnings level or some other performance measure agreed upon earlier. The terms of the earnout are stipulated in the agreement of purchase and sale. A subscription warrant, or simply **warrant**, is a type of security—often issued with a bond or preferred stock—that entitles the holder to purchase an amount of common stock at a stipulated price. The exercise price is usually higher than the price at the time the warrant is issued. Warrants may be converted over a period of many months to many years.

EXHIBIT 3-1 Balance Sheet Adjustments ($ Millions)

	Purchase Price		Purchase Price Reduction	Purchase Price Increase
	At Time of Negotiation	At Closing		
If Working Capital Equals	110	100	10	
If Working Capital Equals	110	125		15

In contrast, a rights offering to buy common shares usually has an exercise price below the current market value of the stock and a life of four to eight weeks.

The earnout typically requires that the acquired business be operated as a wholly owned subsidiary of the acquiring company under the management of the former owners or key executives. Both the buyer and seller are well advised to keep the calculation of such goals and resulting payments as simple as possible because the difficulty of measuring actual performance against the goals often creates disputes.

Earnouts may take many forms. Some are payable only if a certain performance threshold is achieved; others depend on average performance over several periods; and still others may involve periodic payments depending on the achievement of interim performance measures rather than a single, lump-sum payment at the end of the earnout period. The value of the earnout is often capped. In some cases, the seller may have the option to repurchase the company at some predetermined percentage of the original purchase price if the buyer is unable to pay the earnout at maturity.

Exhibit 3-2 illustrates how an earnout formula could be constructed reflecting these considerations. The purchase price has two components. At closing, the seller receives a lump-sum payment of $100 million. The seller and buyer agree to a baseline projection for a three-year period and that the seller will receive a fixed multiple of the average annual performance of the acquired business in excess of the baseline projection. Thus, the earnout provides an incentive for the seller to operate the business as effectively as possible. Normally, the baseline projection is what the buyer uses to value the seller's business. Shareholder value for the buyer is created whenever the actual performance of the acquired business exceeds the baseline projection and the multiple applied by investors at the end of the three-year period exceeds the multiple used to calculate the earnout payment. This assumes that the baseline projection accurately values the business and that the buyer does not overpay. When the anticipated multiple investors will pay for operating cash flow at the end of the three-year period is multiplied by projected cash flow, it is possible to estimate the potential increase in shareholder value.

Earnouts tend to shift risk from the acquirer to the seller in that a higher price is paid only when the seller has met or exceeded certain performance criteria. Earnouts may also create some perverse results during implementation. Management motivation may be lost if the acquired firm does not perform well enough to achieve any payout under the earnout

EXHIBIT 3-2 Hypothetical Earnout as Part of the Purchase Price

Purchase Price:

1. Lump sum payment at closing: The seller receives $100 million.

2. Earnout payment: The seller receives four times the excess of the actual average annual net operating cash flow over the baseline projection at the end of three years not to exceed $35 million.

Base Year (First Full Year of Ownership)	Year 1	Year 2	Year 3
Baseline Projection (Net Cash Flow)	$10	$12	$15
Actual Performance (Net Cash Flow)	$15	$20	$25

Earnout at the end of three years:[1]

$$\frac{(\$15 - \$10) + (\$20 - \$12) + (\$25 - \$15)}{3} \times 4 = \$30.67$$

Potential increase in shareholder value:[2]

$$\left[\frac{(\$15 - \$10) + (\$20 - \$12) + (\$25 - \$15)}{3} \times 10\right] - \$30.67 = \$46$$

[1] The cash flow multiple of 4 applied to the earnout is a result of negotiation before closing.
[2] The cash flow multiple of 10 applied to the potential increase in shareholder value for the buyer is the multiple the buyer anticipates that investors would apply to a three-year average of actual operating cash flow at the end of the three-year period.

formula or if the acquired firm exceeds the performance targets substantially, effectively guaranteeing the maximum payout under the plan.

Moreover, the management of the acquired firm may have an incentive to take actions not in the best interests of the acquirer. For example, management may cut back on advertising and training expenses to improve the operation's current cash flow performance, or make only those investments that improve short-term profits while ignoring those that may generate immediate losses but favorably affect profits in the long term. As the end of the earnout period approaches, managers may postpone investments to maximize their own bonuses under the earnout plan.

Earnouts may also be based on share of equity ownership when the business is sold, as Exhibit 3-3 illustrates.

To avoid various pitfalls associated with earnouts, you might find it appropriate to establish more than one target. For example, it may be appropriate to include a revenue, income, and investment target, although

EXHIBIT 3-3 Earnouts Based on Ownership Distribution

Distribution of ownership equity if average annual free cash flow is less than $5 million in years 3–5[1]

Entrepreneur:	75%
Private Investor:	25%
Total:	100%

Distribution of ownership equity if average annual free cash flow is greater than $5 million in years 3–5

Entrepreneur:	80%
Private Investor:	20%
Total:	100%

[1] A three-year average cash flow figure is used to measure performance to ensure that the actual performance is sustainable as opposed to an aberration.

this adds to the earnout's complexity.[6] New IRS rules may make earnouts less attractive than in the past.[7]

Contingent Value Rights

In M&A transactions, *contingent value rights* (CVRs) are commitments by the issuing company (i.e., the acquirer) to pay additional cash or securities

[6] Earnouts accounted for roughly 2.5 percent of total transactions in the 1990s. Kohers and Ang (2000) and Srikant, Frankel, and Wolfson (2001) found that earnouts are more commonly used when the targets are small, private firms or subsidiaries of larger firms, rather than for large, publicly traded firms. Such contracts are more easily written and enforced when there are relatively few shareholders. Earnouts tend to be most common in high–tech and service industries, when the acquirer and target firms are in different industries, when the target firm has a significant number of assets not recorded on the balance sheet, when buyer access to information is limited, and when little integration will be attempted. Kohers and Ang (2000) also showed that earnouts on average account for 45 percent of the total purchase price paid for private firms and 33 percent for subsidiary acquisitions, and that target firm shareholders tend to realize about 62 percent of the potential earnout amount. In transactions involving earnouts, acquirers earn abnormal returns of 5.39 percent around the announcement date, in contrast to transactions not involving contingent payments in which abnormal returns to acquirers tend to be zero or negative. The authors argue that the positive abnormal returns to acquiring company shareholders are a result of investor perception that with an earnout the buyer is less likely to overpay and more likely to retain key target firm talent.

[7] Revisions to accounting standards (Statement of Financial Accounting Standards 141R) that apply to business combinations went into effect on January 1, 2009. The fair value of earnouts and other contingent payouts must be estimated and recorded on the acquisition closing date. Changes in fair value resulting from changes in the likelihood or amount of the contingent payout must be recorded as charges to the income statement at that time. Under earlier accounting standards, contingent payments were charged against income only when they were actually paid.

to the holder of the CVR (i.e., the seller) if the share price of the issuing company falls below a specified level at some future date. CVRs provide a guarantee of future value of one of various forms of payment made to the seller—such as cash, stock, or debt—as of a given time. Although relatively rare, CVRs are sometimes granted when the buyer and seller are far apart on the purchase price, or when the target firm wants protection for any remaining minority shareholders fearful of being treated unfairly by the buyer.[8]

CVRs are not earnouts. Whereas earnouts represent call options for the target representing claims on future upside performance and are employed when there is substantial disagreement between the buyer and seller on price, CVRs are put options limiting downside loss on the form of payment received by sellers.[9]

Distributed or Staged Payouts

The purchase price payments can be contingent on the target satisfying an agreed-upon milestone, such as achieving a profit or cash flow target, successfully launching a new product, obtaining regulatory or patent approval, and so on. Distributing the payout over time manages risk to the acquirer by reducing some of the uncertainty about future cash flows. An acquirer

---

[8] Chatterjee and Yan (2008) argue that CVRs are issued most often when the acquiring firm issues stock to the target firm's shareholders that it believes it is undervalued—in what is often called information asymmetry, where one party has access to more information than others. The CVR represents a declaration by the acquirer that its current share price represents a floor and that it is confident it will rise in the future. Firms offering CVRs in their acquisitions tend to believe their shares are more undervalued than those acquirers using cash or stock without CVRs as a form of payment. The authors found that most CVRs are issued in conjunction with either common or preferred stock. Acquirers offering CVRs experience announcement period abnormal returns of 5.3 percent. Targets receiving CVRs earn abnormal announcement period returns of 18.4 percent. The size of the abnormal announcement period return is greater than that of firms not offering CVRs. The authors argue that investors view acquirers who offer CVRs as having knowledge of the postmerger performance of the acquired business not available to the broader market. Hence, the issuance of the CVR expresses buyer confidence in the future success of the transaction.

[9] These examples illustrate the use of CVRs. In Tembec. Inc.'s 1999 acquisition of Crestbrook Forest Products, Ltd., each Crestbrook shareholder received a contingent value right, enabling the shareholder to receive a one-time payment on March 31, 2000, the size of which (up to a maximum of $1.50 per share) depended on the amount by which the average price of wood pulp for 1999 exceeded $549/ton. In a 1995 transaction, MacAndrews & Forbes provided each shareholder of Abex Inc. a CVR per common share equal to $10.00 to ensure that Abex shareholders would receive at least that amount per share. In 2008, French utility EDF overcame resistance from certain British Energy shareholders by offering a combination of cash and a CVR that enabled investors to share in future profits whenever electrical output and energy prices rise. The amount of future payouts to shareholders would depend on the amount of the increase in profits.

could also avoid having to finance the entire cash purchase price in a large transaction at one time.[10]

Rights, Royalties, and Fees

The rights to intellectual property, royalties from licenses, and fee-based consulting or employment agreements are other forms of payment that can be used to close the gap between what the buyer is willing to offer and what the seller expects. The right to use a proprietary process or technology free or at a rate below that prevailing in the market may interest former owners considering business opportunities in which it would be useful. Note that such an arrangement, if priced at below-market rates or free to the seller, would represent taxable income to the seller. Obviously, such arrangements should be coupled with reasonable agreements not to compete in the same industry as their former firm. Contracts may be extended to both the former owners and their family members. By spreading the payment of consulting fees or salary over a number of years, the seller may be able to reduce the income tax liability that might have resulted from receiving a larger lump-sum purchase price.

Exhibit 3-4 summarizes the advantages and disadvantages of these various forms of payment. Note the wide range of options available to satisfy the various needs of the parties to the transaction.

USING COLLAR ARRANGEMENTS TO PRESERVE SHAREHOLDER VALUE

The period between announcement of the merger and the transaction close can be tumultuous for many M&A deals involving an exchange of stock. Unlike with all-cash deals, significant fluctuations in the acquirer's share price can threaten to change the terms of the deal or even to derail it altogether. Parties may need to renegotiate price as they approach closing.

A solution is for the acquirer and target firms to agree on a range or collar within which the stock price can change. By setting floors and caps on the stock portion of an acquisition's price, a collar gives both sides some assurance that the deal will retain its value despite share price fluctuations. Whereas most stock mergers have a fixed share exchange ratio, some transactions do allow the share exchange ratio to fluctuate within

---

[10] In 2008, the Swiss pharmaceuticals firm Novartis acquired Nestlé's controlling interest in eye care company Alcon for $39 billion. The deal called for Novartis to pay $11 billion for 25 percent of Alcon at closing and $28 billion in 2010 or 2011 for Nestlé's remaining 52 percent stake. Thus, Novartis deferred having to finance the bulk of the transaction amid the 2008 credit crisis.

EXHIBIT 3-4 Form of Payment Risk Evaluation

Form of Payment	Advantages	Disadvantages
Cash (including highly marketable securities)	*Buyer*: Simplicity.	*Buyer*: Must rely solely on protections afforded in contract to recover claims.
	Seller: Ensures payment if acquirer's creditworthiness questionable.	*Seller*: Creates immediate tax liability.
Stock – Common – Preferred – Convertible Preferred	*Buyer*: High P/E relative to seller's P/E may increase value of combined businesses.	*Buyer*: Adds complexity; potential EPS dilution.
	Seller: Defers taxes and provides potential price increase. Retains interest in the business.	*Seller*: Potential decrease in purchase price if the value of equity received declines. May delay closing because of registration requirements.
Debt – Secured – Unsecured – Convertible	*Buyer*: Interest expense tax deductible.	*Buyer*: Adds complexity and increases leverage.
	Seller: Defers tax liability on principal.	*Seller*: Risk of default.
Performance-Related Earnouts	*Buyer*: Shifts some portion of risk to seller.	*Buyer*: May limit integration of businesses.
	Seller: Potential for higher purchase price.	*Seller*: Increases uncertainty of sales price.
Purchase Price Adjustments	*Buyer*: Protection from eroding values of working capital before closing.	*Buyer*: Audit expense.
	Seller: Protection from increasing values of working capital before closing.	*Seller*: Audit expense. (Note that buyers and sellers often split the audit expense.)

(Continued)

EXHIBIT 3-4 (Continued)

Form of Payment	Advantages	Disadvantages
Real Property – Real Estate – Plant and Equipment – Business or Product Line	*Buyer:* Minimizes use of cash. *Seller:* May minimize tax liability.	*Buyer:* Opportunity cost. *Seller:* Real property may be illiquid.
Rights to Intellectual Property – License – Franchise	*Buyer:* Minimizes cash use. *Seller:* Gains access to valuable rights and spreads taxable income over time.	*Buyer:* Potential for setting up new competitor. *Seller:* Illiquid; income taxed at ordinary rates.
Royalties from – Licenses – Franchises	*Buyer:* Minimizes cash use. *Seller:* Spreads taxable income over time.	*Buyer:* Opportunity cost. *Seller:* Income taxed at ordinary rates.
Fee-Based – Consulting Contract – Employment Agreement	*Buyer:* Uses seller's expertise and removes seller as potential competitor for a limited time. *Seller:* Augments purchase price and allows seller to stay with the business.	*Buyer:* May involve demotivated employees. *Seller:* Limits ability to compete in same line of business. Income taxed at ordinary rates.
Contingent Value Rights	*Buyer:* Minimizes upfront payment. *Seller:* Provides for minimum payout guarantee.	*Buyer:* Commits buyer to minimum payout. *Seller:* Buyer may ask for purchase price reduction.
Staged or Distributed Payouts	*Buyer:* Reduces amount of upfront investment. *Seller* Reduces buyer angst about certain future events.	*Buyer:* May result in underfunding of needed investments. *Seller:* Lower present value of purchase price.

limits or boundaries to compensate for the uncertain value of the deal. These limits are the "collar," and such arrangements have become more common in recent years, with about 20 percent of stock mergers employing some form of collar as part of the bid structure.

A *share exchange ratio* is the number of shares of acquirer stock offered for each share of target stock. A *fixed or constant share exchange agreement* is one in which the number of acquirer shares exchanged for each target share is unchanged between the signing of the agreement of purchase and sale and closing. However, the value of the buyer's share price is allowed to fluctuate. Although the buyer will know exactly how many shares will have to be issued to consummate the transaction, both the acquirer and target will be subject to significant uncertainty about the final purchase price. The acquirer may find that the transaction will be much more expensive than anticipated if the value of its shares rises; in contrast, the seller may be greatly disappointed if the acquirer's share price declines.

A *fixed value agreement* fixes the value of the price per share by allowing the number of acquirer shares issued to vary so as to offset fluctuations in the buyer's share price. For example, an increase in the value of the acquirer's share price would result in the issuance of fewer acquirer shares to keep the value of the deal unchanged, whereas a decrease would require that new shares be issued. Because of potential dilution to acquirer shareholders if more shares than originally anticipated have to be issued, the buyer usually wants a reduction in the purchase price in exchange for a *collar agreement*, which provides for certain changes in the exchange ratio contingent on the level of the acquirer's share price around the effective date of the merger. This date is often defined as the average acquirer share price during a 10- to 20-day period preceding the closing date.

There are two primary types of collar agreements. A *floating collar agreement* may involve a fixed exchange ratio as long as the acquirer's share price remains within a narrow range, calculated as of the effective date of merger. For example, the acquirer and target may agree that the target would receive 0.5 shares of acquirer stock for each share of target stock, as long as the acquirer's share price remains between $20 and $24 per share during a 10-day period just prior to closing. This implies a collar around the bid price of $10 to $12 (i.e., 0.5 × $20 to 0.5 × $24) per target share. The collar arrangement may further stipulate that the target shareholder will receive $10 per share if the acquirer's share price falls below $20 per share, and that if the acquirer's share price exceeds $24 per share, the target shareholder will receive $12 per share. The acquirer and target shareholders can thus be assured that the actual bid or offer price will be between $10 and $12 per target share.

A *fixed payment collar agreement* (or *fixed value collar agreement*) guarantees that the target firm shareholder receives a certain dollar value of acquirer stock as long as the stock remains within a narrow range, and a fixed exchange ratio if the acquirer's average stock price is outside the bounds around the effective date of the merger. For example, the acquirer and target may agree that target shareholders would receive $40 per share, as long as the acquirer's share price remains within a range of $30 to $34 per share. This would be achieved by adjusting the number of acquirer shares exchanged for each target share; that is, the number of acquirer shares exchanged for each target share increases if the acquirer share price declines toward the lower end of the range and decreases if the acquirer share price increases. If the acquirer share price increases above $34 per share, target shareholders would receive 1.1765 shares of acquirer stock (i.e., $40/$34); if the acquirer share price drops below $30 per share, target shareholders would receive 1.333 shares of acquirer stock (i.e., $40/$30) for each target share they own.

Exhibit 3-5 identifies the advantages and disadvantages of various types of collar arrangements.

If the acquirer's share price has historically been highly volatile, the target may demand a collar to preserve the agreed-upon share price. Similarly, the acquirer may demand a collar if the target's share price has shown great variation in the past so as to minimize the potential for overpaying if the target's share price declines significantly relative to the acquirer's share price.[11]

The boards of directors of both the acquirer and target have a fiduciary responsibility to demand that merger terms be renegotiated if the value of the offer made by the bidder changes materially relative to the value of the target's stock, or if there has been any other material change in the target's operations. Merger contracts routinely contain "material adverse effects clauses" that provide a basis for buyers to withdraw from or renegotiate the contract. For example, in 2006, Johnson & Johnson (J&J) demanded that Guidant Corporation, a leading heart pacemaker manufacturer, accept a lower purchase price than the one agreed to in their merger agreement.

---

[11] From an evaluation of 1,127 stock mergers between 1991 and 1999, approximately one-fifth of which had collar arrangements, Officer (2004) concluded that collars are more likely to be used the greater the volatility of the acquirer share price compared to that of the target share price. He further concluded that the use of collars reduces substantially the likelihood that merger terms will have to be renegotiated—a costly proposition in terms of management time and legal and investment banking advice.

EXHIBIT 3-5 Advantages and Disadvantages of Alternative Collar Agreements

Agreement Type	Advantages	Disadvantages
Fixed Share Exchange Agreement	*Buyer*: Number of acquirer shares to be issued known with certainty; minimizes potential for overpaying.	*Buyer*: Actual value of transaction uncertain until closing; may necessitate renegotiation.
	Seller: Share exchange ratio known with certainty.	*Seller*: Same.
Fixed Value Agreement	*Buyer*: Transaction value known; protects acquirer from overpaying.	*Buyer*: Number of acquirer shares to be issued uncertain.
	Seller: Transaction value known; prevents significant reduction in purchase price due to acquirer share price variation.	*Seller*: May have to reduce purchase price to get acquirer to fix value.
Floating Collar Agreement	*Buyer*: Number of acquirer shares to be issued known within a narrow range.	*Buyer*: Actual value of transaction subject to some uncertainty.
	Seller: Greater certainty about share exchange ratio.	*Seller*: May have to reduce purchase price to get acquirer to float exchange ratio.
Fixed Payment Collar Agreement	*Buyer*: Reduces uncertainty about transaction value and potential for renegotiation.	*Buyer*: May still result in some overpayment.
	Seller: Same.	*Seller*: May still result in some underpayment.

J&J was reacting to news of government recalls of Guidant pacemakers and federal investigations that could materially damage the value of the firm, and had such a clause in its agreement. (This situation is discussed in more detail in the case example at the end of this chapter.)

Northrop Grumman's bid for TRW in 2002 illustrates how collars may be used to reduce risk to both acquirer and target shareholders. On March 5, 2002, Northrop Grumman initiated a tender offer for 100 percent of TRW's common shares by offering to exchange $47.00 in market value of Northrop Grumman common stock for each share of TRW common stock. The tender offer would expire at the end of the month. Implicitly, Northrop was offering to exchange 0.4352 (i.e., $47.00/$108.00) of its own common shares (based on its March 5 share price of $108.00) for each share of TRW stock. However, the actual share exchange ratio would be based on the average Northrop share price during the last five business days of the month. The $47.00 offer price was assured within a narrow range to TRW shareholders by placing a collar of plus 5 percent ($113.40) or minus 5 percent ($102.60) around the $108.00 Northrop share price on the tender offer announcement date.

The range of share exchange ratios implied by this collar is as follows:

$$0.4581 \text{ (i.e., } \$47.00/\$102.60) < 0.4352 \text{ (i.e., } \$47.00/\$108.00)$$
$$< 0.4145 \ (\$47.00/\$113.40)$$

The 0.4581 and 0.4145 share exchange ratios represent the maximum and minimum fraction of a share of Northrop stock that would be offered for each TRW share during this tender offer period. The collar gave TRW shareholders some comfort that they would receive $47 per share and enabled Northrop to determine the number of new shares it would have to issue within a narrow range to acquire TRW and the resulting impact on EPS of the combined firms.

CALCULATING SHARE EXCHANGE RATIOS

For public companies, the exchange of the acquirer's shares for the target's shares requires calculating the appropriate exchange ratio. The share exchange ratio (SER) is calculated by the following equation:

$$\text{SER} = P_{TO}/P_A$$

Defined in this manner, the SER can be less than, equal to, or greater than 1, depending on the value of the acquirer's shares relative to the offer price on the date set during the negotiation for valuing the transaction. The SER can be negotiated as a fixed number of shares of the acquirer's stock to be exchanged for each share of the target's stock. Alternatively, SER can be defined in terms of the ratio of the dollar value of the negotiated offer price per share of target stock (P_{TO}) to the dollar value of the acquirer's share price (P_A).

Exhibit 3-6 illustrates a calculation of the SER.

EXHIBIT 3-6 Calculating Share Exchange Ratios (SERs)

The price offered and accepted by the target company is $40 per share, and the acquiring company's share price is $60. What is the SER?

$$SER = \$40/\$60 = 0.6667$$

Implication: To complete the merger, the acquiring company will give 0.6667 shares of its own stock for each share of the target company.

★ ★ ★

The form of payment or total consideration may consist of cash, common stock, debt, or some combination of all three. When buyers and sellers cannot reach agreement on purchase price, they typically use post-closing price adjustment mechanisms.

Significant fluctuations in the acquirer's share price can threaten to change the terms of a deal or even derail it together. In share-for-share exchanges, acquirer and target firms often solve this problem by agreeing to a range within which the stock price can change to be able to preserve the value of the deal.

A Case in Point: Boston Scientific Overcomes Johnson & Johnson to Acquire Guidant: A Lesson in Bidding Strategies

Johnson & Johnson (J&J), the behemoth American pharmaceutical company, announced an agreement in December 2004 to acquire Guidant for $25.4 billion with a combination of cash and stock. Guidant is a leading manufacturer of products used in angioplasty procedures, including implantable heart defibrillators—the market for which has been growing at 20 percent annually. The move reflected J&J's desire to reenergize its slowing growth rate by diversifying into a more rapidly growing market.

Soon after the agreement was signed, Guidant became embroiled in a regulatory scandal over failure to inform doctors about rare malfunctions with its defibrillators, which ultimately led to a serious erosion of market share when five models had to be recalled. J&J would be absorbing risks from federal investigations and civil lawsuits. Citing its material adverse change clause, which is common in most M&A agreements, J&J set out to renegotiate—and succeeded in getting Guidant to accept a lower price of $63 a share in mid-November 2005.

This renegotiated agreement was not without its own risk. It gave Boston Scientific, a leading supplier of heart stents, an opportunity to intervene with a more attractive, informal offer—$72 per share. The offer price consisted of 50 percent stock and 50 percent cash. Boston Scientific saw the proposed acquisition as a vital step in the company's strategy of diversifying into a high-growth market. Stents prop open arteries leading to the heart, potentially preventing heart attacks; implantable defibrillators regulate heart beats through a series of electrical impulses. The bid pitted Boston Scientific against its major competitor in the drug-coated stent market. The two firms had been embroiled in litigation over stent technology.

Despite the more favorable offer, Guidant's board rejected Boston Scientific's offer in favor of an upwardly revised offer of $71 per share made by J&J on January 11, 2005. The board continued to support J&J's lower bid despite the furor it caused among big Guidant shareholders. J&J's market capitalization was nine times the size of Boston Scientific; along with its relative industry position, this kept the Guidant board enamored with J&J. The board argued that a J&J combination would result in much more rapid growth than merging with the much smaller Boston Scientific.

Boston Scientific realized it would win only if it made an offer that Guidant could not refuse without risking major shareholder lawsuits. J&J had greater borrowing capacity, and Boston Scientific knew that J&J also had the option of converting its combination stock and cash bid to an all-cash offer. Such an offer could be made a few dollars lower than Boston Scientific's bid because Guidant investors might view such an offer more favorably than one consisting of both stock and cash whose value could fluctuate between the signing of the agreement and the actual closing. This was indeed a possibility because the J&J offer did not include a collar arrangement.

Boston Scientific decided to boost the new bid to $80 per share, believing it would deter any further bidding from J&J, which had made public pronouncements that Guidant was already "fully valued." By doing so, Boston Scientific believed, J&J had created a public relations nightmare for itself. Raising its bid would upset J&J shareholders and make the company look like an undisciplined buyer.

According to its agreement with Guidant, J&J had five days to respond to the sweetened Boston Scientific bid. J&J refused to up its offer, saying that such an action would not be in the best interests of its shareholders. Boston Scientific had calculated correctly.

A side deal with Abbott Laboratories (Abbott) made the lofty Boston Scientific offer possible. The firm entered into an agreement with Abbott, in which Boston Scientific would divest Guidant's stent business while retaining the rights to Guidant's stent technology. In return, Boston Scientific received $6.4 billion in cash on the closing date: $4.1 billion for the divested assets, a loan of

$900 million, and Abbott's purchase of $1.4 billion of Boston Scientific stock. The additional cash helped fund the purchase price. This deal also helped Boston Scientific gain regulatory approval by enabling Abbott to become a competitor in the stent business. Merrill Lynch and Bank of America each lent $7 billion to fund a portion of the purchase price and provide the combined firms with additional working capital.

To complete the transaction, Boston Scientific paid $27 billion in cash and stock to Guidant shareholders and another $800 million as a breakup fee to J&J—and took $14.9 billion in new debt. Within days of Boston Scientific's winning bid, the firm was warned by the U.S. Food and Drug Administration to delay the introduction of new products until safety procedures improve. Longer term, whether the deal earns Boston Scientific shareholders an appropriate return on their investments depends largely on the continued rapid growth in the defibrillator market and the outcome of civil suits surrounding the recall of Guidant products.

Things to Think About:

1. What might J&J have done differently to avoid igniting a bidding war?
2. What evidence is given that J&J may not have taken Boston Scientific as a serious bidder?
3. How did Boston Scientific finance the deal?
4. How did Boston Scientific's financing strategy help the firm obtain regulatory approval for the transaction?
5. Explain how differing assumptions about market growth, potential synergies, and the size of the potential liability related to product recalls affected the bidding.

Answers can be found at:
www.elsevierdirect.com/companion.jsp?ISBN=9780123749499

CHAPTER 4

Selecting the Form of Acquisition

Acquirers may purchase the stock or assets of a target firm; the mechanism for transferring ownership is called the *form of acquisition*. Each form affects the negotiation and deal-structuring process differently, and each has a number of advantages and disadvantages depending on the point of view—whether buyer or seller.[1]

FORM OF ACQUISITION

The form of acquisition describes the mechanism for conveying or transferring ownership of assets or stock and associated liabilities from the target to the acquiring firm. There are several commonly used methods.

An *asset purchase* involves the sale of all or a portion of the assets of the target to the buyer or its subsidiary in exchange for buyer stock, cash, or debt. The buyer may assume all, some, or none of the target's liabilities. The purchase price is paid directly to the target firm. A *stock purchase* involves the sale of the outstanding stock of the target to the buyer or its subsidiary by the target's shareholders. The target's shareholders may receive acquirer stock, cash, debt, or some combination for their shares. Unlike in an asset purchase, the purchase price in a stock purchase is paid to the target firm's shareholders. This is the biggest difference between the two methods, and has significant tax implications for the seller's shareholders (as detailed in the following chapter).

A *statutory merger* involves the combination of the target with the buyer or a subsidiary formed to complete the merger. The corporation surviving the merger can be the buyer, target, or buyer's subsidiary. The assets and liabilities of the corporation that ceases to exist are merged into the surviving firm as a matter of law governed by the statutes of the state in which the combined businesses will be incorporated. State statutes typically address the percentage of total voting stock required for approval of

---

[1] For more information on this topic, see DePamphilis (2009), Chapter 11.

Mergers and Acquisitions Basics
ISBN: 978-0-12-374949-9, DOI: 10.1016/B978-0-12-374949-9.00004-X

the transaction, who is entitled to vote, how the votes are counted, and the rights of dissenting voters. In a statutory merger, dissenting or minority shareholders are required to sell their shares, although some statutes may grant them the right to be paid the appraised value of their shares. Minority shareholders are forced out to avoid a holdout problem in which a minority of shareholders can delay the completion of a transaction unless they receive compensation in excess of the acquisition purchase price. *Stock-for-stock* or *stock-for-assets* transactions represent alternatives to a merger.

An asset purchase has an important advantage over a purchase of stock: no minority shareholders remain. Shareholders cannot be forced to sell their shares in an asset purchase. The acquirer may choose to operate the target firm as a subsidiary, in which some target shareholders—albeit a minority—could remain. Consequently, the buyer's subsidiary must submit annual reports to these shareholders, hold shareholder meetings, and elect a board of directors by allowing shareholder votes, all while being exposed to potentially dissident shareholders. Moreover, a new owner may void a previously existing labor contract if less than 50 percent of the newly created firm belongs to the union. However, if the employer and union negotiated a "successor clause" into their collective bargaining agreement covering the workforce in the target firm, the terms of the agreement may still apply to the workforce of the new business.

Exhibit 4-1 highlights the primary advantages and disadvantages of these alternative forms of acquisition.

Purchase of Assets

In an asset purchase, a buyer acquires all rights a seller has to an asset for cash, stock, or some combination. Many state statutes require shareholder approval of a sale of "substantially all" of the target's assets. An asset purchase may be the most practical way to complete the transaction when the acquirer is interested only in a product line or division of a parent firm with multiple product lines or divisions that are not organized as separate legal subsidiaries. The seller retains ownership of the shares of stock of the business. The buyer must either create a new entity or use another existing business unit as the acquisition vehicle for the transaction. Only assets and liabilities specifically identified in the agreement of purchase and sale are transferred to the buyer.

Asset purchases are generally more complicated than mergers or stock purchases because ownership of the assets and liabilities and any related contracts must actually be transferred, often by filing documents with government offices. This may involve additional fees. Other considerations that

EXHIBIT 4-1 Advantages and Disadvantages of Alternative Forms of Acquisition

Alternative Forms	Advantages	Disadvantages
Cash Purchase of Assets	*Buyer:* • Allows targeted purchase of assets • Asset writeup • May renegotiate union and benefits agreements, assuming no successor clause in union contract • May avoid need for shareholder approval • No minority shareholders *Seller:* • Maintains corporate existence and ownership of assets not acquired • Retains NOLs and tax credits	*Buyer:* • Lose NOLs[1] and tax credits (see Chapter 5) • Lose rights to intellectual property • May require consents to assignment of contracts • Exposed to liabilities transferring with assets (e.g., warranty claims) • Subject to taxes on any gains resulting in asset writeup • Subject to lengthy documentation of assets in contract *Seller:* • Potential double taxation if shell liquidated • Subject to state transfer taxes • Necessity of disposing of unwanted residual assets • Requires shareholder approval if substantially all the firm's assets sold

(Continued)

EXHIBIT 4-1 (Continued)

Alternative Forms	Advantages	Disadvantages
Cash Purchase of Stock	*Buyer:* • Assets/liabilities transfer automatically • May avoid need to get consents to assignment of contracts • Less documentation • NOLs and tax credits pass to buyer • No state transfer taxes • May insulate from target liabilities if kept as subsidiary • No shareholder approval if funded by cash or debt • Enables circumvention of target's board in hostile tender offer • May be less complex than asset purchase if target has relatively few shareholders *Seller:* • Liabilities generally pass to the buyer • May receive favorable tax treatment if acquirer stock received in payment	*Buyer:* • Responsible for known and unknown liabilities • No asset writeup unless 338 election taken by buyer[2] • Union and employee benefit agreements do not terminate • Potential for minority shareholders[3] *Seller:* • Loss of NOLs and tax credits • Favorable tax treatment lost if buyer adopts 338 election (see Chapter 5)
Statutory Merger	*Buyer:* • Flexible form of payment (stock, cash, or debt) • Assets and liabilities transfer automatically, without lengthy documentation	*Buyer:* • May have to pay dissenting shareholders' appraised value of stock

	Advantages	Disadvantages
	• No state transfer taxes • No minority shareholders as shareholders required to tender shares (minority freeze-out) • May avoid shareholder approval *Seller:* • Favorable tax treatment if purchase price primarily in acquirer stock • Allows for continuing interest in combined companies • Flexible form of payment	• May be time consuming because of the need for target shareholder and board approvals, which may delay closing *Seller:* • May be time consuming • Target firm often does not survive • May not qualify for favorable tax status
Stock-for-Stock Transaction	*Buyer:* • May operate target company as a subsidiary • See cash purchase of stock above *Seller:* • See cash purchase of stock above	*Buyer:* • May postpone realization of synergies • See cash purchase of stock above *Seller:* • See cash purchase of stock above
Stock-for-Assets Transaction	*Buyer:* • See cash purchase of assets above *Seller:* • See cash purchase of assets above • Provides greater strategic flexibility	*Buyer:* • May dilute buyer's ownership position • See cash purchase of assets above *Seller:* • See cash purchase of assets above
Staged Transactions		• May postpone realization of synergies

[1] Net operating loss carry forwards or carry backs which can be used to offset future tax liabilities or to recover taxes paid in the past.

[2] In Section 338 of the U.S. tax code, the acquirer in a purchase of 80 percent or more of the stock of the target may elect to treat the acquisition as if it were an acquisition of the target's assets.

[3] Minority shareholders in a subsidiary may be eliminated by a so-called "back-end" merger following the initial purchase of target stock. As a result of the merger, minority shareholders are required to abide by the majority vote of all shareholders and sell their shares to the acquirer. If the acquirer owns more than 90 percent of the target's shares, it may be able to use a short form merger, which does not require any shareholder vote.

must be addressed include the possible transfer of the corporate name and the rehiring of the employees by the acquirer of the assets. These employees are needed to operate the acquired assets.

In a *cash-for-assets* acquisition, the acquirer pays cash for the seller's assets and may choose to accept some or all of the seller's liabilities. Seller shareholders must approve the transaction whenever the seller's board votes to sell all or "substantially all" of the firm's assets. For example, when Valero Oil and Gas purchased substantially all of the assets of bankrupt ethanol manufacturer VeraSun for $280 million in early 2009—five refineries and one under construction—it required VeraSun shareholder approval. Despite that the purchase was fewer than half of VeraSun's total number of refineries, it represented about three-quarters of the firm's production capacity.

Selling "substantially all" assets does not necessarily mean that most of the firm's assets have been sold; rather, it could mean that even a relatively small percentage of the firm's total assets are critical to the ongoing operation of the business. Hence, the firm may be forced to liquidate if a sale of assets does not leave the firm with "significant continuing business activity"—that is, at least 25 percent of total pretransaction operating assets and 25 percent of pretransaction income or revenue. Unless required by the firm's bylaws, the buyer's shareholders do not vote to approve the transaction.

After receiving the cash from the buyer, the selling firm may reinvest it all in its operations, reinvest some and pay some as a dividend to shareholders, or pay it out in a single liquidating distribution. When substantially all of the selling firm's assets are acquired, the selling firm's shares are extinguished if shareholders approve the liquidation of the firm. After any liabilities not assumed by the buyer are paid, the assets remaining with the seller and the cash received from the acquiring firm are transferred to the seller's shareholders in a liquidating distribution.

In a *stock-for-assets* transaction, when approved by the seller's board and shareholders, the seller's shareholders receive buyer stock in exchange for the seller's assets and liabilities. In a second stage, the seller dissolves the corporation following shareholder ratification of such a move, leaving its shareholders with buyer stock. Consequently, the shareholders of the two firms have effectively pooled their ownership interests in the buyer's corporation, which holds the combined assets and liabilities of both firms. Many states and public stock exchanges give acquiring firm shareholders the right to approve a stock-for-assets transaction if the new shares issued by the buyer exceed more than 20 percent of the firm's total shares outstanding before the transaction.

Advantages and Disadvantages from the Buyer's Perspective

There are both advantages and disadvantages to a purchase of assets from the buyer's perspective. The *advantages* are many. Buyers can be selective as to which assets of the target to purchase. The buyer is generally not responsible for the seller's liabilities, unless specifically assumed under the contract. However, the buyer can be held responsible for certain liabilities such as environmental claims, property taxes, and, in some states, substantial pension liabilities and product liability claims. To protect against such risks, buyers usually insist on **indemnification** that holds the seller responsible for payment of damages resulting from such claims. Of course, this is of value only as long as the seller remains solvent. Indemnification is explained in more detail later in this chapter.[2]

The October 7, 2007, takeover of ABN Amro illustrates the advantages of being able to purchase only certain assets. The buyer consortium—The Royal Bank of Scotland, Spain's Banco Santander, and Belgium's Fortis Bank—won control of ABN, the largest bank in the Netherlands, in a buyout valued at $101 billion. The deal was made possible by a buyer group banding together to buy the firm after reaching agreement as to which of the target's assets would be owned by each member of the consortium after closing.

Another advantage is that asset purchases also enable buyers to revalue acquired assets to market value on the closing date under the purchase method of accounting (a form of financial reporting of business combinations detailed in Chapter 6). This increase, or **step-up**, in the tax basis of the acquired assets to fair market value provides for higher depreciation and amortization expense deductions for tax purposes. Such deductions are said to shelter pretax income from taxation (detailed in Chapter 5). Buyers are generally free of any undisclosed or contingent liabilities. Absent successor clauses in the contract, the asset purchase results in the termination of union agreements, thereby providing an opportunity to renegotiate agreements viewed as too restrictive. Benefits plans may be maintained or terminated at the acquirer's discretion. Buyers, though, may be reluctant to terminate contracts and benefits plans because of the potential undermining of employee morale and productivity.

Even with all these advantages, there are still several *disadvantages* to a purchase of assets from the buyer's perspective. The buyer loses the seller's net operating losses and tax credits. Rights to assets such as licenses, franchises,

---

[2] Note that in most agreements of purchase and sale, buyers and sellers agree to indemnify each other from claims for which they are directly responsible. Liability under such arrangements usually is subject to specific dollar limits and is in force only for a specific period.

and patents cannot be transferred to buyers. Such rights are viewed as belonging to the owners of the business—the target shareholders. These rights can be difficult to transfer because of the need to obtain consent from the U.S. Patent Office or other agency issuing the rights. The buyer must seek the consent of customers and vendors to transfer existing contracts to the buyer. The transaction often is more complex and costly because acquired assets must be listed in appendices to the definitive agreement, the sale of and titles to each asset transferred must be recorded, and state title *transfer taxes* must be paid. Moreover, a lender's consent may be required if the assets to be sold are being used as collateral for loans.

The acquisition by Cadbury Schweppes plc (a confectionary and beverage company headquartered in London, England) of Adams Inc. from Pfizer in 2003 illustrates the complexity of an asset purchase. Cadbury bought 100 percent of Adams for $4.2 billion. Many Adams employees had positions with both the parent and operating unit, and the parent supplied numerous support services to its subsidiary. Adams also operated in 40 countries, representing 40 different legal jurisdictions—quite typical in the purchase of a unit of a larger company.

Whether to transfer assets or stock was a decision that depended on which form gave Cadbury and Pfizer optimum tax advantages. The decision was made to execute a single asset and stock sale and purchase agreement (i.e., the master agreement), which transferred the relevant U.S. assets and stock in Adams's subsidiaries to Cadbury. The master agreement contained certain overarching terms, including closing conditions, representations and warranties, covenants, and indemnification clauses that applied to all legal jurisdictions. However, the master agreement required Pfizer or Adams to enter into separate local "implementation" agreements—done to complete the transfer of either Adams's assets in non-U.S. jurisdictions or shares in non-U.S. Adams's subsidiaries to local Cadbury subsidiaries, depending on which provided the most favorable tax advantages and, where necessary, to accommodate differences in local legal conditions. The parties entered into more than 20 such agreements to transfer asset and stock ownership, all using the master agreement as a template. Written in English, the various contracts were governed by the laws of New York State, where Pfizer is headquartered, except where there was a requirement that the law governing the contract be that of the local country.

Advantages and Disadvantages from the Seller's Perspective
As for the buyer, there are both advantages and disadvantages to a purchase of assets for the seller. Among the *advantages*, sellers are able to maintain

their corporate existence and hence ownership of tangible assets not acquired by the buyer and of intangible assets such as licenses, franchises, and patents. The seller retains the right to use the corporate identity in subsequent marketing programs, unless ceded to the buyer as part of the transaction. The seller also retains the right to use all tax credits and accumulated net operating losses, which can be used to shelter future income from taxes. Such tax considerations remain with the holders of the target firm's stock.

The *disadvantages* for the sell included several issues related to taxes, including that the seller may be subject to double taxation. If the tax basis in the assets or stock is low, the seller may experience a sizable gain on the sale. In addition, if the corporation subsequently is liquidated, the seller may be responsible for the recapture of taxes deferred as a result of the use of accelerated rather than straight-line depreciation. If the number of assets transferred is large, the amount of state transfer taxes may become onerous. Whether the seller or buyer actually pays the transfer taxes or they are shared is negotiable. If substantially all of the target's assets are to be sold, approval must be obtained from the target's shareholders.

Purchase of Stock

Stock purchases often are viewed as the purchase of all of a target firm's outstanding stock. In effect, the buyer replaces the seller as owner; the business continues to operate without interruption; and the seller has no ongoing interest in, or obligation with respect to, the assets, liabilities, or operations of the business.

In *cash-for-stock* or *stock-for-stock* transactions, the buyer purchases the seller's stock directly from the seller's shareholders. If the target is a private firm, the purchase is completed by a stock purchase agreement signed by the acquirer and target's shareholders, if they are few in number. For a public company, the acquiring firm making a tender offer to the target firm's shareholders would consummate the purchase. A tender offer is employed because public company shareholders are likely to be too numerous to deal with individually. The tender offer would be considered friendly or hostile depending on whether it was supported by the board and management of the target firm.

This is in marked contrast to a statutory merger in which the boards of directors of the firms involved must first ratify the proposal before submitting it to their shareholders for approval. Consequently, a purchase of stock is the approach most often taken in hostile takeovers. If the buyer is unable to convince all of the seller's shareholders to tender their shares, then a minority of seller shareholders remains outstanding. The target firm would then be viewed not as a wholly owned but rather as a partially owned subsidiary of the buyer or acquiring company. No seller shareholder approval is required in such transactions because the seller's shareholders are expressing approval by tendering their shares. As required by most major stock exchanges, acquiring company shareholders have the right to approve a stock-for-stock transaction if the amount of new acquirer shares issued exceeds 20 percent of the firm's total outstanding shares before the transaction takes place.

Advantages and Disadvantages from the Buyer's Perspective

When it comes to the purchase of stock, there are a number of *advantages* for the buyer. All assets are transferred with the target's stock, resulting in less need for documentation to complete the transaction. State asset transfer taxes may be avoided with a purchase of shares. Net operating losses and tax credits pass to the buyer with the purchase of stock. The right of the buyer to use the target's name, licenses, franchises, patents, and permits also is preserved. Furthermore, the purchase of the seller's stock provides for the continuity of contracts and corporate identity, which obviates the need to renegotiate contracts and enables the acquirer to employ the brand recognition that may be associated with the name of the target firm. However, the consent of some customers and vendors may be required before a contract is transferred; this may apply as well to some permits.

Although the acquirer's board normally approves any major acquisition, approval by shareholders is not required if the purchase is financed primarily with cash or debt. If stock that has not yet been authorized is used, shareholder approval is likely to be required. Neither the target's board nor shareholders need to approve a sale of stock; however, shareholders may simply refuse to sell their stock.

Among the *disadvantages*, the buyer is liable for all unknown, undisclosed, or contingent liabilities. The seller's tax basis is carried over to the buyer at historical cost, unless the seller consents to take certain tax code elections. These elections potentially can create a tax liability for the seller and therefore are used infrequently. Consequently, there is no step-up in the cost basis of assets, and no tax shelter is created. Dissenting shareholders have the right to have their shares appraised, with the option of being paid the appraised value of their shares or remaining minority shareholders. The purchase of stock does not terminate existing union agreements or employee benefit plans.

The existence of minority shareholders creates significant administrative costs and practical concerns. The parent incurs significant additional expenses to submit annual reports, hold annual shareholder meetings, and conduct a formal election process. Furthermore, implementing strategic business moves may be inhibited. The obstacle minority shareholders can represent is illustrated in DaimlerChrysler's effort to sell its MTU Friedrichshafen diesel engine assembly operations. Unable to reach agreement with enough shareholders to enable it to sell the business, DaimlerChrysler had to purchase the holdings of these minority shareholders, comprising less than 10 percent of the firm's outstanding stock.

Advantages and Disadvantages from the Seller's Perspective

Sellers generally prefer a stock purchase rather than an asset purchase because of its *advantages*. First, this type of purchase allows them to step away from the business and be completely free of future obligations. The seller is able to defer paying taxes. If stock is received from the acquiring company, the target's shareholders pay taxes only when the stock is sold. All obligations, disclosed or otherwise, transfer to the buyer. This advantage for the seller usually is attenuated by the buyer's insistence that it be indemnified from damages resulting from any undisclosed liability. However, as previously noted, indemnification clauses in contracts generally are in force for only a limited time. Finally, the seller is not left with the problem of disposing of assets that the seller does not wish to retain but that were not purchased by the acquiring company.

There are, though, *disadvantages* for the seller. For instance, the seller cannot pick and choose the assets to be retained. Furthermore, the seller loses all net operating losses, tax credits, and potential tax savings. Chapter 5 discusses net operating loss carry forwards and tax credits in detail.

Mergers

When a **merger** is used to consummate the transaction, the legal structure may take on one of many forms. In a merger, two or more firms combine, and all but one legally cease to exist. The combined organization continues under the original name of the surviving firm. Typically, shareholders of the target firm exchange their shares for those of the acquiring firm after a shareholder vote approving the merger. The minority shareholders who vote against the merger are required to accept it and exchange their shares for those of the acquirer.

In most states, if the parent firm is the primary shareholder in the subsidiary, the merger—this type is called a *short form merger*—does not require approval of the parent's shareholders. The principal requirement is that the parent's ownership exceeds the minimum threshold set by the state. For example, Delaware allows a parent corporation to merge with a subsidiary without a shareholder vote if the parent owns at least 90 percent of the outstanding voting shares.

Statutory and Subsidiary Mergers

In a *statutory merger*, the acquiring company assumes the assets and liabilities of the target in accordance with the statutes of the state in which the combined companies will be incorporated. A *subsidiary merger* involves the target becoming a subsidiary of the parent. To the public, the target firm may be operated under its brand name, but will be owned and controlled by the acquirer.

Most mergers are structured as subsidiary mergers in which the acquiring firm creates a new corporate subsidiary that merges with the target, with the target surviving. By using a reverse triangular merger, the acquirer may be able to avoid seeking approval from its shareholders. Although merger statutes require approval by shareholders of both the target and acquiring firms, the parent of the acquisition subsidiary is the shareholder. Just as in a stock purchase, an assignment of contracts is generally not necessary because the target survives. In contrast, an assignment is required in a forward triangular merger because the target is merged into the subsidiary with the subsidiary surviving.

Statutory Consolidations

Although the terms *merger* and *consolidation* often are used interchangeably, this is not always accurate. Technically, a *statutory consolidation*, which involves two or more companies joining to form a new company, is not a merger. All legal entities that are consolidated are dissolved as the new company is formed, usually with a new name, whereas in a merger either the acquirer or target survives. The 1999 combination of Daimler-Benz and Chrysler to form DaimlerChrysler is an example of a consolidation.

The new corporate entity created as a result of consolidation, or the surviving entity following a merger, usually assumes ownership of the assets and liabilities of the merged or consolidated organizations. Stockholders in merged companies typically exchange their shares for shares in the new company.

Mergers of Equals

A *merger of equals* is a merger framework usually applied whenever the participants are comparable in size, competitive position, profitability, and market capitalization—which can make it unclear whether one party is ceding control to the other and which party provides the greatest synergy. Consequently, target firm shareholders rarely receive any significant premium for their shares. It is common for the new firm to be managed by the former CEOs of the merged firms as co-equals, and for the new firm's board to have equal representation from the boards of the merged firms.[3] In such transactions, it is relatively uncommon for the ownership split to be equally divided.[4]

The 1998 formation of Citigroup from Citibank and Travelers is an example of a merger of equals.

Tender Offers

Tender offers refer to solicitations to buy stock. When a firm extends an offer to its own shareholders to buy back stock, it is called a *self-tender offer*. A *hostile tender offer* is a takeover tactic in which the acquirer bypasses the target's board and management and goes directly to the target's shareholders with an offer to purchase their shares. Unlike a merger in which the minority must agree to the terms of the agreement negotiated by the board after the majority of the firms' shareholders (i.e., 50.1 percent or more) approve the proposal, the tender offer specifically allows for minority shareholders to approve or deny the merger. In a traditional merger, minority shareholders are said to be frozen out of their positions because they ultimately must tender their shares (although they may have appraisal rights). The majority approval requirement of mergers is intended to prevent minority shareholders from stopping a merger until they are paid a premium over the purchase price agreed to by the majority.

An alternative to a traditional merger that accomplishes the same objective is the *two-step acquisition*. The acquirer first buys through a stock purchase the majority of the target's outstanding stock from the target's shareholders in a tender offer and then follows up with a *squeeze-out merger* or *back-end merger* approved by the acquirer as majority shareholder. Minority shareholders are required to take the acquisition consideration in

---

[3] Research by Wulf (2004) suggests that the CEOs of target firms often negotiate to retain a significant degree of control in the merged firm for both their board and management in exchange for a lower premium for their shareholders.

[4] According to Mallea (2008), only 14 percent have a 50/50 split.

the back-end merger because of the state statutory provisions designed to prevent a minority from delaying completion of a merger until they receive better terms. Two-step acquisitions sometimes are used to make it more difficult for another firm to make a bid because the merger can be completed quickly. In summary, whether a one-step (i.e., the traditional merger) or two-step merger involving a stock purchase followed by a back-end merger, all stock held by each target shareholder gets converted into the merger consideration, regardless of whether the shareholder voted for the merger.

In March 2009, Merck Pharmaceuticals—seeking to close the deal quickly—acquired much smaller rival Schering-Plough through a two-step merger. Merck wanted to prevent a potential bidding war with Johnson & Johnson and the loss of profits from a joint venture Schering had with Johnson & Johnson. The deal was constructed as a reverse triangular merger in which a wholly owned shell subsidiary (i.e., a merger subsidiary) of Schering would be merged into Merck, with Merck surviving as a wholly owned Schering subsidiary. Thus, Schering is viewed as the acquiring firm, even though the combined firms were renamed Merck; the Merck CEO became the CEO of the merged firms; and Merck put up all the money to finance the transaction. Merck was merged into Schering subsequent to closing. By positioning Schering as the acquirer, Merck wanted to avoid triggering a change of control provision in a longstanding drug distribution agreement between Johnson & Johnson and Schering, under which J&J would be able to cancel the agreement and take full ownership of the drugs.

In contrast, the Swiss pharmaceutical giant Roche reached agreement on March 12, 2009, to acquire the remaining 44 percent of Genentech it did not already own, but was unable to employ the back-end merger approach. Roche was bound by an affiliation agreement between the two firms that governed prior joint business relationships. It required, in the event of a merger with Genentech, that Roche must receive a favorable vote from the majority of the remaining Genentech shares it did not already own or offer the remaining Genentech shareholders a price equal to or greater than the average of fair values of such shares as determined by two investment banks appointed by the Genentech board of directors.

Board Approvals

Unlike purchases of target stock, mergers require approval of both the acquirer's and the target's board of directors and the subsequent submission of the proposal to the shareholders of both firms. Unless otherwise required by a firm's bylaws, a simple majority of all the outstanding voting shares must ratify the proposal. The merger agreement must then be filed with the appropriate authorities of the state in which the merger is to be consummated.

There are three exceptions under which no vote is required by the acquirer's (i.e., surviving firm) shareholders. The first involves a transaction not considered material, in that the acquirer issues new shares to the target's shareholders in an amount comprising less than 20 percent of the acquirer's voting shares outstanding before the transaction. The second is when a subsidiary is being merged into the parent and the parent owns a substantial majority (over 90 percent in some states) of the subsidiary's stock before the transaction. The third exception involves use of a triangular merger, in which the acquirer establishes a merger subsidiary in which it is the sole shareholder. The subsidiary is funded by the consideration to be used in the merger, and the target firm and the subsidiary merge. Because the acquirer is the sole shareholder in the operating subsidiary, the only approval required might be that of the board of directors of the subsidiary, which may be essentially the same as that of the parent or acquiring company. However, acquirer shareholders may still be required by the firm's bylaws to vote to authorize creation of new shares of stock to be offered in the transaction. The subsidiary may be merged with the parent at a later date.

Form of Payment

The purchase price in a merger can consist of cash, stock, or debt, giving the acquiring company more latitude in how it will pay for the purchase of the target's stock. If the seller receives acquirer shares in exchange for their shares (with the seller's shares subsequently canceled), the merger is a *stock-for-stock* or *stock swap*. If the shareholders of the selling firm receive cash or some form of nonvoting investment (e.g., debt, or nonvoting preferred or common stock) for their shares, the merger is referred to as a *cash-out statutory merger*.

Mergers generally are not suitable for hostile transactions because they require the approval of the target's board.

Advantages of Mergers

The primary advantage of a merger is that the transfer of assets and exchange of stock between the acquirer and the target happen automatically by "rule of law"—that is, under applicable federal and state laws and legal precedents resulting from numerous court cases that establish when and how ownership is transferred. As previously noted, when a majority of target shareholders has approved the merger, all shareholders—even those who did not support the transaction—are required to sell their shares. As with the purchase of stock, the statutes of many states allow dissenting shareholders the right to have their shares appraised and to be paid the appraised value rather than what is offered by the acquiring firm. Transfer taxes are not paid because there are no asset transfer documents. Contracts, licenses, patents, and permits automatically transfer, unless they require "consent to assignment"; that is, the buyer must convince all parties to the contracts to consign them to the new owner. This transfer can be accomplished by merging a subsidiary set up by the buyer with the target, which can then be merged with the parent immediately following closing.

Disadvantages of Mergers

Mergers of public corporations can be costly and time consuming because of the need to obtain shareholder approval and comply with proxy regulations. Delays can open the door to other bidders, create an auction environment, and boost the purchase price.

Staged Transactions

An acquiring firm may choose to complete a takeover of another firm in stages spread over an extended period. Staged transactions may be used to structure an earnout, enable the target to complete development of a technology or process, await regulatory approval, eliminate the need to obtain shareholder approval, and minimize cultural conflicts with the target. A potential acquirer may assume a minority investment in the target with an option to acquire the company at a later date.

As part of an earnout agreement, the acquirer may agree to allow the target to operate as a wholly owned but largely autonomous unit until the earnout period expires. This suggests that there will be little attempt to integrate facilities, overhead operations, and distribution systems during the earnout period.

The value of the target may depend considerably on the target developing a key technology or production process, receiving approval of whatever is developed from a regulatory authority (e.g., the Federal Communications Commission), or signing a multiyear customer or vendor contract. The target's ability to realize these objectives may be enhanced if it is aligned with a larger company or receives a cash infusion to fund the required research. When these dependencies exist, the target may be well advised to wait. The two parties may enter into a letter of intent, with the option to exit the agreement without any liability to either party if certain key objectives are not realized within a stipulated time.

ACQUISITION AGREEMENTS

Although the form (or structure) of acquisition in which ownership is conveyed from one party to another can be an asset purchase, stock purchase, or merger, all acquisition agreements share certain elements in common. These elements include representations and warranties, preclosing covenants, conditions precedent to closing, and indemnification.

Representations and Warranties

The acquisition agreement will include representations (i.e., claims) and warranties (i.e., guarantees) made by the acquirer and target to each other. The target firm's "reps and warranties" include statements made about various aspects of the business being sold. Reps and warranties give the buyer an opportunity to walk away from or renegotiate the deal if facts are discovered between signing and closing that are contrary to representations and warranties made by the seller. They also provide the basis for the seller's indemnification obligations to the acquirer following closing. Common reps and warranties include those pertaining to corporate organization, authority, and capitalization; assets; liabilities; financial statements; and taxes. Other common reps and warranties include the following: contracts, leases, and other commitments; environmental protection; compliance with prevailing laws; product liability; and employment issues.

Preclosing Covenants

Covenants are promises that something will or will not be done during the period between signing and closing. Although generally absolute, they also may be expressed in terms of "best or reasonable efforts." Preclosing covenants are either negative or affirmative.

Negative covenants protect the acquirer from the target firm taking actions between the signing and closing that somehow change the business the acquirer expects to be buying. For example, they typically prevent the seller from changing accounting practices, entering into transactions or incurring liabilities outside the ordinary course of business, making cash outlays in excess of certain amounts, and paying dividends or making distributions to shareholders. Other negative covenants might include amending or terminating contracts or doing anything that would make untrue the representations and warranties that apply to the seller.

Affirmative covenants obligate the acquirer or seller to do certain things before closing, such as giving the buyer full access to all records, obtaining required board and regulatory approvals, and obtaining consent from customers and vendors to transfer contracts to the new owner.

Closing Conditions

Closing conditions are obligations that must be satisfied to require the other party to close the deal. Typical closing conditions relate to approvals from corporate boards, shareholders, and relevant regulators. All M&A agreements include closing conditions requiring that all representations and warranties of both parties must be true as of the closing date. Furthermore, closing conditions also require that all preclosing covenants be satisfied before closing. Other typical closing conditions include the receipt of necessary third-party consents, government approvals, signed employment and non-compete agreements, and satisfactory completion of the buyer's due diligence.

Preclosing covenants and closing conditions are interconnected. If an issue is addressed only as a covenant, the acquirer's only remedy for any breach of the covenant is to receive monetary compensation. However, if the issue is also addressed as a closing condition, the acquirer can walk away from the deal or attempt to renegotiate the terms of the transaction.

Indemnification

Indemnification provisions protect the parties to the agreement from matters that occur after closing and distribute the risks and responsibilities associated with these events between the acquirer and the seller. Indemnification covers breaches or violations of preclosing covenants and representations and warranties that are uncovered after closing. It also addresses issues disclosed in the seller's reps and warranties, for which the seller is responsible. Examples include pending litigation, infractions of environmental laws, the seller's failure to pay all tax obligations, and other occurrences whose impact and damages cannot be determined until after closing.

The seller will attempt to limit the period after closing during which the indemnification provision applies. In practice, it is common for such indemnification periods to be one to three years long. In some instances, they may be longer if the potential impact—such as an environmental cleanup—is likely to be distributed over a longer period. The seller may also want to cap or limit its total indemnification liability to an amount less than the total purchase price for the target's business. Furthermore, sellers often try to negotiate a deductible or a basket for obligations incurred as a result of indemnification provisions. With a deductible, the seller has no liability to the buyer until the amount of the buyer's losses exceeds a stipulated amount, after which the seller is responsible only for the amount of the loss in excess of the deductible. With a basket, when the buyer's losses exceed the agreed–upon basket amount, the seller is liable for the total amount of the losses.

★ ★ ★

The form of acquisition—the mechanism for conveying or transferring ownership of assets or stock and associated liabilities from the target to the acquiring firm—is typically either an asset purchase, stock purchase, or statutory merger. Acquisition agreements share many common elements, from representations and warranties to preclosing covenants and from closing conditions to indemnification.

A Case in Point: Teva Pharmaceuticals Buys Barr Pharmaceuticals to Create a Global Generic Drugs Powerhouse

Teva Pharmaceutical Industries, Ltd., is headquartered in Israel, leads the world in generic pharmaceuticals and is among the world's top-20 drug companies overall. It also is the world's leading generic pharmaceutical company. The firm develops, manufactures, and markets pharmaceutical ingredients called biologics, as well as animal health pharmaceutical products, generating more than 80 percent of its business in North America and Europe. On December 23, 2008, Teva completed its acquisition of U.S.-based Barr Pharmaceuticals, Inc., also one of the world's leading generic drug companies operating in more than 30 countries—primarily in North America and Europe, with key markets in the United States, Croatia, Germany, Poland, and Russia. Barr also actively develops generic biologics, an area with strong prospects for long-term earnings and profitability.

Teva was seeking, through the merger, to achieve increased economies of scale through better utilization of manufacturing facilities, economies of scope through more effective sharing of common resources, and greater geographic coverage with significant growth potential in emerging markets. The two companies had highly complementary generic drug offerings, and Teva stood to extend into new and attractive product categories such as a substantial women's healthcare business. The merger was part of a global consolidation trend spurred by governments—key purchasers of pharmaceutical products in general—increasingly becoming the primary purchasers of generic drugs.

The combined business has a significant presence in 60 countries worldwide and about $14 billion in annual sales (on a pro forma—or hypothetical—basis).

The form of payment, or merger consideration (the amount and composition of what was paid to Barr shareholders in exchange for their shares), for this merger included both Teva shares and cash. The form of acquisition was a purchase of Barr stock.

The merger agreement provided that each share of Barr common stock issued and outstanding immediately prior to the effective time of the merger would be converted into the right to receive 0.6272 ordinary shares of Teva (which would trade in the United States as American Depository Shares, or ADSs) and $39.90 in cash. The 0.6272 represented the share exchange ratio (i.e., the number of shares of Teva stock to be exchanged for each Barr share) stipulated in the merger agreement. Each ADS represented one share of Teva common stock deposited with a custodian bank.[5] Under Delaware law, Barr shareholders could exercise appraisal rights in connection with the merger.

The value of the portion of the merger consideration composed of Teva ADSs was such that it could increase or decrease as the trading price of Teva ADSs increased or decreased, based on a negotiated fixed exchange ratio. Thus it was possible that the value of Teva shares could be different on the closing date than on the contract signing date.

By most measures, the offer price for Barr shares constituted an attractive premium over the value of Barr shares just prior to the merger announcement—some 43 percent. The premium totaled approximately 53 percent over the average closing price of Barr common stock for the 30 trading days prior to the announcement. Because the merger qualified as a reorganization under U.S. federal income tax laws, a U.S. holder of Barr common stock generally would not have recognized any gain or loss on the exchange of Barr common stock for Teva ADSs but would have recognized a gain (but not a loss) on cash received in exchange for the holder's Barr common stock.

---

[5] ADSs may be issued in uncertificated form or certified as an American Depositary Receipt, or ADR. ADRs provide evidence that a specified number of ADSs have been deposited by the acquirer commensurate with the number of new ADSs issued to shareholders of the target.

The merger agreement established a wholly owned Teva corporate subsidiary—the Boron Acquisition Corp.—as the acquisition vehicle. It merged with Barr, with Barr surviving the merger as a wholly owned subsidiary of Teva. Immediately following the closing of the merger, Barr was then merged with and into a newly formed limited liability company (the postclosing organization), also wholly owned by Teva, which became the surviving company in the second step of the merger. Hence, Barr became a wholly owned subsidiary of Teva and ceased to be traded on the New York Stock Exchange.

The merger agreement had standard preclosing covenants in which Barr agreed to conduct its business only in the ordinary course and not to alter any supplier, customer, or employee agreements or declare any dividends or buy back any outstanding stock. Barr also agreed not to engage in one or more transactions or investments or assume any debt exceeding $25 million. The firm also promised not to change any accounting practices in any material way or in a manner inconsistent with Generally Accepted Accounting Principles, or to solicit alternative bids from any other possible investors between the signing of the merger agreement and closing.

Teva, for its part, agreed to conduct business in the ordinary course and use its best efforts to preserve the business organization as it was prior to signing the merger agreement, along with other covenants similar to those made by Barr. Furthermore, Teva agreed not to take any action that would materially affect the value of the ADSs that traded on the NASDAQ exchange. Teva also agreed that for one year following closing it would continue the Barr compensation, benefit, and bonus plans at the same levels that existed prior to closing.

Key closing conditions applying to both Teva and Barr included satisfaction of required regulatory and shareholder approvals, compliance with all prevailing laws, and that no representations and warranties were found to have been breached. Moreover, both parties had to provide a certificate signed by the chief executive officer and the chief financial officer attesting that their firms had met, in all material respects, all obligations required to be performed in accordance with the merger agreement prior to the closing date and that neither business had suffered any material damage between the signing and closing.

The merger agreement required approval by a majority of the outstanding voting shares of Barr common stock. Shareholders failing to vote or abstaining were counted as votes against the merger agreement. Because the shares issued by Teva in exchange for Barr's stock had already been authorized and did not exceed 20 percent of Teva's shares outstanding (i.e., the threshold on some public stock exchanges at which firms are required to obtain shareholder approval), the merger was not subject to a vote of Teva's shareholders.

Notification of the proposed transaction was filed by each company, as required by law, with the U.S. Federal Trade Commission and the Antitrust

Division of the U.S. Department of Justice. Given the global nature of the merger, the two firms also had to file with the European Union Antitrust Commission as well as with other country regulatory authorities.

Based on the average closing price of Teva ADSs on NASDAQ on July 16, 2008, the last trading day in the United States before the merger's announcement, the total purchase price was approximately $7.4 billion, consisting of a combination of Teva shares and cash. Barr shareholders ended up owning approximately 7.3 percent of Teva after the merger.

Things to Think About:

1. Why do you think Teva chose to acquire the outstanding stock of Barr rather than selected assets? Explain your answer.

2. Mergers of businesses with operations in many countries must seek approval from a number of regulatory agencies. How might this affect the time between the signing of the agreement and the actual closing? How might the ability to realize synergy following the merger of the two businesses be affected by actions required by the regulatory authorities before granting their approval? Be specific.

3. What it the importance of the preclosing covenants signed by both Teva and Barr?

4. What is the importance of the closing conditions in the merger agreement? What could happen if any of the closing conditions are breached?

5. Speculate as to why Teva offered Barr shareholders a combination of Teva stock and cash for each Barr share outstanding and why Barr was willing to accept a fixed share exchange ratio rather than some type of collar arrangement.

Answers can be found at:
www.elsevierdirect.com/companion.jsp?ISBN=9780123749499

CHAPTER 5

Tax Structures and Strategies

Taxes are an important consideration in almost any transaction—but they seldom are the primary motivation for an acquisition. The fundamental economics of the transaction should always be the deciding factor, and any tax benefits that might accrue to the buyer should simply reinforce a purchase decision.

From the viewpoint of the seller or target company shareholder, transactions may be tax free or entirely or partially taxable. The sale of stock, rather than assets, is generally preferable to the target firm shareholders to avoid double taxation, if the target firm is structured as a C corporation.[1] The composition of the purchase price usually determines whether a transaction will be taxable or nontaxable for target company shareholders. In early 2006, Disney Corporation exchanged its stock for 100 percent of Pixar Animation's outstanding stock in a deal valued at $7.4 billion—and Pixar shareholders did not have to pay taxes until they sold the Disney shares. More recently, in mid-2008, Belgian brewer InBev acquired all of iconic U.S. brewer Anheuser-Busch in an all-cash transaction valued at $52 billion. Anheuser-Busch shareholders were subject to taxes on any capital gains realized in exchanging their stock for cash.

This chapter focuses on the implications of tax structures and strategies for M&A negotiations and deal structuring. As noted in Chapter 1, tax considerations can affect the amount, timing, and composition of the purchase price. If a transaction is taxable, target shareholders typically will demand a higher purchase price to offset the anticipated tax liability, and the increase in the purchase price may cause the acquirer to defer some portion of the purchase price by altering the terms to include more debt or installment payments to maintain the same purchase price in present value terms.

Which organizational structure is appropriate for the combined businesses is affected by factors such as the desire to minimize taxes and to pass through losses to owners. The subchapter S corporation, limited liability

---

[1] For a detailed discussion of the application of the tax code to M&As, see CCH Tax Law Editors (2005); Ginsburg and Levin (2004); Hurter, Petersen, and Thompson (2005); and PricewaterhouseCoopers (2006).

Mergers and Acquisitions Basics
ISBN: 978-0-12-374949-9, DOI: 10.1016/B978-0-12-374949-9.00005-1

EXHIBIT 5-1   Alternative Taxable and Nontaxable Structures

Taxable Transactions: Immediately Taxable to Target Shareholders	Nontaxable Transactions: Tax Deferred to Target Shareholders
1. Purchase of assets with cash 2. Purchase of stock with cash 3. Statutory cash merger or consolidation 4. Triangular statutory cash mergers 　a. Forward 　b. Reverse	1. Type A reorganization (statutory stock merger or consolidation) 2. Type B reorganization (stock for stock) 3. Type C reorganization (stock for assets) 4. Triangular statutory stock mergers 　a. Forward 　b. Reverse

---

company (LLC), and partnership eliminate double taxation problems. Current operating losses, loss carry forwards or carry backs, or tax credits generated by the combined businesses can be passed through to the owners if the postclosing organization is a partnership or LLC. The legal status of the seller also will affect the form of acquisition preferred by the seller.

Exhibit 5-1 summarizes various taxable and tax-free structures, including both statutory mergers (two-party transactions) and triangular mergers (three-party transactions).

TAXABLE TRANSACTIONS

A transaction generally is considered taxable to the target firm's shareholders if it involves the purchase of the target's stock or assets for substantially all cash, notes, or some other nonequity consideration. In this type of transaction, the term *cash* often is synonymous with the use of notes or other nonequity consideration as part of or as the entire purchase price. Using the term *cash* to represent all forms of nonequity payment, such transactions may take the form of a cash purchase of target assets, a cash purchase of target stock, a statutory cash merger or consolidation, or a triangular statutory cash merger. There are both *forward triangular mergers* and *reverse triangular mergers* (detailed later). In a triangular cash merger, the target firm may either be merged into an acquirer's operating or shell acquisition subsidiary with the subsidiary surviving (called a forward triangular cash merger), or the acquirer's subsidiary is merged into the target firm with the target surviving (called a reverse triangular cash merger).

The major advantages of using a triangular structure are that it limits the voting rights of acquiring shareholders and gives the acquirer control of the target through a subsidiary without making the acquirer directly responsible for the target's known and unknown liabilities. Recall that the acquiring firm is not required to obtain shareholder approval if the stock used to purchase the target represents less than 20 percent of the firm's total shares outstanding or if it has been previously authorized. This advantage, though, may be nullified if the stock is newly issued and if the firm's bylaws require such approval.

Taxable Purchase of Target Assets with Cash

If a transaction involves a cash purchase of target assets, the target company's tax cost or basis in the acquired stock or assets is increased or "stepped up" to their fair market value (FMV), which is equal to the purchase price paid by the acquirer. The resulting additional depreciation and amortization in future years reduce the present value of the tax liability of the combined companies. The target firm realizes an immediate gain or loss on assets sold equal to the difference between the FMV of the asset and the asset's adjusted tax basis (i.e., book value less accumulated depreciation).

The target's shareholders could be taxed twice: once when the firm pays taxes on any gains and again when the proceeds from the sale are paid to the shareholders either as a dividend or distribution following liquidation of the corporation. A liquidation of the target firm may occur if a buyer acquires enough of the assets of the target to cause it to cease operations. To compensate the target company shareholders for any tax liability they may incur, the buyer usually will have to increase the purchase price.[2] Buyers are willing to do this only if the present value of the tax savings resulting from the step-up of the target's assets is greater than the increase in the purchase price required to compensate the target's shareholders for the increase in their tax liability.

There is little empirical evidence that the tax shelter resulting from the ability of the acquiring firm to increase the value of acquired assets to their

---

[2] Ayers, Lefanowicz, and Robinson (2003).

FMV is a highly important motivating factor for a takeover.[3] However, taxable transactions have become somewhat more attractive to acquiring firms since 1993, when a change in legislation allowed acquirers to amortize certain intangible assets.[4]

Taxable Purchase of Target Stock with Cash

Taxable transactions often involve the purchase of the target's voting stock because the purchase of assets automatically will trigger a taxable gain for the target if the FMV of the acquired assets exceeds the target firm's tax basis in the assets. All stockholders are affected equally in a taxable purchase of assets because the target firm is paying the taxes. In contrast, double taxation does not occur in a taxable stock purchase because the transaction takes place between the acquirer and the target firm's shareholders. The target firm pays no taxes on the transaction.

The target firm does not restate (i.e., revalue) its assets and liabilities for tax purposes to reflect the amount that the acquirer paid for the shares of common stock. Rather, the tax basis of assets and liabilities of the target (i.e., their value on the target's financial statements) before the acquisition carries over to the acquirer after the acquisition. This represents a potential problem for the buyer in a purchase of stock because the buyer loses the additional tax savings that would result from acquiring assets and writing them up to fair market value. Consequently, the buyer may want to reduce what it is willing to pay to the seller.

Section 338 Election

The acquirer and target firms can jointly elect Section 338 of the Internal Revenue Code and thereby record assets and liabilities at their fair market value for tax purposes. This allows a purchaser of 80 percent or more of the stock of the target to treat the acquisition as an asset purchase for tax purposes. The acquiring corporation avoids having to transfer assets and obtain consents to assignment of all contracts (as would be required in a direct purchase of assets), while still benefiting from the write-up of assets.

---

[3] Auerbach and Reishus (1988).

[4] Assets must qualify under Section 197 of the Internal Revenue Service Code. Such assets include goodwill, going concern value, books and records, customer lists, licenses, permits, franchises, and trademarks. A "197" intangible must be amortized over 15 years for tax purposes. Moreover, the current tax code allows operating losses (including those resulting from the write down of impaired goodwill) to be used to recover taxes paid in the preceding 2 years and to reduce future tax liabilities up to 20 years.

Asset transfer, sales, and use taxes may also be avoided. However, the 338 election generates an immediate tax liability for the target firm, which is viewed by the IRS as an "old" corporation selling its assets to a "new" corporation. Hence, the target must recognize and pay taxes on any gains of the sale of assets. To compensate for the immediate tax liability, the target firm may demand a higher selling price.

Triangular Cash-Out Mergers

The IRS generally views forward triangular cash mergers as a purchase of target assets followed by a liquidation of the target for which target shareholders will recognize a taxable gain or loss as if they had sold their shares. The target firm often is liquidated after it has, in effect, sold its operating assets; its tax attributes—in the form of any tax loss carry forwards or carry backs or investment tax credits—do not carry over to the acquirer. However, its assets and liabilities do transfer because it is a merger. The target firm pays taxes on any gain on the sale of its assets and again by target shareholders, who receive a liquidating dividend. With the merger, no minority shareholders remain because all shareholders are required to accept the terms of the merger, although dissident shareholders may have appraisal rights for the stock they are required to sell. Exhibit 5-2 illustrates the forward triangular cash merger.

In contrast, the IRS treats the reverse triangular cash merger as a purchase of target shares, with the target firm surviving—along with its assets,

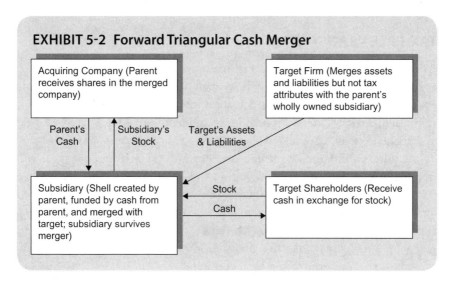

EXHIBIT 5-2 Forward Triangular Cash Merger

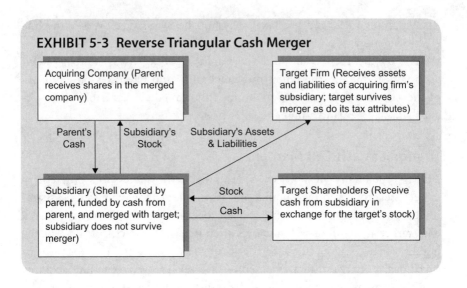

EXHIBIT 5-3 Reverse Triangular Cash Merger

liabilities, and tax attributes. Consequently, the cash is taxed only once—when the target firm's shareholders pay taxes on any gain on the sale of their stock. However, if the acquirer and target agree to invoke a 338 election, the target will have to pay taxes on any gains on assets written up to their fair market value. Exhibit 5-3 illustrates the reverse triangular cash merger, and Exhibit 5-4 summarizes the key characteristics of taxable transaction structures.

TAX-FREE TRANSACTIONS

As a general rule, a transaction is tax free if the form of payment is primarily acquirer's stock. Transactions may be partially taxable if the target shareholders receive some nonequity consideration, such as cash or debt, in addition to the acquirer's stock. This nonequity consideration or *boot* is taxable if paid as a dividend to all shareholders, and it is taxed as ordinary income.

Acquirers and targets planning to enter into a tax-free transaction will frequently seek an *advance ruling* from the IRS to determine its tax-free status, which is formal and binding. However, the certainty of the formal letter may diminish if any of the key assumptions underlying the transaction change prior to closing. Moreover, the process of requesting and receiving a letter may take five or six months. Alternatively, acquirers may rely on the opinion of trusted legal counsel.

EXHIBIT 5-4 Key Characteristics of Alternative Taxable (to Target Shareholders) Transaction Structures

Transaction Structure	Form of Payment	Acquirer Retains Tax Attributes of Target	Target Survives?	Parent Exposure to Target Liabilities	Shareholder Vote Required? Acquirer	Shareholder Vote Required? Target	Minority Freeze Out?	Automatic Transfer of Contracts?[2]
Purchase of Stock	Mostly cash, debt, or other nonequity payment	Yes, but no asset step-up without 338 election[1]	Yes	High	No[4]	No, but shareholder may not sell shares	No	Yes
Purchase of Assets	Mostly cash, debt, or other nonequity payment	No, but can step up assets	Perhaps[3]	Low, except for assumed liabilities	No[4]	Yes, if sale of assets is substantial	No minority created	No
Statutory Merger or Consolidation	Mostly cash, debt, or other nonequity payment	Yes	No	High	No[4]	Yes	Yes[5]	Yes
Forward Triangular Cash Merger (Treated as an asset purchase by IRS as target generally liquidated)	Mostly cash, debt, or other nonequity payment	No	No	Low—limited by subsidiary	No[4]	Yes	Yes	No

(Continued)

EXHIBIT 5-4 (Continued)

Transaction Structure	Form of Payment	Acquirer Retains Tax Attributes of Target	Target Survives?	Parent Exposure to Target Liabilities	Shareholder Vote Required?		Minority Freeze Out?	Automatic Transfer of Contracts?[2]
					Acquirer	Target		
Reverse Triangular Cash Merger (Treated as a stock purchase by IRS)	Mostly cash, debt, or other nonequity payment	Yes	Yes	Low—limited by subsidiary	No[4]	Yes	Yes	Yes

[1] An acquirer may treat a stock purchase as an asset purchase if it and the target agree to invoke Section 338 (of the Tax Code) election.

[2] Contracts, leases, licenses, and rights to intellectual property automatically transfer unless contracts stipulate consent to assignment required.

[3] The target may choose to liquidate if the sale of assets is substantial, to distribute the proceeds to its shareholders, or to continue as a shell.

[4] Shareholder voting may be required by public stock exchanges or by legal counsel if deemed material to the acquiring firm or if the parent needs to authorize new stock. In practice, most big mergers require shareholder approval.

[5] Target shareholders must accept terms due to the merger, although in some states dissident shareholders have appraisal rights for their shares.

If the transaction is tax free, the acquiring company is able to transfer or carry over the target's tax basis to its own financial statements. There is no increase or step-up in assets to fair market value. A tax-free reorganization envisions the acquisition of all or substantially all of a target company's assets or shares. Consequently, the tax-free structure generally is not suitable for the acquisition of a division within a corporation.

Continuity of Interests and Continuity of Business Enterprise Requirements

Under U.S. law, tax-free transactions require substantial continuing involvement of the target company's shareholders. To demonstrate continuity of interests (COI), target shareholders must continue to own a substantial part of the value of the combined target and acquiring firms. To demonstrate continuity of business enterprise (COBE), the acquiring corporation must either continue the acquired firm's "historic business enterprise" or use a significant portion of the target's "historic business assets" in a business.[5] This continued involvement is intended to demonstrate a long-term or strategic commitment on the part of the acquiring company to the target.

Nontaxable or tax-free transactions usually involve mergers, with the acquirer's stock exchanged for the target's stock or assets. Nontaxable transactions also are called *tax-free reorganizations*. The continuity of interests requirement serves to prevent transactions that more closely resemble a sale from qualifying as a tax-free reorganization.

Alternative Tax-Free Reorganizations

Eight principal forms of tax-free reorganizations are described in Section 368 of the Internal Revenue Code. Five are discussed here: Types A, B, and C, as well as forward and reverse triangular subsidiary mergers. Three are excluded because they do not fall under the definition of "merger" or "acquisition": Type D, transfers between related corporations (typically, one corporation has some level of investment in the other); Type E, the restructuring of a firm's capital structure; and Type F, a reorganization in which the firm's name or location is changed.

---

[5] The IRS is vague about exactly how it is determined that these criteria are being met. The acquirer must purchase the assets that are key to continuing the operation of the target's business, but such assets may not necessarily represent a majority of the target's total assets. However, acquirers often purchase at least 80 percent of the target's assets to ensure that they are in compliance with IRS guidelines.

Type A and B are the most common tax-free reorganizations for mergers in which a combination of stock, cash, or debt is used to acquire the target's stock or assets. Forward and reverse triangular mergers are used primarily when the acquirer stock is the predominant form of payment used to purchase the target's stock or assets. The U.S. tax code and case law define what constitutes the "substantial equity interest" target shareholders are required to hold in the acquiring company; the definition varies with the type of tax-free reorganization used. Reorganizations under the tax code may be wholly (all stock) or partially tax free (stock and other nonequity consideration). Triangular mergers are commonly used for tax-free transactions.

A *Type A reorganization* is either a statutory merger or consolidation governed by state law. There are no limitations on the type of consideration involved: target company shareholders may receive cash, voting or nonvoting common or preferred stock, notes, or real property. Nor must target shareholders all be treated equally: some may receive all stock, others all cash, and others a combination of the two.

The acquirer may choose not to purchase all of the target's assets. Unlike a direct statutory merger in which all known and unknown target assets and liabilities transfer to the buyer by law, a subsidiary merger often results in the buyer acquiring only a majority interest in the target and then carrying the target as a subsidiary of the parent. The target may later be merged into the parent in a back-end merger (discussed in Chapter 4). To ensure the target does not resemble an actual sale (thereby making the transaction taxable), at least 40 percent of the purchase price must be acquiring company stock to satisfy the IRS continuity of interests requirement. For forward and reverse triangular stock mergers, the acquirer must purchase at least 80 percent of the fair market value of the target's net assets.

Type A reorganizations are used widely because of their great flexibility. Because there is no requirement to utilize voting stock, acquiring firms enjoy more options. By issuing nonvoting stock, the acquiring corporation may acquire control of the target without diluting control of the combined or newly created company. Moreover, there is no stipulation as to the amount of target net assets that must be acquired. Finally, there is no maximum amount of cash that may be used in the purchase price, and the limitations articulated by both the IRS and the courts allow significantly more cash than Type B and C reorganizations. In fact, this flexibility with respect to cash may be the most important consideration because it enables the acquirer to satisfy better the disparate requirements of the target's shareholders. Some will want cash, and some will want stock.

In a *Type B stock-for-stock reorganization*, the acquirer must use its voting common stock to purchase an amount of voting stock that comprises at least 80 percent of the voting power of all voting stock outstanding (recall that some voting shares may have multiple voting rights). In addition, the acquirer must purchase at least 80 percent of each class of nonvoting shares. Any cash or debt will disqualify the transaction as a Type B reorganization. However, cash may be used to purchase fractional shares.

Type B reorganizations are used as an alternative to a merger or consolidation. The target's stock may be purchased over 12 months or less as part of a formal acquisition plan. Type B reorganizations may be appropriate if the acquiring company wishes to conserve cash or its borrowing capacity. Because shares are being acquired directly from shareholders, there is no need for a target shareholder vote. Finally, contracts, licenses, and so on, transfer with the stock, thereby obviating the need to receive consent to assignment, unless specified in the contract.

The *Type C stock-for-assets reorganization* is used when it is essential for the acquirer not to assume any undisclosed liabilities. It requires that at least 80 percent of the FMV of the target's assets, as well as the assumption of certain specified liabilities, be acquired solely in exchange for acquirer voting stock. Because the cash portion of the purchase price must be reduced by assumed liabilities (which the IRS views as equivalent to cash), cash may be used to purchase the remainder of the stock only if the assumed liabilities amount to less than 20 percent of the fair market value of the acquired assets. Since assumed liabilities frequently exceed 20 percent of the FMV of the acquired assets, the form of payment, as a practical matter, generally is 100 percent stock. As part of the reorganization plan, the target subsequent to closing dissolves and distributes the acquirer's stock to the target's shareholders for the now-canceled target stock.

The requirement to use only voting stock is a major deterrent to the use of Type C reorganization. Although a purchase of assets will allow the acquirer to step up the basis of the acquired assets, asset purchases will result in the target recognizing a taxable gain if the purchase price exceeds the firm's tax basis in the assets. If the target is liquidated to enable the firm to pay the sale proceeds to its shareholders, target shareholders will then have to pay taxes on these payouts. The potential for double taxation will generally make the purchase of stock more attractive than an asset purchase. Unlike a stock-for-stock reorganization in which the target remains a wholly owned subsidiary of the buyer, the stock-for-assets reorganization will result in the assessment of sales, use, and other transfer taxes.

A forward triangular stock merger is the most commonly used form of reorganization for tax-free asset acquisitions in which the form of payment is acquirer stock. It involves three parties: the acquiring firm, the target firm, and a shell subsidiary of the acquiring firm (see Exhibit 5-5).

As with the forward triangular cash merger described earlier, the parent funds the shell corporation by buying stock issued by the shell with its own stock. All of the target's stock is acquired by the subsidiary with the stock of the parent, and the target's stock is canceled, with the acquirer subsidiary surviving. The target company's assets and liabilities are merged into the acquirer's subsidiary in a statutory merger. The parent's stock may be voting or nonvoting, and the acquirer must purchase substantially all of the target's assets and liabilities (defined as 80 percent of the FMV of the target's net assets, i.e., assets minus liabilities).[6]

Asset sales by the target firm just prior to the transaction may threaten the tax-free status of the deal. Moreover, tax-free deals are disallowed within two years of a spinoff. The IRS imposes these limitations to preclude sellers from engaging in restructuring activities that make them more

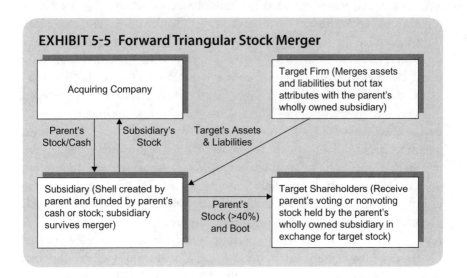

EXHIBIT 5-5 Forward Triangular Stock Merger

[6] In 2006, the IRS announced new rules establishing that the "substantially all" requirement may not apply if a so-called disregarded unit, such as a limited liability company, is used as the acquiring subsidiary and the target firm (structured as a C corporation) ceases to exist. As such, no limitations would be placed on the amount of target net assets that would have to be acquired to qualify as a tax-free reorganization. This is explained in more detail later in this chapter.

EXHIBIT 5-6 Reverse Triangular Stock Merger

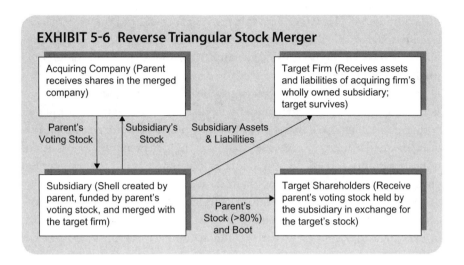

attractive to potential acquirers that might be willing to consummate a tax-free deal if the target firm were smaller. At least 40 percent of the purchase price must consist of acquirer stock, with the remainder consisting of boot tailored to meet the needs of the target's shareholders. The transaction qualifies as a Type A tax-free reorganization. The parent indirectly owns all of the target's assets and liabilities because it owns the subsidiary's entire voting stock.

The advantages of the forward triangular merger may include the avoidance of approval by the parent firm's shareholders. However, public exchanges on which the parent firm's stock trades still may require parent shareholder approval if the amount of the parent stock used to acquire the target exceeds some predetermined percentage of parent voting shares outstanding. Other advantages include the possible insulation of the parent from the target's liabilities, which remain in the subsidiary, and the avoidance of asset recording fees and transfer taxes, because the target's assets go directly to the parent's wholly owned subsidiary.

The reverse triangular stock merger is used most commonly to effect tax-free stock acquisitions in which the form of payment is predominantly the acquirer's voting stock (see Exhibit 5-6). The acquirer forms a new shell subsidiary, which is merged into the target in a statutory merger. The target is the surviving entity and must hold substantially all (again, at least 80 percent of the FMV) of the assets and liabilities of both the target and shell subsidiary.[7] The target firm's shares are canceled, and the target shareholders receive the acquirer's or parent's shares. The parent corporation, which owned all of the subsidiary stock, now owns all of the new target stock and, indirectly, all of the target's assets and liabilities.

To qualify as a tax-free transaction, at least 80 percent of the total consideration paid to the target must be in the form of the acquirer's parent voting stock. This stock may be common or preferred equity. Like the forward triangular merger, a reverse triangular merger precludes asset sales or spinoffs just prior to the completion of the transaction. This transaction qualifies as a Type A tax-free reorganization.

Although the reverse triangular merger is similar to a Type A reorganization in which the acquiring company purchases the target's stock in exchange for its stock, it permits the acquirer to use up to 20 percent cash. The reverse merger also may eliminate the need for parent company shareholder approval. Because the target firm remains in existence, the target can retain any nonassignable franchise, lease, or other valuable contract rights. Also, the target's liabilities are isolated in a subsidiary of the acquirer. By avoiding the dissolution of the target firm, the acquirer avoids the possible acceleration of loans outstanding. Insurance, banking, and public utility regulators may require the target to remain in existence to be granted regulatory approval.

Exhibit 5-7 summarizes the key characteristics of alternative tax-free deal structures.

Expanding the Role of Mergers in Tax-Free Reorganizations

In late 2006, the IRS finalized regulations[8] defining the term *statutory merger or consolidation* for purposes of using tax-free reorganizations. The new regulations offer more flexibility to businesses in using the statutory merger or consolidation with respect to transactions involving so-called disregarded entities, which include separate limited liability companies, a corporation that is a qualified real estate investment trust subsidiary, and a corporation that is a qualified subchapter S subsidiary), as well as transactions completed under the laws of foreign jurisdictions.

---

[7] Note that unlike in a forward triangular merger, the "substantially all" requirement cannot be circumvented by merging a LLC created by a parent corporation with a target C corporation and exchanging parent stock for target stock.

[8] Under U.S. Treasury Regulation Section 1.368-2. The new rules apply to transactions taking place on or after January 22, 2006.

EXHIBIT 5-7 Key Characteristics of Alternative Tax-Free (to Target Shareholders) Transaction Structures[1]

Transaction Structure (Type of Reorganization)	Form of Payment	Limitations[2]	Acquirer Retains Target Tax Attributes	Target Survives?	Parent Exposure to Target Liabilities	Shareholder Vote Required?		Minority Freeze Out?	Automatic Transfer of Contracts?[3]
						Acquirer	Target		
Statutory Merger or Consolidation (Type A Reorganization)	At least 40% parent voting or nonvoting stock	No limitations on target net assets purchased	Yes, but no asset step-up	No	High, unless merged into subsidiary[4]	No[6, 7]	Yes	Yes	Yes
Forward Triangular Stock Merger (Type A Reorganization)	At least 40% parent voting or nonvoting stock	Must purchase as least 80% of FMV of net assets unless LLC acquiring sub	Yes, but no asset step-up	No	Low, limited by subsidiary	No[6, 7]	Yes	Yes	No
Reverse Triangular Stock Merger (Type A Reorganization)	At least 80% parent voting stock (common/preferred)	Must purchase at least 80% of FMV of net assets	Yes, but no asset step-up	Yes	Low, limited by subsidiary	No[6, 7]	Yes	Yes	Target retains nonassignable contracts, etc.

(Continued)

EXHIBIT 5-7 (Continued)

Transaction Structure (Type of Reorganization)	Form of Payment	Limitation[2]	Acquirer Retains Target Tax Attributes	Target Survives?	Parent Exposure to Target Liabilities	Shareholder Vote Required? Acquirer	Shareholder Vote Required? Target	Minority Freeze Out?	Automatic Transfer of Contracts?[3]
Purchase of Stock—Without a Merger (Type B Reorganization)	100% parent voting stock (common/ preferred)	Must purchase at least 80% of voting power and of nonvoting shares	Yes, but no asset step-up	Yes	Low, limited by subsidiary	No[6]	No, as shares bought directly from shareholders	No	Yes
Purchase of Assets (Type C Reorganization)	100% voting stock[8]	Must purchase at least 80% FMV of net assets	No, and no asset step-up	No	Low,[5] except for assumed liabilities	No[6]	Yes, if sale of assets substantial	No minority created	No

[1] Target shareholders are taxed at ordinary rates on any "boot" received (i.e., anything other than acquiring company stock).

[2] Asset sales or spinoffs two years prior (may reflect effort to reduce size of purchase) or subsequent to (violates continuity requirement) closing may invalidate tax-free status. Forward triangular mergers do not require any limitations on purchase of target net assets if a so-called disregarded unit such as an LLC is used as the acquiring entity and the target is a C corporation that ceases to exist as a result of the transaction.

[3] Contracts, leases, licenses, and rights to intellectual property automatically transfer with the stock unless contracts stipulate consent to assignment required. Moreover, the target retains any nonassignable franchise, lease, or other contract right, as long as the target is the surviving entity as in a reverse triangular merger.

[4] Acquirer may be insulated from a target's liabilities as long as it is held in a subsidiary, except for liabilities such as unpaid taxes, unfunded pension obligations, and environmental liabilities.

[5] The parent is responsible for those liabilities conveying with the assets such as warranty claims.

[6] Shareholder voting may be required by public stock exchanges or by legal counsel if deemed material to the acquiring firm or if the parent needs to authorize new stock.

[7] Mergers are generally ill-suited for hostile transactions because they require approval of both the target's board and shareholders.

[8] Although cash may be used to pay for up to 20 percent of the FMV of net assets, it must be offset by assumed liabilities, making the purchase price usually 100 percent stock.

Under the new regulations, only the continuity of interests and the continuity of business enterprise tests and not the more restrictive "substantially all" requirement must be satisfied. Previously, two-party statutory Type A mergers offered greater flexibility than three-party transactions because they did not place any restriction on the amount of target net assets that could be acquired and allowed the use of nonvoting stock.

It is now possible for a merger of a corporation into a single-member limited liability company (i.e., the parent is the only member) established by the parent corporation in a triangular merger to qualify as a two-party Type A merger, with no limit on the amount of target net assets the buyer may acquire. However, the target firm must be a C corporation that ceases to exist after the transaction is completed. Because three parties are involved in the forward triangular merger, the target firm can be operated as a subsidiary, thereby insulating the parent from its liabilities. Also, no vote of parent firm shareholders is required because the parent firm is the sole owner of the subsidiary, unless the increase in shares issued to complete the transaction exceeds 20 percent of total parent shares outstanding. All of this can be accomplished without endangering the tax-free status of the transaction.

For years, the IRS had contended that a foreign corporation could not participate in a Type A tax-free reorganization because the term *statutory merger* referred only to a merger completed under the laws of the United States, an individual state, or the District of Columbia. The new regulations change this restriction.[9] The new regulations also make its easier to qualify foreign acquisitions—both unrelated party transactions and internal restructurings and reorganizations—as Type A tax-free reorganizations. Therefore, if a U.S. firm buys a foreign firm having U.S. shareholders, the transaction can be structured so that the purchase is free of U.S. taxes to the U.S. shareholders.

Tax-Free Transactions Arising from 1031 "Like-Kind" Exchanges

The prospect of being able to defer taxable gains indefinitely is often associated with 1031 exchanges of real estate property. The potential benefits are significant, with capital gains taxes (at this writing) of 15 percent at

---

[9] With the advent of the new regulations, the merger of a foreign corporation into another foreign corporation (or the creation of a new corporation in a consolidation) in accordance with the host country's laws will qualify as a Type A reorganization. As such, the exchange will be tax free for any U.S. shareholders in the target firm receiving acquirer shares or shares in the new company formed as a result of the consolidation.

the federal level and between 10 percent and 15 percent at the state level. Furthermore, depreciation recapture taxes (i.e., taxes applied to the difference between accelerated and straight-line depreciation) also may be postponed, with applicable federal income tax rates as high as 35 percent and some state income tax rates approaching 10 percent.

The concept involves selling one property and buying another, subject to certain restrictions and time limitations. The 1031 exchange is relevant to M&As in that it represents a means of using "like-kind" assets (allowed under section 1031 of the U.S. tax code) to finance all or a portion of the purchase price of the target firm, while deferring the payment of taxes. A wide variety of investment properties can be swapped, such as an apartment complex for land or an oil and gas property for a commercial strip mall. Investors can continue exchanging existing properties for new properties of equal or greater value, while deferring any tax consequences.[10]

By postponing the tax payments, investors have more money to reinvest in new properties. For example, assume a property was purchased 10 years ago for $5 million, and it is now worth $15 million. If the property were sold with no subsequent purchase of a substantially similar property within the required period, the federal capital gains tax bill would be $1.5 million (i.e., ($15 − $5) × 0.15). This ignores the potential for state taxes or depreciation recapture taxes that could be owed if the owner took deductions for depreciation. However, by entering into a 1031 exchange, the owner could use the entire $15 million from the sale of the property as a down payment on a more expensive property. If the investor acquires a property of a lesser value, taxes are owed on the difference. With tax rates likely to rise in the next few years, the value of tax-free exchanges will increase.

Two examples illustrate the use of the 1031 regulations. In a tax-free asset swap, News Corp. reached an agreement in early 2007 to buy

---

[10] To qualify for a 1031 exchange, the property must be an investment property or one used in a trade or business (e.g., a warehouse, store, or commercial office building). Delayed exchanges are the most common means of implementing this type of a tax strategy. When a property is sold, a replacement property must be identified within 45 days of the closing, and the deal for the replacement property must be closed within 180 days. An independent party not involved directly in the transaction—the "qualified intermediary"—must hold the proceeds of the sale until the next property is purchased; this intermediary might be a real estate broker, lawyer, or accountant. Moreover, if the taxpayer were to take control of the proceeds of the sale, it would invalidate the "like-kind" exchange. Qualified intermediaries can be found by contacting the Federation of Exchange Accommodators through the website http://www.1031.org.

Liberty Media's 19 percent—or $11 billion—stake in the media giant in exchange for News Corp's 38.6 percent stake in satellite TV firm DirecTV Group, $550 million in cash, and three sports TV channels. Although the two investments were approximately equal in value, Liberty's management believed that DirecTV's stock was inflated by speculation about the impending deal. The cash and media assets were added to ensure that Liberty Media was exchanging its stake in News Corp for "like-kind" assets of an equivalent or higher value to qualify as a tax-free exchange. Because the deal was structured in this manner, the transaction was viewed as an asset swap rather than a sale of assets, and Liberty Media stood to save billions of dollars in taxes that would have been owed due to its low basis in its investment in News Corp. Had the assets been divested, the two companies would have had to pay an estimated $4.5 billion in taxes due to likely gains on the sale of these assets.[11]

Similarly, Berkshire Hathaway Inc. traded its 16.3 percent stake in White Mountains Insurance Group for two of the firm's subsidiaries and $751 million in cash. The terms of the deal valued Berkshire's White Mountains stock at $836 million. Because the deal was structured as an asset swap, neither firm expected to record a taxable gain on the transaction.

OTHER TAX CONSIDERATIONS AFFECTING CORPORATE RESTRUCTURING ACTIVITIES

Many parts of the tax code affect corporate restructuring activities. They include treatment of net operating losses, corporate capital gains taxes, the alternative corporate minimum tax, the treatment of greenmail for tax purposes, Morris Trust transactions, and leveraged partnerships.

Net Operating Losses

Net operating loss (NOL) carry backs and carry forwards are provisions in the tax laws that allow firms to carry NOLs generated in the past back 2 years to obtain a tax refund (if those years were profitable) and forward 20 years to offset future taxable income. There are annual limits to carry forwards and carry backs, introduced as part of the Tax Reform Act of

---

[11] Angwin and Drucker (September 16, 2006).

1986.[12] Still, NOLs may represent a potentially significant source of value to acquirers that should be considered during the process of valuing an acquisition target. For instance, Lucent Technologies had accumulated numerous losses after the Internet bubble burst in 2000. By acquiring Lucent in 2006, Alcatel obtained $3.5 billion in NOLs that could be used to shelter future income for many years.[13]

Exhibit 5-8 illustrates how an analyst might value NOLs on the books of a target corporation.

The use of NOLs must be monitored carefully to realize the full value that could potentially result from deferring income taxes. An acquirer must be highly confident that the expected future pretax income stream will be realized. Without the future income, the NOLs will expire worthless. Because the acquirer can never be certain that future income will be sufficient to realize fully the value of the NOLs, loss carry forwards alone rarely justify an acquisition.[14]

In late 2007, General Motors Corporation announced a $39 billion noncash charge on its income statement (and the addition of an equivalent reserve to its balance sheet) to write down deferred-tax assets that had resulted from cumulative losses. They could be used to offset taxes on current or future profits for a number of years. However, the write-down suggested that GM, experiencing huge operating losses, did not expect to return to profitability any time soon. Consequently, it was likely that some portion of the tax deferrals would expire before they could be used to offset future taxable income. Were the corporation to return to profitability, the firm could reverse (i.e., remove) the valuation reserve and utilize some portion of the unexpired deferred tax credits to reduce its tax liability. Continued losses in 2008 and 2009 resulted in the firm's NOLs growing to $87 billion. This tax asset was transferred from the "Old GM" to the "New GM" following the firm's emergence from bankruptcy in late 2009.

---

[12]   The limits take effect if there is change in ownership exceeding 50 percent in a corporation that generated cumulative losses during the three years preceding the change. Such a corporation is referred to as a "loss corporation," and the maximum amount of the NOL that can be used annually to offset earnings is limited to the value of the loss corporation on the date of the acquisition, multiplied by the long-term tax-exempt bond rate. Furthermore, a loss corporation cannot use an NOL carry forward or carry back unless it remains viable and in essentially the same business for at least two years following the closing of the acquisition.

[13]   Drucker and Silver (April 26, 2006).

[14]   Studies show that it is easy to overstate the value of loss carry forwards because of their potential to expire before they can be fully used. Empirical analyses indicate that the actual tax savings realized from loss carry forwards tend to be about one-half of their expected value (Auerbach and Poterba, 1987).

EXHIBIT 5-8 Valuing Net Operating Losses

Acquiring Company is contemplating buying Target Company, which has a tax-loss carry forward of $8,000,000. Acquiring Company has a 40 percent tax rate. Assume the tax-loss carry forward is within the limits of the Tax Reform Act of 1986 and that the firm's cost of capital is 15 percent. The following information is given for the two firms:

Years Remaining in Loss Carry Forward	Amount ($ 000)	Years After Acquisition	Earnings Before Tax ($ 000)
1	2,000	1	1,800
2	2,000	2	2,000
3	800	3	1,000
4	1,200	4	1,000
5	800	5	2,000
Total	6,800	Total	7,800

Calculate Acquiring Company's tax payments without the acquisition.

Years	Tax Benefit
1	720
2	800
3	400
4	400
5	800

Calculate Acquiring Company's tax payment for each year with the proposed acquisition.

Year	Earnings Before Taxes ($ 000)	Tax Loss ($ 000)	Amount Carried Forward ($ 000)	Use of Tax Loss ($ 000)	Taxable Income ($ 000)	Tax Payment ($ 000)
1	1,800	2,000		1,800	0	0
2	2,000	2,000	200	2,000	0	0
3	1,000	800	0	1,000	0	0
4	1,000	1,200	200	1,000	0	0
5	2,000	800	0	1,000	1,000	400

(Continued)

EXHIBIT 5-8 (Continued)

What is the most Acquiring Company should pay for Target Company if its only value is its tax loss?

Answer: Acquiring Company should not pay more than the present value of the net tax benefit: $720,000; $800,000; $400,000; $400,000; and $400,000. The present value of the cumulative tax benefits discounted at a 15 percent cost of capital is $1,921,580.

Notes:

1. Tax benefits are equal to earnings before tax times the 40 percent marginal tax rate of Acquiring Company. Therefore, the tax benefit in Year 1 is $1,800,000 × .4 = $720,000.

2. The net tax benefit in Year 5 is equal to the $800,000 tax benefit less the $400,000 in tax payments required in Year 5.

Corporate Capital Gains Taxes

Because both short- and long-term corporate capital gains are taxed as ordinary income and are subject to a maximum federal corporate tax rate of 34 percent, acquirers often adopt alternative legal structures with more favorable tax attributes for making acquisitions. These include master limited partnerships (MLPs), subchapter S corporations, and limited liability companies; in these structures, partners, shareholders, and members, respectively, are taxed at their personal tax rates for the profits distributed to them directly.

Alternative Corporate Minimum Tax

Under certain circumstances in which corporate taxes have been significantly reduced, corporations may be subject to an alternative minimum tax with a flat rate of 20 percent. The introduction of the alternative minimum tax has proven to be particularly burdensome for leveraged buyouts, which—by intent—are highly leveraged and have little (if any) taxable income because of their high annual interest expense. Consequently, the alternative minimum tax reduced the potential returns to equity investors that could be achieved as a result of highly leveraged transactions.

Greenmail Payments

Greenmail refers to payments made to "corporate raiders" to buy back positions they had taken in target companies (see Chapter 8 for more detail). Greenmail has been made more expensive by changes in the tax code that sharply reduced the amount of such payments that can be deducted from before-tax profits.

Morris Trust Transactions

Tax code rules for Morris Trust transactions (named for a precedent established in tax court case law involving the Morris Family Trust) restrict how certain types of corporate deals can be structured to avoid taxes. Assume Firm A sells an operating unit to Firm B and makes a profit on the transaction on which it would owe taxes. To avoid paying those taxes, Firm A spins off the operating unit as a dividend to its shareholders. The operating unit, still owned by Firm A's shareholders, is subsequently merged with Firm B, and shareholders in Firm A thus become shareholders in Firm B. By spinning off the operating unit, Firm A avoided paying corporate taxes on taxable gains, and Firm A's shareholders defer paying personal taxes on any gains until they sell their stock in Firm B.

To make such transactions less attractive, the tax code was amended in 1997 to require that taxes be paid unless no cash changed hands and Firm A's shareholders end up as majority owners in Firm B. The practical effect of this requirement is that merger partners such as Firm B in these types of transactions must be significantly smaller than Firm A, which reduces significantly the number of potential deal candidates.

Absent maintaining "continuity of ownership" in the operating unit, the IRS views this type of transaction as a sale having taken place. The 1997 tax code change was a response to deals done on a tax-free basis that appeared to be sales in disguise. In some instances, a parent company would borrow money through a subsidiary, keep the money, leave responsibility for the debt with the subsidiary, and then spin off the subsidiary to the parent's shareholders. Later, the former subsidiary would be merged with another company. The cash was effectively transferred from the merger partner to the former parent company tax-free, even if the parent would have earned a profit on the transaction had it sold the business outright.[15]

---

[15] Note that if a corporation borrows and retains the funds but later transfers responsibility for repayment to another entity, the IRS views those funds as taxable income to the original borrower.

The change in the law has had a material impact on the way M&A business is conducted. For example, in 2005, Alltel announced it was getting rid of its local telephone business. Although Alltel had been in talks with phone companies, its size made the prospects of a tax-free transaction more complicated. In the end, Alltel sold the business to a far smaller firm, Valor Communications Group Inc., to meet the tax code requirements.

Leveraged Partnerships

Leveraged partnerships may permit a C corporation to sell appreciated assets for cash without incurring an immediate tax liability. Assume Firm A wants to sell appreciated assets to Firm B but also wishes to defer the payment of taxes on the resulting profit from the sale. Firm A may be able to avoid recognizing the gain immediately by forming a partnership with B. Here is how it would work.

The two firms form a partnership called AB. Firm A contributes the appreciated assets to AB and retains a minimal ownership position in AB. Firm B contributes a substantial amount of assets to AB in exchange for the remaining ownership equity. AB subsequently borrows from a third-party lender an amount equal to the value of the assets contributed by Firm A, with Firm A guaranteeing the debt. The proceeds of the debt are distributed to Firm A. As guarantor, Firm A has effectively borrowed the funds. Therefore, the transaction is not viewed as a sale and no gain must be recorded for tax purposes. The debt is structured as annual interest payments and a single payment of principal at maturity paid by the partnership. Immediately before the debt is retired, Firm B will also acquire Firm A's interest in AB for a small amount of money, and Firm A will be released from the loan guarantee. Firm B, as the sole owner of AB, will own the assets initially contributed by Firm A. This appears to be the structure employed in the Cablevision Systems Corporation (CVC) deal with Tribune Company in 2008.

Under the terms of the transaction, CVC and Tribune will have equity ownerships of about 97 percent and 3 percent, respectively, in the partnership. Tribune contributed the Newsday assets, and CVC contributed newly issued parent company bonds with a fair market value of $650 million of senior debt maturing in 10 years. The CVC debt is equivalent to contributing a deferred cash payment, with the cash actually paid to the partnership when the bonds mature. The partnership planned to borrow $650 million for 10 years from Bank of America, guaranteed by Tribune Company and with the proceeds distributed to Tribune.

Despite earning a profit on the "deferred sale" of Newsday, Tribune had no capital gains taxes to pay on that $650 million. In 2007, turnaround specialist Sam Zell, after taking Tribune Company private, converted the firm from a C to a subchapter S corporation to take advantage of favorable tax treatment. By structuring the transaction as a leveraged partnership, Tribune was not required to recognize the contribution of Newsday as a sale on which it would have to pay capital gains taxes because CVC will not own Newsday outright until the debt matures. Then, the 10-year holding period following the conversion of Tribune from a C to a subchapter S corporation will have expired, and Tribune will not be required to recognize the gain on the sale of Newsday as a taxable event.

LEGAL FORM OF SELLING ENTITY

As noted in Chapter 4, taxes can be an important factor in determining the form of acquisition. As Exhibit 5-9 illustrates, whether the seller will care about the form of the transaction may depend on the seller's own legal form: subchapter S corporation, limited liability company, partnership, or C corporation.

★ ★ ★

Taxes are an important, but rarely overarching, consideration in most M&A transactions. The deciding factor in any transaction—which may be either partly or entirely taxable to the target firm's shareholders, or tax free—should be whether it makes good business sense. Tax benefits simply provide an additional reason for doing the deal.

EXHIBIT 5-9 How the Legal Form of the Seller Affects Form of Payment

Assume a business owner, beginning with an initial investment of $100,000, sells her business for $1,000,000. Different legal structures have different tax impacts.

1.   After-tax proceeds of a stock sale:

$$(\$1,000,000 - \$100,000) \times (1 - 0.15) = \$765,000$$

The subchapter S corporation shareholder or LLC member holding shares for more than one year pays a maximum capital gains tax equal to 15 percent of the gain on the sale.*

EXHIBIT 5-9 (Continued)

2. After-tax proceeds from an asset sale:

$$(\$1,000,000 - \$100,000) \times (1 - 0.4) \times (1 - 0.15) = \$900,000 \times 0.51 = \$459,000$$

A C corporation typically pays tax equal to 40 percent (i.e., 35 percent federal and 5 percent state and local) and the shareholder pays a maximum capital gains tax equal to 15 percent, resulting in double taxation of the gain on sale.

Implications

1. C corporation shareholders generally prefer acquirer stock for their stock or assets to avoid double taxation.

2. Subchapter S corporation and LLC owners often are indifferent to an asset sale or stock sale because 100 percent of the corporation's income passes through the corporation untaxed to the owners, who are subject to their own personal tax rates. Subchapter S corporation shareholders or LLC members may still prefer a share-for-share exchange if they are interested in deferring their tax liability, or if they are attracted by the long-term growth potential of the acquirer's stock.

*The current capital gains tax as of this writing.

A Case in Point: "Grave Dancer" Takes Tribune Company Private in an Ill-Fated Transaction

At the closing in late December 2007, well-known real estate investor Sam Zell described the takeover of Tribune Company as "the transaction from hell." His comments were prescient: what had appeared to be a cleverly crafted deal from a tax standpoint, albeit highly leveraged, could not withstand the credit malaise of 2008. The end came swiftly when the 161-year-old Tribune, unable to refinance its outstanding debt, filed for bankruptcy that December.

The story began on April 2, 2007, when Tribune Company—then owner of nine newspapers (accounting for 75 percent of the firm's total $5.5 billion annual revenue), 23 TV stations, a 25 percent stake in Comcast's SportsNet Chicago, and the Chicago Cubs baseball team—announced that the firm's publicly traded shares would be acquired in a multistage transaction valued at $8.2 billion. Advertising and circulation revenue had fallen by 9 percent at the firm's three largest newspapers—the *Los Angeles Times*, *Chicago Tribune*, and *Newsday* in New York—between 2004 and 2006. Even aggressive cost cutting could not keep Tribune's stock from falling more than 30 percent from its 2005 price.

The deal involved the famed Sam Zell, the self-proclaimed "grave dancer" (for his skill in restructuring failing businesses), fresh from earning as much as

$900 million in the sale of Equity Office Properties to the Blackstone Group for $39 billion (including debt) in March 2007. It would be Zell's second investment in the media industry; in 1992, he acquired a failing radio station operator for $79 million and sold it seven years later for $4.4 billion. He became Tribune's CEO.

There were two stages to the transaction. First, Tribune initiated a cash tender offer for 126 million shares (51 percent of total shares) for $34 per share, totaling $4.2 billion. The tender was financed using $250 million of the $315 million provided by Sam Zell in the form of subordinated debt, plus additional borrowing to cover the balance. Zell thus acquired a controlling interest. The second stage was triggered when regulators approved the deal. An employee stock ownership plan (ESOP) bought the rest of the shares at $34 a share (totaling about $4 billion), with Zell providing the remaining $65 million of his pledge. Most of the 121 million shares the ESOP purchased were financed by debt guaranteed by the firm on its behalf. At that point, the ESOP held all of the remaining stock outstanding, valued at about $4 billion. In exchange for his commitment of funds, Zell received a 15-year warrant to acquire 40 percent of the common stock (newly issued) at a price set at $500 million.

Following closing in December 2007, all company contributions to employee pension plans were funneled into the ESOP in the form of Tribune stock. Over time, the ESOP would hold all of the stock. Furthermore, Tribune was converted from a C corporation to a subchapter S corporation, allowing the firm to avoid corporate income taxes. However, it would have to pay taxes on gains resulting from the sale of assets held less than 10 years after the conversion from a C to a subchapter S corporation.

The purchase of Tribune's stock was financed almost entirely with debt, with Zell's equity contribution amounting to less than 4 percent of the purchase price. Along with $5 billion already owed by Tribune, this created a $13 billion debt burden for Tribune; at 10 times EBITDA (earnings before interest, tax, depreciation, and amortization), it was more than 2.5 times that of the average media company. Annual interest and principal repayments reached $800 million (almost three times their preacquisition level), about 62 percent of the firm's previous EBITDA cash flow of $1.3 billion. Although the ESOP owned the company, it was not liable for the debt guaranteed by Tribune.

The conversion of Tribune into a subchapter S corporation eliminated the firm's then annual tax liability of $348 million. Such entities pay no corporate income tax but must pay all profit directly to shareholders who then pay taxes on these distributions. Because the ESOP is the sole shareholder, the restructured Tribune was expected to be largely tax exempt, since ESOPs are not taxed.

In an effort to reduce the firm's debt burden, the Tribune Company announced in early 2008 the formation of a partnership in which Cablevision Systems Corporation would own 97 percent of Newsday for $650 million, with Tribune owning the remaining 3 percent. Tribune needed to reduce its debt when the 2008 credit crisis hit, but could not find a buyer either for the Chicago Cubs (an asset that had been expected to fetch as much as $1 billion) or for its minority interest in SportsNet Chicago. As the recession worsened, it accelerated the decline in newspaper and TV advertising revenue, and the firm's ability to meet its obligations eroded even further. Finally, filing for Chapter 11 bankruptcy protection became the option of choice.

Bankruptcy protection was meant to give Tribune a reprieve from its creditors as it attempted to restructure its business. Although the extent of the losses to employees, creditors, and other stakeholders are difficult to determine at this writing, some things are clear. Any pension funds set aside prior to the closing remain with the employees, but it is likely that equity contributions made to the ESOP on behalf of the employees since the closing would be lost. The employees became general creditors of Tribune. As a holder of subordinated debt, Zell enjoyed priority over the employees were the firm to be liquidated and the proceeds distributed to the creditors.

Those benefiting from the acquisition by Zell included Tribune's public shareholders, including the Chandler family, which owned 12 percent of Tribune as a result of its prior sale of the *Times-Mirror* to Tribune, and Dennis FitzSimons, the firm's former CEO, who received $17.7 million in severance and $23.8 million for his Tribune shares. Citigroup and Merrill Lynch walked away with $35.8 million and $37 million, respectively, in advisory fees. Morgan Stanley received $7.5 million for writing a fairness opinion letter. Finally, Valuation Research Corporation received $1 million for providing a solvency opinion indicating that Tribune could satisfy its loan covenants.

What appeared to be one of the most complex deals of 2007 designed to reap huge tax advantages soon became a victim of the downward-spiraling economy, the credit crunch, and of its own leverage. A lawsuit filed in late 2008 on behalf of Tribune employees contended that the transaction was flawed from the outset and was intended to benefit Sam Zell, his advisors, and the Tribune board. Even if the employees were to win, they would simply have to stand in line with other Tribune creditors awaiting the resolution of the bankruptcy court proceedings. The Chicago Cubs baseball team was eventually sold to the billionaire Ricketts family for $900 million in mid-2009.

Things to Think About:

1. What were the acquisition vehicle, postclosing organization, form of payment, form of acquisition, and tax strategy in the deal?
2. Describe the firm's strategy to finance the transaction?
3. Is this transaction best characterized as a merger, acquisition, leveraged buyout, or spinoff? Explain your answer.
4. Is this transaction taxable or nontaxable to Tribune's public shareholders? To its posttransaction shareholders? Explain your answer.

5. How fair was this transaction to the various stakeholders involved? How would you apportion the responsibility for Tribune's eventual bankruptcy among Sam Zell and his advisors, the Tribune board, and the largely unforeseen collapse of the credit markets in late 2008? Be specific.

Answers can be found at:
www.elsevierdirect.com/companion.jsp?ISBN=9780123749499

CHAPTER 6

Accounting Considerations

By substantially overpaying for acquisitions, acquirers condemn themselves to having to improve profitability dramatically just to earn the financial returns required by investors. If they have significantly overestimated potential synergy, they will be unable to realize these returns. The tendency in the late 1990s was to overpay, and so many firms have been forced to write off goodwill in line with current accounting practices associated with prior acquisitions or major portions of the acquired assets.

The decline in the stock market in 2000 and 2001 took many firms' share prices to levels significantly less than book value. Announcing in the first quarter of 2002 that it would reduce the value of goodwill associated with its acquisition of Time Warner by an eye-popping $60 billion, AOL was effectively admitting it had overpaid by more than one-half. By 2005, Time Warner had paid out as much as $3 billion to settle fraud claims by shareholders who lost money after the company's 2001 merger with AOL.

In 2004, MCI took a record-setting $75 billion write-off for acquisitions made by the company when it was named WorldCom. In 2009, private equity investors across the globe were slashing the value of their investments in their portfolio companies, many of which were made at inflated prices in 2007 and early 2008.

With the elimination of pooling of interests as an alternative to purchase accounting in 2001 and further changes in financial reporting standards that took effect in late 2008, acquirers are likely to be more circumspect in making acquisitions. Overpayment for target firms and the use of contingent payout mechanisms can result in significant increases in future earnings volatility for acquiring firms. Furthermore, equity may become less attractive as a form of payment because of the requirement to record business combinations on the closing, rather than the announcement date—although these concerns may be mitigated by the use of collar arrangements. The ever-present threat of these factors may exert some discipline into the negotiating process, affecting both the amount and timing of offer prices and the length and intensity of M&A due diligence.

Mergers and Acquisitions Basics
ISBN: 978-0-12-374949-9, DOI: 10.1016/B978-0-12-374949-9.00006-3

Financial data in the valuation of the target firm and in the negotiation process have limitations. Recent developments in financial reporting requirements for business combinations could affect the M&A process. The impending convergence of Generally Accepted Accounting Principles and International Financial Reporting Standards and recapitalization accounting methods are important factors for the future. These points are the focus of this chapter.[1]

LIMITATIONS OF FINANCIAL DATA

Financial models often are constructed to value target firms and simulate the impact of alternative scenarios discussed during the negotiation process. The output of models is only as good as the accuracy and timeliness of the numbers used to create them and the quality of the assumptions used in making projections. Consequently, analysts must understand the basis on which numbers are collected and reported. Consistency and adherence to uniform standards become exceedingly important.

Imaginative accounting tricks threaten to undermine an analyst's ability to gain a proper understanding of a firm's underlying dynamics. The tales of inordinate accounting abuses in recent years are many, including the well-known examples of WorldCom, Tyco, Enron, Sunbeam, Waste Management, and Cendant.

Generally Accepted Accounting Principles and International Accounting Standards

U.S. public companies prepare their financial statements in accordance with the rules-based system known as Generally Accepted Accounting Principles (GAAP), which has explicit instructions for every situation anticipated by the Financial Accounting Standards Board (FASB) that developed GAAP.[2] In contrast, the International Financial Reporting Standards (IFRS) is a principles-based system, established by the International Accounting Standards Board (IASB) to promote consistency across countries. All European Union publicly traded companies had to adopt the IFRS system in 2007. The more than 400 foreign firms also listed on U.S. exchanges continue to display their books in accordance with GAAP as well. Although the two systems have significant differences, those are expected to narrow in the coming years.

---

[1] Stickney et al. (2007) and Gale et al. (2006) provide excellent discussions of financial reporting and statements analysis. For an in-depth discussion of tax accounting for mergers and acquisitions, see Carrington (2007).

[2] The FASB is an independent organization funded entirely by the private sector.

Few would argue that GAAP ensures transactions are recorded accurately. Nevertheless, the scrupulous application of GAAP does ensure consistency in comparing the financial performance of firm with another. Customarily, definitive agreements of purchase and sale require that a target company represent that its financial books are kept in accordance with GAAP. This ensures that the acquiring company at least understands how the financial numbers were assembled. During due diligence, the acquirer can look for discrepancies between the target's reported numbers and GAAP practices, which could indicate potential problems.

Pro Forma Accounting

Although public companies still are required to file their financial statements with the Securities and Exchange Commission (SEC) in accordance with GAAP, companies increasingly are using pro forma financial statements to portray their current or projected financial performance in what they argue is a more realistic (and usually more favorable) manner. Pro forma statements frequently are used to show what the combined financial performance of an acquirer and target would look like were they to merge. Because there are no accepted standards for this type of accounting, however, pro forma statements may deviate substantially from standard GAAP statements.

Companies maintain that such statements provide investors with a better view of a company's core performance than GAAP reporting. Although pro forma statements do provide useful insight into how a proposed combination of businesses might look, such liberal accounting techniques easily can be abused so as to hide a company's poor performance.

Exhibit 6–1 suggests some ways in which an analyst can tell whether a firm is engaging in inappropriate accounting practices.[3]

FINANCIAL REPORTING OF BUSINESS COMBINATIONS

Since 2001, all M&As must be accounted for using the purchase method (also called the acquisition method) as required by the FASB. A company maintaining its financial statements under IFRS or GAAP needs to account for its business combinations.[4]

According to the **purchase method of accounting**, the purchase price or acquisition cost is determined and then, using a cost allocation approach, assigned first to tangible and then intangible net assets, at their value on

---

[3] For a more detailed discussion of these issues, see Sherman and Young (2001).
[4] According to IFRS 3 and SFAS (Statements of Financial Accounting Standards) 141, respectively.

EXHIBIT 6-1 Accounting Discrepancy Red Flags

1. The source of the revenue is questionable. Beware of revenue generated by selling to an affiliated party, selling something to a customer in exchange for something other than cash, or the receipt of investment income or cash received from a lender.

2. Income is inflated by nonrecurring gains. Gains on the sale of assets may be inflated by an artificially low book value of the assets sold.

3. Deferred revenue shows an unusually large increase. Deferred revenue increases as a firm collects money from customers in advance of delivering its products. It is reduced as the products are delivered. A jump in this balance sheet item could mean the firm is having trouble delivering its products.

4. Reserves for bad debt are declining as a percentage of revenue. This implies the firm may be boosting revenue by not reserving enough to cover probable losses from customer accounts that cannot be collected.

5. Growth in accounts receivable exceeds substantially the increase in revenue or inventory. This may mean that a firm is having difficulty selling its products (and hence inventories are accumulating) or that it is having difficulty collecting what it is owed.

6. The growth in net income is significantly different from the growth in cash from operations. Because it is more difficult to "manage" cash flow than net income (which is subject to distortion due to improper revenue recognition), this could indicate that net income is being deliberately misstated. Potential distortion may be particularly evident if the analyst adjusts end-of-period cash balances by deducting cash received from financing activities and adding back cash used for investment purposes. Consequently, changes in the adjusted cash balances should reflect changes in reported net income.

7. An increasing gap exists between a firm's income reported on its financial statements and its tax income. Although it is legitimate for a firm to follow different accounting practices for financial reporting and tax purposes, the relationship between book and tax accounting is likely to remain constant over time, unless there are changes in tax rules or accounting standards.

8. Unexpected large asset write-offs exist. This may reflect management inertia in incorporating changing business circumstances into its accounting estimates.

9. Related-party transactions are used extensively. Such transactions may not be subject to the same discipline and high standards of integrity as transactions between unrelated parties.

10. Changes in auditing firms are not well justified. The firm may be seeking a firm that will accept its aggressive accounting positions.

the date of the signing of the agreement of purchase and sale, and recorded on the books of the acquiring company. Net assets refer to acquired assets less assumed liabilities. Any excess of the purchase price over the fair value of the acquired net assets is recorded as goodwill. Goodwill is an asset representing future economic benefits arising from acquired assets that were not identified individually.

Revised accounting rules (SFAS 141R) have changed the standards covering business combinations to require the acquiring entity to recognize, separately from goodwill, identifiable assets and assumed liabilities at their acquisition date (closing date) fair values and to account for future changes in fair value. The intent was to achieve greater conformity with international accounting standards as applied to business combinations.[5] Another recent accounting standard change (SFAS 157) introduces a new definition of fair value, which could have a significant impact on the way mergers and acquisition are done. Previously, the definition of fair value was ambiguous, and it often was used inconsistently.[6]

SFAS 141R: The Revised Standards

The revised standards in SFAS 141R require an acquirer to recognize the assets acquired, the liabilities assumed, and any noncontrolling interest in the target, measured at their fair value as of the acquisition/closing date. Previous guidance had resulted in failure to recognize items on the date of the acquisition, such as acquisition-related expenses.

The revised standards retain the fundamental requirements that the applicable acquisition method of accounting for all business combinations be the purchase method of accounting and that an acquirer be identified for each business combination. The acquirer is defined as the entity that obtains control of one or more businesses in the business combination and the acquisition date is established as the date the acquirer achieves control. The acquisition date generally corresponds to the closing date rather than the announcement or signing date as was true previously.

A business is defined as an integrated set of activities and assets utilized in such a way as to provide a stream of benefits such as dividends, increasing share price, lower costs, and so on. As such, a business does not actually have to generate outputs. Consequently, what had been classified previously

---

[5] SFAS 141R applies to transactions with acquisition dates on or after December 15, 2008.
[6] The effective date for SFAS 157 was November 15, 2007, for financial assets and liabilities on financial statements and November 15, 2008, for nonfinancial assets and liabilities.

as asset purchases, such as pipeline purchases, or assets that were still in their development stage, such as reserves of natural resources, must now be treated as business combinations.

Recognizing Acquired Net Assets and Goodwill at Fair Value

To increase the ability to compare different transactions, Statement 141R requires the acquirer to recognize goodwill as of the acquisition date, measured as the excess of the purchase price plus the fair value of any noncontrolling (i.e., minority) interest in the target at the acquisition date over the fair value of the acquired net assets.

Statement 141R requires recognizing 100 percent of the assets acquired and liabilities assumed, even if less than 100 percent of the target's ownership interests are acquired by the buyer. In other words, this results in the recognition of the target's business in its entirety regardless of whether 51 percent, 100 percent, or any amount in between of the target is acquired. Consequently, the portion of the target that was not acquired (i.e., the noncontrolling or minority interest) is also recognized, causing the buyer to account for both the goodwill attributable to it as well as to the noncontrolling interest. Minority interest is reported in the consolidated balance sheet within the equity account, separately from the parent's equity. Moreover, the revenues, expenses, gains, losses, net income or loss, and other income associated with the noncontrolling interest should be reported on the consolidated income statement.

A "bargain" purchase is a business combination in which the total acquisition date fair value of the acquired net assets exceeds the fair value of the purchase price plus the fair value of any noncontrolling interest in the target. Such a purchase may arise due to forced liquidation or distressed sales. Statement 141R requires the acquirer to recognize that excess on the consolidated income statement as a gain attributable to the acquirer.

Recognizing and Measuring Net Acquired Assets in Step or Stage Transactions

The revised standards require an acquirer in a business combination undertaken in stages (i.e., a stage or step transaction) to recognize the acquired net assets as well as the noncontrolling interest in the target firm, at the full amounts of their fair values. Net acquired assets at each step must be revalued to the current fair market value. The acquirer is obligated to disclose gains or losses that arise due to the reestimation of the formerly noncontrolling interests on the income statement. Furthermore, if prior gains or losses on the noncontrolling interests were reported under "other comprehensive income," the acquirer is required to reclassify such gains or losses and report their impact on earnings.

Recognizing Contingent Considerations

Revised standards pertaining to contingencies and contingent considerations also may affect how deals are done. Contingencies are uncertainties—such as potential legal, environmental, and warranty claims about which the future may not be fully known at the time a transaction is consummated—that may result in future assets or liabilities. Under the new standards, the acquirer must recognize an asset or liability arising from a contingency at its acquisition date fair value absent new information about the possible outcome. However, as new information becomes available, the acquirer must revalue the asset or liability to its current fair value reflecting the new information and record the impact of changes in the fair values of these assets or liabilities on earnings. This is likely to encourage more rigorously defined limits on liability in acquisitions, with indemnification clauses that cover specific issues rather than general indemnification clauses.

Contingent consideration or payments are an important component of many transactions and include the transfer of additional equity or cash to the previous owners of the target firm (e.g., earnouts). Payment of contingent consideration depends on the acquired business achieving certain prespecified performance benchmarks over some period. Statement 141R treats contingent consideration as part of the total consideration paid (i.e., purchase price) for the acquired business, and it is measured at the acquisition date fair value. The revised standard also requires the reporting entity to reestimate the fair value of the contingent consideration at each reporting date until the amount of the payout (if any) is determined, with changes in fair value during the period reported as a gain or loss on the income statement. The potential for increased earnings volatility due to changes in the value of contingent liabilities may reduce the attractiveness of earnouts as a form of consideration.

In-Process Research & Development Assets

Under the new standards, the acquirer must recognize separately from goodwill the acquisition date fair values of R&D assets acquired in the business combination. Such assets will remain on the books as an asset with an indefinite life until the project's outcome is known. If the specific project is deemed a success, the firm will begin to amortize the asset over the estimated useful life of the technology; if the research project is abandoned, the R&D asset booked at the date of the acquisition will be considered impaired and expensed.

Expensing Deal Costs

Under the new standard, transaction-related costs such as legal, accounting, and investment banking fees are recorded as an expense on the closing date and charged against current earnings. As such, firms may need to explain the nature of the costs incurred in closing a deal and the impact of such costs on the earnings of the combined firms. This could result in downward pressure on such fees as acquirers become more aggressive in negotiating the cost of legal and advisory services. Financing costs, such as expenses incurred as a result of new debt and equity issues, will continue to be capitalized and amortized over time.

SFAS 157: The New Fair Value Framework

The purpose of SFAS 157 is to establish a single definition of fair value and a consistent framework for measuring fair value under GAAP to increase consistency and comparability in fair value estimates. The new definition of fair value under SFAS 157 is the price that would be received to sell an asset or paid to transfer a liability in an orderly transaction (i.e., not a forced liquidation or distress sale) between market participants on the date the asset or liability is to be estimated. This new definition introduces the notion that fair value is an "exit" price a market participant would pay the seller for a company, asset, or investment. An asset's "entry" price will always be the price paid, but the asset's exit price can fluctuate dramatically, reflecting changing market, industry, or regulatory conditions.

SFAS 157 allows acquirers to use the market approach (i.e., valuation based on prices paid for comparable assets or in recent transactions), income approach (i.e., discounted cash flow), or replacement cost approach (which involves estimating what it would cost to physically replace an asset). When a valuation approach is selected, SFAS 157 requires sufficient disclosure to enable users of financial statements to understand how an asset was valued. So-called Level 1 assets are those whose valuation is based on quoted prices for identical assets or liabilities in an active or liquid market. Level 2 assets and liabilities are valued based on either a quote for an identical item in an inactive or illiquid market or a quote for similar items in an active or liquid market. Level 3 assets and liabilities are valued using the firm's own data and valuation models.

IMPACT OF PURCHASE ACCOUNTING ON FINANCIAL STATEMENTS

A long-term asset is impaired if its fair value falls below its book or carrying value. Impairment could occur due to loss of customers, loss of contracts, loss of key personnel, obsolescence of technology, litigation, patent expiration, failure to achieve anticipated cost savings, overall market slowdown, and so on. In a case of *asset impairment*, the firm is required to report a loss equal to the difference between the asset's fair value and its carrying value.

The write down of assets associated with an acquisition constitutes a public admission by the firm's management of having substantially overpaid for the acquired assets. In an effort to minimize goodwill, auditors often require that factors underlying goodwill be tied to specific intangible assets for which fair value can be estimated, such as customer lists and brand names. These intangible assets must be capitalized and shown on the balance sheet. Consequently, if the anticipated cash flows associated with an intangible asset, such as a customer list, have not materialized, the carrying value of the customer list must be written down to reflect its current value.

Balance Sheet Considerations

For financial reporting purposes, the purchase price (PP) paid (including the fair value of any noncontrolling interest in the target at the acquisition date) for the target company consists of the fair market value of total identifiable acquired tangible and intangible assets (FMV_{TA}) less total assumed liabilities (FMV_{TL}) plus goodwill (FMV_{GW}). The difference between FMV_{TA} and FMV_{TL} is called *net asset value*.

These relationships can be summarized as follows:

Purchase price (total consideration): $PP = FMV_{TA} - FMV_{TL} + FMV_{GW}$

Calculation of goodwill: $FMV_{GW} = PP - FMV_{TA} + FMV_{TL} = PP - (FMV_{TA} - FMV_{TL})$

From this equation, it should be noted that as net asset value increases, FMV_{GW} decreases. Also note that the calculation of goodwill can result either in a positive (i.e., PP > net asset value) or negative (i.e., PP < net asset value). Negative goodwill arises if the acquired assets are purchased at a discount to their FMV and is referred to under Statement 141R as a "bargain purchase."

Exhibit 6–2 illustrates the calculation of goodwill in a transaction in which the acquirer purchases less than 100 percent of the target's

EXHIBIT 6-2 Estimating Goodwill

On January 1, 2009, Acquirer Inc. purchased 80 percent of Target Inc.'s 1,000,000 shares outstanding at $50 per share, for a total value of $40,000,000 (0.8 × 1,000,000 shares outstanding × $50/share). On that date, the fair value of the net assets acquired from Target was estimated to be $42,000,000. Acquirer paid a 20 percent control premium, which was already included in the $50 per share purchase price. The implied minority discount of the minority shares is 16.7 percent [i.e., $1 - (1/(1 + 0.2))$].*

What is the value of the goodwill shown on Acquirer's consolidated balance sheet? What portion of that goodwill is attributable to the minority interest retained by the Target's shareholders? What is the fair value of the 20 percent minority interest measured on a fair value per share basis?

Goodwill shown on Acquirer's balance sheet

From the equation in the chapter text, goodwill (FMV_{GW}) can be estimated as follows:

$$FMV_{GW} = PP - (FMV_{TA} - FMV_{TL}) = \$50,000,000 - \$42,000,000 = \$8,000,000,$$

where $50,000,000 = $50/share × 1,000,000 shares outstanding.

Goodwill attributable to the minority interest

Note that 20 percent of the total shares outstanding equals 200,000 shares with a market value of $10,000,000 ($50/share × 200,000). Therefore, the amount of goodwill attributable to the minority interest is calculated as follows:

Fair Value of Minority Interest:	$10,000,000
Less: 20% fair value of net acquired assets (0.2 × $42,000,000):	$ 8,400,000
Equals: Goodwill attributable to minority interest:	$ 1,600,000

Fair value of the minority interest per share

Because the fair value of Acquirer's interest in Target and Target's retained interest are proportional to their respective ownership interest, the value of the ownership distribution of the majority and minority owners is as follows:

Acquirer Interest (0.8 × 1,000,000 × $50/share)	$40,000,000
Target Minority Interest (0.2 × 1,000,000 × $50/share)	$10,000,000
Total Market Value	$50,000,000

Were the minority interest to be sold, the fair market value per share of the minority interest is $41.65 [(($10,000,000/200,000) × (1−0.167))]. The minority share value is less than the share price of the controlling shareholders (i.e.,

(Continued)

EXHIBIT 6-2 (Continued)
$50/share) because it must be discounted for the relative lack of influence on the firm's decision-making process of minority shareholders.

*Control premiums represent the amount an investor is willing to pay in excess of the current market price of a firm to gain the benefits of control. Such benefits include being able to make important strategic and tactical business decisions. Minority investors, those with a less-than-controlling interest, would value a minority position at a discount from the firm's current market value to reflect the potential erosion in the value of their investment that might occur if the controlling investors made decisions not in their best interests. Such decisions could include the payment of dividends, assumption of excessive amounts of debt, the payment of above-market prices to vendors owned by the controlling shareholders, or the receipt of below-market prices for products sold to customers owned by the controlling shareholders. The minority discount (MD) can be approximated as follows:

$$MD = 1 - (1/1 + MI), \text{ where MI represents the minority interest.}$$

This implies that the smaller the minority ownership interest in a business, the larger the reduction in the fair market value of the minority interest.

---

outstanding shares. Exhibit 6–3 lists valuation guidelines for each major balance sheet category.

Many assets, such as intangibles, are not specifically identified on the firm's balance sheet. In the United States, companies expense the cost of investing in intangibles in the year in which the investment is made; the rationale is the difficulty in determining whether a particular expenditure results in a future benefit (i.e., an asset, not an expense). For example, the value of the Coca-Cola brand name clearly has value extending over many years, but there is no estimate of this value on the firm's balance sheet.

Firms capitalize (i.e., value and display as assets on the balance sheet) the costs of acquiring identifiable intangible assets. The value of such assets can be ascertained from similar transactions made elsewhere. The acquirer must consider the future benefits of the intangible asset to be at least equal to the price paid. Specifically, identifiable assets must have a finite life. Intangible assets are listed as identifiable if the asset can be separated from the firm and sold, leased, licensed, or rented—such as patents and customer lists. Intangible assets also are viewed as identifiable if they are contractually or legally binding. An example is the purchase of a firm that has a leased manufacturing facility whose cost is less than the current cost of a comparable lease. The difference would be listed as an intangible asset on the consolidated balance sheet of the acquiring firm.

EXHIBIT 6-3 Guidelines for Valuing Acquired Assets and Liabilities

1. Cash and accounts receivable, reduced for bad debt and returns, are valued at their values on the books of the target on the acquisition date.

2. Marketable securities are valued at their realizable value after any transaction costs.

3. Inventories are broken down into finished goods and raw materials. Finished goods are valued at their liquidation value; raw material inventories are valued at their current replacement cost. Last-in, first-out inventory reserves maintained by the target before the acquisition are eliminated.

4. Property, plant, and equipment are valued at fair market value on the acquisition date.

5. Accounts payable and accrued expenses are valued at the levels stated on the target's books on the acquisition date.

6. Notes payable and long-term debt are valued at their net present value of future cash payments discounted at the current market rate of interest for similar securities.

7. Pension fund obligations are booked at the excess or deficiency of the present value of the projected benefit obligations over the present value of pension fund assets. This may result in an asset or liability being recorded by the consolidated firms.

8. All other liabilities are recorded at their net present value of future cash payments.

9. Intangible assets are booked at their appraised values on the acquisition date.

10. Goodwill is the difference between the purchase price less the fair market value of the target's net asset value. Positive goodwill is recorded as an asset, whereas negative goodwill (i.e., a bargain purchase) is shown as a gain on the acquirer's consolidated income statement.

Firms must amortize the value of the asset over this estimated lifespan. Firms must test the value of intangible assets that are amortized periodically for impairment, following a procedure similar to that used for goodwill. The test compares the "carrying value" (i.e., value as shown on the firm's financial statements) to the fair value of the intangible asset and requires recognition of an impairment loss whenever the carrying value exceeds the fair value.

The test for intangibles not requiring amortization (e.g., goodwill) is different from that of tangibles. The test for assets requiring amortization necessitates comparison of the undiscounted cash flows of the asset to the asset's carrying value. Intangibles not requiring amortization have an indefinite life and thus no defined period over which to project cash flows. Therefore, determining the fair value of goodwill is often difficult. It entails estimating the fair value of the reporting unit that resulted from a previously acquired firm for which the purchase price exceeded the fair value of net acquired assets, resulting in the creation of goodwill. Generally, the reporting unit does not have shares trading on a public exchange. Firms often employ comparable company valuation methods (e.g., price to earnings ratios for similar companies) to value the reporting unit.

Intangible assets can be classified into three categories. **Operational intangibles** are the ability of a business to continue to function and generate income without interruption because of a change in ownership. **Production intangibles** or **product intangibles** are values placed on the accumulated intellectual capital resulting from the production and product design experience of the combined entity. **Marketing intangibles** are those factors that help a firm to sell a product or service. Exhibit 6–4 details these categories.[7]

Exhibit 6–5 illustrates the balance sheet impacts of purchase accounting on the acquirer's balance sheet and the effects of impairment subsequent to closing. Assume that Acquirer Inc. purchases Target Inc. on 12/31/2009 (the acquisition date) for $500 million. Identifiable acquired assets and assumed liabilities are shown at their fair value on the acquisition date. The excess of the purchase price over the fair value of net acquired assets is shown as goodwill. The fair value of the "reporting unit" (i.e., Target Inc.) is determined annually to ensure that its fair value exceeds its carrying value. As of December 31, 2010, it is determined that the fair value of Target Inc. has fallen below its carrying value due largely to the loss of a number of key customers.

---

[7] For tax and financial reporting purposes, goodwill is a residual item equal to the difference between the purchase price for the target company and fair market value of net assets, including identifiable operational, production, and marketing intangible assets. In most cases, intangible assets, like tangible assets, have separately determinable values with limited useful lives. In certain cases, the useful lives are defined by the legal protection afforded by the agency issuing the protection, such as the U.S. Patent Office. In contrast, the useful life of intangible assets such as customer lists is more difficult to define. See DePamphilis (2009), Chapters 7 and 8, for a detailed discussion of alternative valuation methods to value both tangible and intangible assets.

EXHIBIT 6-4 Intangible Asset Categories

Intangible Asset Categories	Examples
Operating Intangibles	Assembled and trained workforce*
	Operating and administrative systems*
	Corporate culture*
Production or Product Intangibles	Patents
	Technological know-how
	Production standards
	Copyrights
	Software
	Favorable leases and licenses
Marketing Intangibles	Customer lists and relationships
	Price lists and pricing strategies*
	Marketing strategies, studies, and concepts*
	Advertising and promotional materials*
	Trademarks and service marks
	Trade names
	Covenants not to compete
	Franchises

*Intangible assets often included as part of goodwill because they are not easily separable from other assets or contractually/legally binding.

EXHIBIT 6-5 Balance Sheet Impacts of Purchase Accounting

Target Inc. Purchase Price, 12/31/2009 (Total Consideration)		$500,000,000
Fair Values of Target Inc.'s Net Assets on 12/31/2009		
Current Assets	$40,000,000	
Plant and Equipment	$200,000,000	
Customer List	$180,000,000	
Copyrights	$120,000,000	
Current Liabilities	($35,000,000)	
Long-Term Debt	($100,000,000)	

(Continued)

EXHIBIT 6-4 (Continued)

Value Assigned to Identifiable Net Assets		$405,000,000
Value Assigned to Goodwill		$95,000,000
Carrying Value as of 12/31/2009		$500,000,000
Fair Values of Target Inc.'s Net Assets on 12/31/2010		$400,000,000*
Current Assets	$30,000,000	
Plant and Equipment	$175,000,000	
Customer List	$100,000,000	
Copyrights	$120,000,000	
Current Liabilities	($25,000,000)	
Long-Term Debt	($90,000,000)	
Fair Value of Identifiable Net Assets		$310,000,000
Value of Goodwill		$90,000,000
Carrying Value After Impairment on 12/31/2010		$400,000,000
Impairment Loss (Difference between 12/31/2010 and 12/31/1009 carrying values)		$100,000,000

*Note that the 12/31/2010 carrying value is estimated based on the discounted value of projected cash flows of the reporting unit and therefore represents the fair market value of the unit on that date. The fair value is the sum of the fair value of identifiable net assets plus goodwill.

Income Statement and Cash Flow Considerations

For financial reporting purposes, an upward valuation of tangible and intangible assets, other than goodwill, raises depreciation and amortization expenses, which lowers operating and net income. For tax purposes, goodwill created after July 1993 may be amortized up to 15 years and is tax deductible. Goodwill booked before July 1993 is not tax deductible. Cash flow benefits from the tax deductibility of additional depreciation and amortization expenses that are written off over the useful lives of the assets. This assumes that the acquirer paid more than the target's net asset value. If the purchase price paid is less than the target's net asset value, the acquirer records a one-time gain equal to the difference on its income statement. If the carrying value of the net asset value subsequently falls below its fair market value, the acquirer records a one-time loss equal to the difference.

INTERNATIONAL ACCOUNTING STANDARDS

Ideally, financial reporting would be the same across the globe, but at this writing it is not yet the case, although the bodies responsible for setting standards have pledged to work diligently to achieve that objective as soon as practical. The discussion of financial reporting for business combinations focuses on the application of GAAP in the United States. Many of the same challenges are addressed in the application of the International Financial Reporting Standards (IFRS) of the International Accounting Standards Board (IASB). When financial information is compared for companies operating in multiple countries, it is important to achieve comparability of the reporting methods and accounting principles employed by the acquisition and merger targets.

The overarching objective of the IASB is the convergence of accounting standards worldwide and the establishment of global standards, sometimes referred to as "global GAAP." Since 2005, firms across the European Union have to conform to the above-mentioned IFRS directives.

Non-U.S. firms that have debt or equity securities trading in the United States must either file a Form 10-K using GAAP or a Form 20-F report with the U.S. Securities and Exchange Commission. The Form 20-F report must include a reconciliation of shareholders' equity and net income as reported in the firm's local country with GAAP in the United States. Such information enables the translation of the financial statements of a non-U.S. firm to achieve comparable accounting principles in the United States.

RECAPITALIZATION ACCOUNTING

An acquisition resulting in a change in control (i.e., a change in majority voting power) must use purchase accounting for recording the net assets of the acquired business on the acquirer's financial statements. However, under certain circumstances that arise with a leveraged buyout (LBO), control may change without changing the basis of the acquired assets and liabilities. In an LBO, some of the target's shareholders will continue to own stock in the postacquisition firm. For example, assume the buyer makes an equity investment in the firm by acquiring new shares issued directly by the target. The target uses this equity infusion to borrow money to repurchase some, but not all, of the target's outstanding shares. Consequently, some old target shareholders continue to own a significant part of the firm.

Recapitalization accounting applies when either of the following two conditions is met. One, there is no change in control of the target firm since the target's old investors continue to own a substantial portion of the target's equity after the acquisition. Two, there is change of control of the target, but the target survives as an entity (e.g., a reverse triangular merger) and the target's shareholders own more than 20 percent of the resulting business.

The advantage of recapitalization accounting is that acquired net assets do not have to be restated for book purposes. If the value of the acquired assets were revised upward, net income would be reduced as a result of an increase in depreciation expense. Furthermore, because the acquired net assets are not restated to their fair market value, no goodwill is created. The absence of goodwill eliminates concern about future goodwill write-offs due to impairment and the potential violation of loan covenants requiring a certain minimum level of debt to total assets. Also, absent an asset write-up, financial returns will be higher because they are calculated on a lower asset base. Therefore, when the target is to be taken public or sold to a strategic buyer, its financials will be more favorable since recapitalization rather than purchase accounting was applied to the target's financial statements when the firm was taken private.

★ ★ ★

Financial data in the valuation of the target firm and in the negotiation process have limitations. The changes in financial reporting requirements and purchase accounting rules on financial statements are all important in the M&A process, as will be the eventual convergence of Generally Accepted Accounting Principles and International Financial Reporting Standards.

A Case in Point: JDS Uniphase-SDL Merger Results in Huge Write-off

It began as the biggest technology merger ever when it was proposed on July 10, 2000. Then a declining stock market, weakening economy, and concerns about cash flow in the wake of actions to win regulatory approval saw its value plummet.

The deal in question involved JDS Uniphase (JDSU) and SDL. JDSU was the dominant supplier in the market for fiberoptic components for telecommunication and cable systems providers worldwide, packaging entire systems into a single integrated unit. SDL's products, including pump lasers, support the transmission of data, voice, video, and Internet information over fiberoptic networks by expanding their fiberoptic communications networks much more quickly and efficiently than would be possible using conventional electronic and optical technologies. JDSU believed a merger with SDL would allow it to add a line of lasers to its JDSU product, offering strengthened signals beamed across fiber-optic networks, and would bolster its capacity to package multiple components into a single product line.

The mega-merger was valued at $41 billion when proposed. The challenge was whether JDSU could win approval for the merger from the U.S. Department of Justice (DoJ); some feared the merger would result in a supplier that could exercise enormous pricing power over the entire range of products, from raw components to packaged products, purchased by equipment manufacturers. Regulators were also concerned that the combined entities could control the market for a specific type of pump laser used in a wide range of optical equipment. Other manufacturers of pump lasers, such as Nortel Networks, Lucent Technologies, and Corning, complained to regulators that they would have to buy some of the chips necessary to manufacture their pump lasers from a supplier (JDSU) that, in combination with SDL, also would be a competitor.

A regulatory review lengthened the period between the signing of the merger agreement and the actual closing to more than seven months. The risk to SDL shareholders was that JDSU shares could decline in price during this period, lessening the value of the deal at closing. But given the size of the premium, JDSU's management was unwilling to protect SDL's shareholders from this possibility by providing a "collar" within which the exchange ratio could fluctuate. This proved particularly devastating to SDL shareholders, who continued to hold JDSU stock well beyond the closing date.

What was originally valued at $41 billion when first announced had fallen, after the seven-month regulatory review, to $13.5 billion on the day of closing. How did this story unfold? A variety of factors played a part.

One was that JDSU agreed, as part of a consent decree with DoJ, to sell a Swiss subsidiary that manufactured pump laser chips to Nortel Networks Corporation, a JDSU customer. This agreement was aimed at satisfying DoJ concerns about the proposed merger. The divestiture of this operation set up an alternative supplier of such chips, thereby alleviating concerns expressed by other manufacturers of pump lasers that they would have to buy such components from a competitor. But it also extended the regulatory review period.

Another factor was how the deal was structured. On July 9, 2000, the JDSU and SDL boards both unanimously approved an agreement to merge SDL with a newly formed, wholly owned subsidiary of JDS Uniphase, K2 Acquisition, Inc.—which was created by JDSU as the acquisition vehicle to complete the merger. In a reverse triangular merger, K2 was merged into SDL, with SDL as the surviving entity. The postclosing organization comprised SDL as a wholly owned subsidiary of JDS Uniphase. The form of payment was an exchange of JDSU common stock for SDL common shares at a share exchange ratio of 3.8 shares of JDSU stock for each SDL common share outstanding—a premium of about 43 percent over the price of SDL's stock on the announcement date. Instead of a fraction of a share, each SDL stockholder received cash, without interest, equal to the dollar value of the fractional share at the average of the closing prices for a share of JDSU common stock for the five trading days before the completion of the merger.

Under the rules of the NASDAQ National Market, JDSU was required to seek stockholder approval for any issuance of common stock to acquire another firm. This requirement is triggered if the amount issued exceeds 20 percent of its issued and outstanding shares of common stock and of its voting power. In connection with the merger, both SDL and JDSU received fairness opinions from advisors employed by the firms.

The merger agreement specified that the merger could be consummated when all of the conditions stipulated in the agreement were either satisfied or waived by the parties to the agreement. Both JDSU and SDL were subject to certain closing conditions specified in JDSU's September 7, 2000, S4 filing with the SEC (required whenever a firm intends to issue securities to the public). The consummation of the merger was to be subject to approval by the shareholders of both companies, the approval of the regulatory authorities as specified under the Hart–Scott–Rodino (HSR) Antitrust Improvements Act of 1976, and any other foreign antitrust law that applied. For both parties, representations and warranties must have been found to be accurate, and both parties must have complied with all of the agreements and covenants (promises) in all material ways.

Some 18 closing conditions were found in the merger agreement. For example, the merger was structured so that JDSU and SDL's shareholders would not recognize a gain or loss for U.S. federal income tax purposes in the merger, except for taxes payable because of cash received by SDL shareholders for fractional shares. Both JDSU and SDL were required to receive opinions of tax counsel that the merger would qualify as a tax-free reorganization (also stipulated as a closing condition). Were the merger agreement to be terminated as a result of an acquisition of SDL by another firm within 12 months of the termination, SDL could be required to pay JDSU a termination fee of $1 billion.

Despite dramatic cost-cutting efforts, JDSU reported a loss of $7.9 billion for the quarter ending June 30, 2001, and $50.6 billion for the 12 months ending June 30, 2001. This compares to the projected pro forma loss reported in the September 9, 2000, S4 filing of $12.1 billion. The actual loss was the largest annual loss ever reported by a U.S. firm to that date. The fiscal year 2000 loss included a reduction in the value of goodwill carried on the balance sheet of $38.7 billion to reflect the declining market value of net assets acquired during a series of previous transactions. Most of this reduction was related to goodwill arising from the merger of JDS FITEL and Uniphase and the subsequent acquisitions of SDL, E-TEK, and OCLI.

The stock continued to tumble in line with the declining fortunes of the telecommunications industry; by mid-2001, it was trading as low as $7.50 per share, about 6 percent of its value the day the merger with SDL was announced.

Thus, the JDS Uniphase–SDL merger achieved two distinctions. At the time, it was the largest purchase price paid for a pure technology company, and it came to be the largest write-off ever (at the time). Both "achievements" took place within 12 months.

Things to Think About:

1. What is goodwill? How is it estimated? Why did JDS Uniphase write down the value of its goodwill in 2001? Why did this reflect a series of poor management decisions with respect to mergers completed between 1999 and early 2001?

2. How might the use of stock, as an acquisition "currency," have contributed to the sustained decline in JDSU's stock through mid-2001? In your judgment, what is the likely impact of the glut of JDSU shares in the market on the future appreciation of the firm's share price? Explain your answer.

3. What are the primary differences between a forward and a reverse triangular merger? Why might JDS Uniphase have chosen to merge its K2 Acquisition Inc. subsidiary with SDL in a reverse triangular merger? Explain your answer.

4. Discuss various methodologies you might use to value assets acquired from SDL such as existing technologies, "core" technologies, trademarks and trade names, assembled workforce, and deferred compensation?

5. Why do boards of directors of both acquiring and target companies often obtain so-called fairness opinions from outside investment advisors or accounting firms? Should stockholders have confidence in such opinions? Why or why not?

Answers can be found at:
www.elsevierdirect.com/companion.jsp?ISBN=9780123749499

CHAPTER 7

Financing Structures and Strategies

Typically, a firm pursues a financing *strategy* that will result in a financing *structure* that maximizes the value of the firm. The financial structure (or capital structure) is the dollar amount of debt compared to equity a firm uses to finance its growth in assets. The strategy for getting there is very important.

A poorly designed financing strategy can have disastrous affects for buyers, sellers, and lenders. When a consortium of three buyout firms purchased Home Depot Inc.'s HD supply business in mid-2007 for $10.3 billion, three banks were involved. The banks agreed to provide the buyers with a $4 billion loan based on the expectation that the loans could be sold to investors. Growing unease in the credit markets later that year, however, raised questions about the potential for default of *all* loans made to finance highly leveraged transactions. Many lenders sought added financial protections, including these three banks. Fearing they would not be able to resell the loans, the banks insisted on stricter covenants. Eventually, the banks agreed to provide financing based on only slightly more restrictive covenants, the buyer consortium agreed to pay higher fees to the lenders, and Home Depot agreed to lower the selling price to $8.5 billion and guarantee a portion of the debt if the buyout firms defaulted on the loans.

A properly structured financing strategy should be sufficiently flexible to allow for the kind of unforeseen event—the collapse of the credit markets—that had such an impact on the Home Depot deal. Flexibility includes not borrowing so much up front that it is impossible to borrow more in an emergency, and not borrowing at terms that become unrealistic if market conditions change unexpectedly—which they often do.

Merger and acquisition financing strategies or plans should be developed before negotiations are completed, and include developing a balance sheet and income and cash flow statements for the combined firms. The financing plan also provides insights into the appropriate composition of the purchase price by projecting the potential for earnings per share dilution if the acquirer issues a substantial number of new shares, as well as the

Mergers and Acquisitions Basics
ISBN: 978-0-12-374949-9, DOI: 10.1016/B978-0-12-374949-9.00007-5
149

potential for higher borrowing costs if leverage is increased significantly. Consequently, by simulating alternative financial structures (e.g., debt-to-equity ratios), the acquirer can gain insight into what might constitute the least costly way of financing the transaction. The financing plan thus serves as a reality check for the buyer.

No matter the size or composition of the offer price, lenders and equity investors will want to see a coherent analysis explaining why the proposed transaction is a good investment opportunity for them. Lenders want assurances of timely repayment at a rate that compensates them for the perceived risk of the deal. Equity investors require some degree of confidence that the risk they assume will come with an adequate reward, especially because they are subordinate to lenders if the firm should ultimately be liquidated.

The focus here is on reasons financing structures matter, the various alternatives for financing transactions, the complex capital structures of highly leveraged transactions, and ways of selecting the appropriate capital structure.[1]

WHY FINANCING STRUCTURES MATTER

A financing structure, also called a capital structure, is the way a firm finances its asset growth using some combination of equity, debt, or hybrid securities (i.e., those displaying both debt and equity characteristics). For example, a firm with $100 million in assets may have financed the purchase of those assets by issuing $30 million in equity and borrowing $70 million in debt. The ratio of the firm's debt to equity is a measure of the firm's leverage (i.e., the number of dollars a firm has borrowed per dollar of equity).

Some economists theorize that the value of a firm is unaffected by how it is financed. They assume, though, a perfect world in which there are no taxes, no transaction or bankruptcy costs, where management decisions are always made in the best interests of the shareholders (i.e., agency costs are zero), and in which all investors have access to the same information as the firm's management.[2] Using debt is considered better than using equity.

The real world is quite different. In the real world, whatever tax advantage there might be to using debt must be balanced—because of

---

[1] See DePamphilis (2009), Chapter 13, for a more detailed discussion of this topic.
[2] The Modigliani–Miller theorem was named for economists Franco Modigliani and Merton Miller, who developed it in the late 1950s. According to the theory, using debt becomes more valuable than equity—because of the tax deductibility of interest—and the best or optimal financing or capital structure would be to have virtually no equity. See Modigliano and Miller (1958).

tradeoffs—against the potential costs of bankruptcy if leverage becomes excessive. These costs can be measured by the increased interest rate lenders will charge as the firm increases its leverage. The amount of leverage acceptable for firms often varies from industry to industry because the predictability of cash flows and the availability of tangible assets to serve as collateral also differ.

Although such tradeoffs tend to explain differences in leverage of firms across industries, it does not explain differences in firms within the same industry, which may be due to perceptions managers have about their firm's future prospects. This so-called pecking order theory argues that managers tend to use equity to finance investments only as a last resort and incorporates the notion that managers have access to more information than investors. In the "pecking order," managers prefer to borrow when they believe their firm's stock is undervalued and issue new stock when they believe their stock is overvalued. When the stock is undervalued, the firm would have to issue more shares to raise the same amount of funds than if its stock were overvalued. Because shares represent ownership claims on the firm's earnings, cash flows, assets, and liabilities, existing shareholders would prefer to issue as few shares as possible to minimize the extent to which their existing ownership interest is diluted.

Not all management actions are necessarily in the best interests of shareholders; these so-called agency costs also help explain the relevance of a company's financing/capital structure. As leverage increases, management has an incentive to undertake increasingly risky investments because, if successful, shareholders will reap all the upside profit after interest and principal on the debt are repaid. Increased leverage, however, may also increase the probability of bankruptcy. Furthermore, managers may have an incentive to grow a firm (e.g., through acquisition) to increase their compensation, perks, and influence—and the increased leverage growth requires may eventually restrain management by reducing the firm's free cash flow (i.e., cash available to reward shareholders) as interest expense increases.

FINANCING STRATEGIES: BORROWING

After a prospective target has been identified, the buyer may choose from a number of financing alternatives. For the risk-averse acquirer, the ideal mechanism might be to finance the transaction with cash held by the target in excess of normal working capital requirements. Such situations, though, are unusual. Venture capital or wealthy individual "angel" investors also may be available to fund the transaction—although this can be quite expensive financing because the buyer may have to relinquish majority ownership of the acquired company. Using the buyer's stock may be an appropriate way to minimize the initial cash outlay, but such an option rarely is available in a management buyout or a buyout by privately held companies.

The seller may be willing to accept debt issued by the buyer if an upfront cash payment is not important. For the buyer, though, this can be highly disadvantageous if the seller places substantial restrictions on how the business may be managed. Using a public issue of long-term debt to finance the transaction may minimize the initial cash outlay, but it is also subject to restrictions on how the business may be operated by the investors buying the issue. Moreover, public issues have high administrative, marketing, and regulatory reporting costs.

For these reasons, asset-based lending has emerged as an attractive alternative to using cash, stock, or public debt issues if the target has sufficient tangible assets to serve as collateral.

Asset-Based or Secured Lending

Under asset-based lending, the borrower pledges certain assets as collateral. Asset-based lenders look at the borrower's assets as their primary protection against the borrower's failure to repay. Such loans are often short term (less than one year in maturity) and secured by assets that can be liquidated easily, such as accounts receivable and inventory. Often, a borrower will seek a *revolving line of credit* to draw upon on a daily basis to run the business.

For a fee, the borrower may choose to convert the revolving credit line into a *term loan*, which typically matures in 2 to 10 years and is secured by the very asset being financed, such as new capital equipment. Borrowers often prefer term loans because they eliminate concerns about renewal, and they can be structured such that the loan period corresponds with the economic life of the item being financed. Term loans sometimes are used in leverage buyout (LBO) transactions to reduce the overall cost of borrowing; because they are negotiated privately between the borrower and the lender, they can be much less expensive than the cost of floating a public debt or stock issue.

Asset-based lenders generally require personal guarantees from the buyer, who must pledge personal assets such as a principal residence. This is especially true in small transactions if the buyer does not have a demonstrated track record buying and operating businesses.

Acquiring firms often prefer to borrow funds on an unsecured basis because the added administrative costs involved in pledging assets as security significantly raise the total cost of borrowing. Secured borrowing also can be onerous because of security agreements that severely limit a company's future borrowing and ability to pay dividends, make investments, and manage working capital aggressively. In many instances, however, borrowers may have little choice but to obtain secured lending for at least a portion of the purchase price.

Loan Documentation

The lending process entails negotiating a **loan agreement** that stipulates the terms and conditions under which the lender will loan the firm funds, a **security agreement**[3] specifying which of the borrower's assets will be pledged to secure the loan, and a **promissory note** that commits the borrower to repay the loan, even if the assets, when liquidated, do not fully cover the unpaid balance. These agreements contain certain security provisions and protective covenants that limit what the borrower may do as long as the loan is outstanding. The security agreement is filed at a state regulatory office in the state where the collateral is located, and future lenders can check to see which assets a firm has pledged and which are free to be used as future collateral.[4]

Pledging Receivables and Inventory

Depending on the extent to which they are collectable, lenders may lend as much as 80 to 90 percent of the book value of the receivables. Asset-based lenders generally are willing to lend only against receivables that are due within 90 days; receivables more than 90 days past due are likely to be difficult to collect. Lenders are not willing to lend the full amount of even the more current receivables because they are aware that some portion will not be collectable.

---

[3] Filing a security agreement legally establishes the lender's security interest in the collateral. If the borrower defaults on the loan or otherwise fails to honor the terms of the agreement, the lender can seize and sell the collateral to recover the value of the loan.

[4] The process of determining which of a firm's assets are free from liens is made easier today by commercial credit reporting repositories such as Dun & Bradstreet, Experian, Equifax, and TransUnion.

Inventories (raw material and finished goods but not work-in-process) also are commonly used to provide collateral for LBO transactions. Like receivables, inventory can be highly liquid. The amount a lender will advance against the book value of inventory depends on its ease of identification and its liquidity; the typical amount is between 50 and 80 percent, and lenders tend to loan less if the inventory is viewed as perishable, subject to rapid obsolescence, or as having relatively few potential buyers.

Pledging Equipment and Real Estate to Support Term Loans

Lenders are frequently willing to lend up to 80 percent of the appraised value of durable equipment and 50 percent of the value of real estate. Lenders are unlikely to lend against special purpose equipment, which is likely to have few potential buyers, and land, which is often difficult to convert to cash rapidly. The cash flows generated by the assets will be used to pay off the loan.

Security Provisions and Protective Covenants

Security provisions and protective covenants in loan documents are intended to ensure timely repayment of the interest and principal of outstanding loans. Typical security features include assigning payments due under a specific contract to the lender, assigning a portion of the receivables or inventories, and a pledge of marketable securities held by the borrower. Other features could include a mortgage on property, plant, and equipment held by the borrower, and assigning the cash surrender value of a life insurance policy held by the borrower on key executives.

An *affirmative covenant* is a portion of a loan agreement that specifies the actions the borrowing firm agrees to take during the term of the loan. These actions typically include furnishing periodic financial statements to the lender, carrying sufficient insurance to cover insurable business risks, maintaining a minimum amount of net working capital, and retaining key management personnel acceptable to the lender. A *negative covenant* restricts the actions of the borrower and may limit the amount of dividends that can be paid, the level of salaries and bonuses for the borrower's employees, the total amount of indebtedness the borrower can assume, investments in plant and equipment and acquisitions, and the sale of certain assets.

All loan agreements have default provisions permitting the lender to collect the loan immediately under certain conditions; they could include the borrower failing to pay interest, principal, or both, according to the terms of the loan agreement; the borrower materially misrepresenting information on the firm's financial statements; and the borrower failing to observe any of the affirmative or negative covenants. Loan agreements also commonly have **cross-default provisions** that allow a lender to collect its loan immediately if the borrower defaults on a loan to another lender.

Cash-Flow or Unsecured Lenders

Cash-flow lenders view the borrower's future ability to generate cash flow as the primary means of recovering a loan; the borrower's assets are a secondary source in the event of default. Cash-flow-based lending for LBOs became more commonplace in the mid-to-late 1980s, as the capital structures of many LBOs assumed increasing amounts of unsecured debt. To compensate for the additional risk, unsecured lenders would receive both a higher interest rate and warrants that were convertible into equity at a future date.

Unsecured debt, often called *mezzanine financing*, includes senior subordinated debt, subordinated debt, bridge financing, and LBO partnership financing. It frequently consists of high-yield junk bonds that may also include zero coupon deferred interest debentures (i.e., bonds whose interest is not paid until maturity) used to increase the postacquisition cash flow of the acquired entity.

In liquidation, this debt lies between the secured or asset-based debt and preferred and common equity. Unsecured financing often consists of several layers of debt, each subordinate in liquidation to the next most senior issue. Those with the lowest level of security normally offer the highest yields to compensate for their higher level of risk in the event of default.

Bridge financing consists of unsecured loans often provided by investment banks or hedge funds to supply short-term financing pending the placement of subordinated debt (i.e., long-term or "permanent" financing). The typical expectation is that bridge financing will be replaced six to nine months after the closing date of the LBO transaction.

Types of Long-Term Financing

Generally, long-term debt is classified according to whether it is secured. *Secured debt* issues usually are called mortgage bonds or equipment trust certificates; issues not secured by specific assets are called **debentures**, and their quality depends on the general creditworthiness of the issuing company. The attractiveness of long-term debt is its relatively low after-tax cost that results from interest being tax deductible. Leverage can also help improve earnings per share and returns on equity. Too much debt, though, can increase the risk of default on loan repayments and bankruptcy.

Convertible Debt and Debentures

Convertible bonds or debentures are types of debt that are convertible into shares of stock of the issuing company; this type of debt is often referred to as a hybrid security because it has both debt and equity characteristics. The conversions are allowed at some predetermined ratio (i.e., a specific number of shares per bond). The fixed number of dollars to be paid each payment period as a percent of the value of the bonds when issued, called the coupon rate, is typically relatively low for this type of debt. The bond buyer is compensated primarily through the ability to convert the bond to common stock at a substantial discount from the stock's market value.

Issuers of such debt benefit by having to pay lower cash interest payments. However, current shareholders will experience earnings or ownership dilution when bondholders convert their bonds into new shares. For example, a shareholder owning 10 percent of the outstanding shares of a firm will see her ownership position reduced to 5 percent if new share issues double the number of shares outstanding because of the conversion of such debt into equity.

Senior and Junior Debt

Long-term debt issues also are classified by whether they are senior or junior in liquidation. Senior debt has a higher priority claim to a firm's earnings and assets than junior debt. Unsecured debt also may be classified according to whether it is subordinated to other types of debt. In general, subordinated debentures are junior to other types of debt, including bank loans, and even may be junior to all of a firm's other debt.

Indentures

An *indenture* is a contract between the firm that issues the long-term debt securities and the lenders. It establishes the restrictions that determine the extent to which a debt issue is junior to other debt. The indenture details the nature of the issue, specifies the way in which the principal must be repaid, and specifies affirmative and negative covenants applicable to the long-term debt issue. Typical covenants include maintaining a minimum interest coverage ratio, a minimum level of working capital, a maximum amount of dividends that the firm can pay, and restrictions on equipment leasing and issuing additional debt.

Bond Ratings

Debt issues are rated by various rating agencies according to their relative degree of risk. The agencies consider a variety of factors, including a firm's earnings stability, interest coverage ratios, the relative amount of debt in the firm's capital structure, the degree of subordination of the issue being rated, and the firm's past performance in meeting its debt service requirements.[5]

Junk Bonds

Junk bonds are high-yield bonds that credit-rating agencies have deemed either to be below investment grade or that they have not rated at all.[6] When originally issued, junk bonds frequently yielded more than four percentage points above the yields on U.S. Treasury debt of comparable maturity.

Junk bond financing exploded at the beginning of the 1980s but dried up by the end of the decade.[7] Although junk bonds were a popular source of financing for takeovers, about three-fourths of the total proceeds of junk bonds issued between 1980 and 1986 were used to finance the capital requirements of high-growth corporations; the remainder was used to finance takeovers.[8] Junk bonds have assumed a subordinate role to other forms of financing for mergers and acquisitions in recent years.

Leveraged Bank Loans

Leveraged loans often are defined as unrated or noninvestment-grade bank loans with interest rates equal to or greater than the London Interbank

---

[5] Rating agencies include Moody's Investors Services and Standard & Poor's Corporation. Each has its own scale for identifying the risk of an issue. For Moody's, the ratings are Aaa (the lowest risk category), Aa, A, Baa, Ba, B, Caa, Ca, and C (the highest risk). For S&P, AAA denotes the lowest risk category, and risk rises progressively through ratings AA, A, BBB, BB, B, CCC, CC, C, and D.

[6] Moody's usually rates noninvestment-grade bonds Ba or lower; for S&P, it is BB or lower.

[7] Rapid growth of the junk bond market coincided with a growing deterioration during the 1980s in their quality, as measured by interest coverage ratios (i.e., earnings before interest and taxes/interest expense), debt/net tangible book value, and cash flow as a percentage of debt (Wigmore, 1994). Cumulative default rates for junk bonds issued in the late 1970s reached as high as 34 percent by 1986 (Asquith, Mullins, and Wolff, 1989), but firms that emerged from bankruptcy managed to recover some portion of the face value of the junk bond. Altman and Kishore (1996) found that recovery rates for senior secured debt averaged about 58 percent of the original principal and that the actual realized spread between junk bonds and 10-year U.S. Treasury securities was actually about four percentage points between 1978 and 1994, rather than more than four percentage points when they were issued originally. This source of LBO financing dried up in the late 1980s after a series of defaults of overleveraged firms, coupled with alleged insider trading and fraud at companies such as Drexel Burnham, the primary market maker for junk bonds at that time.

[8] Yago (1991).

Rate (LIBOR) plus 150 basis points (1.5 percentage points). Leveraged loans include second mortgages, which typically have a floating rate and give lenders a lower level of security than first mortgages. Some analysts include other forms of debt instruments in this market, such as mezzanine or senior unsecured debt, discussed earlier in this chapter, and payment-in-kind notes, for which interest is paid in the form of more debt.

In the United States, the volume of such loans substantially exceeds the volume of junk bond issues. This represents a revival in bank loan financing as an alternative to financing transactions with junk bonds after junk bond issues dried up in the late 1980s; at the time, bank loans were more expensive. Leveraged loans are often less costly than junk bonds for borrowers because they may provide a higher level of security than unsecured junk bonds.

Globally, the syndicated loan market (which includes leveraged loans, senior unsecured debt, and payment-in-kind notes) is growing more rapidly than public markets for debt and equity. Syndicated loans are those typically issued through a consortium of institutions, including hedge funds, pension funds, and insurance companies, to individual borrowers. Because such lending usually avoids the public debt markets, it often is referred to as the "private debt market."

The "Road Show"

To arrange both bridge and permanent financing, the buyer will develop elaborate presentations to convince potential lenders of the attractiveness of the lending opportunity. It is referred to as a "road show" for good reason: immaculately dressed borrowers passionately display confidence in their business plan through carefully rehearsed and choreographed multimedia presentations in stuffy conference rooms throughout the country. The road show is an opportunity for potential lenders to see management and to ask tough questions. If the road show succeeds, at least several lenders will compete for all or a portion of the bond issue, resulting in lower interest rates and less onerous loan covenants.

FINANCING STRATEGIES: EQUITY AND HYBRID SECURITIES

Unlike with debt and preferred equity, income payments on common stock can vary over time. Common stock, of which there are many varieties, represents shareholder ownership in the equity of a corporation. Some common stock pays dividends and offers voting rights entitling the owner to participate in certain corporate decisions such as electing members of the board of directors. Other common shares (often called supervoting shares) have multiple voting rights. The total return on capital stock reflects both the dividends paid as well as any capital appreciation due to increasing expected earnings and cash flow. Common stockholders participate in the firm's future earnings because they may receive a larger dividend if earnings increase.

If the corporation is forced to liquidate, common shareholders have rights to the firm's assets only after bondholders and preferred stockholders have been paid. In addition to voting rights, common shareholders sometimes receive rights offerings. Such rights allow common shareholders to maintain their proportional ownership in the company in the event that the company issues another stock offering. Common shareholders with rights have the right, but not the obligation, to acquire as many new shares of the stock as needed to maintain their proportional ownership in the company.

Like common stock, preferred stock is part of shareholders' equity. Although preferred stockholders receive dividends rather than interest payments, it is considered a fixed income security. Dividends on preferred stock are generally constant over time, like interest payments on debt, but the firm is generally not obligated to pay them at a specific time. Unpaid dividends may cumulate for eventual payment by the issuer if the preferred stock is a special cumulative issue. In liquidation, bondholders are paid first and then preferred stockholders; common stockholders are paid last. Preferred stock often is issued in LBO transactions because its claim is senior to common stock in the event of liquidation, which provides investors a fixed income security. To conserve cash, LBOs frequently issue *paid-in-kind (PIK) preferred stock*, where the dividend obligation can be satisfied by issuing additional par amounts of the preferred security.

FINANCING STRATEGIES: SELLER FINANCING

In some transactions, the seller may defer receipt of a portion of the purchase price until some future date. This so-called seller financing (also known as owner financing or owner carry-back) is a highly important source of financing for buyers.

In effect, the seller provides a loan to the buyer to cover a portion of or the entire purchase price. Typically, in a seller-financed transaction, the buyer contributes a large portion of the purchase price in cash, and the buyer and seller then negotiate a payback schedule and interest rate for the remaining balance. Sellers often are willing to carry a promissory note for some portion of the purchase price when the buyer is unable to get a bank loan or unwilling to put more cash or equity in the purchase price.

Seller financing may be used as way to "close the gap" between what a seller wants and what a buyer is willing to pay. A buyer may be willing to pay the seller's asking price if a portion is deferred because the buyer recognizes that the loan will reduce the purchase price in present or current value terms. Because less capital is needed at the time of closing, a seller-financed deal lowers the overall risk to the buyer, shifting operational risk to the seller if the buyer ultimately defaults on the loan to the seller.

Seller financing typically is unsecured. If the business being purchased is part of a larger parent company, the borrower may be able to obtain certain concessions from the parent. For example, the parent may be willing to continue to provide certain products and services to the business at cost to increase the likelihood that the business is successful and that its note will be repaid in a timely fashion.

Although most businesses do not want to use seller financing because it requires that they accept the risk that the note will not be repaid, such financing is necessary when bank financing is not an option. In the slumping economy of 2008 and 2009, as bank lending dried up and a crisis of confidence unfolded in the credit markets, there was an increase in seller financing to complete the sale of businesses, particularly of small, privately owned companies.

In many instances, a business may have excellent cash flow but very few tangible assets that can serve as collateral. Consequently, banks often are unwilling to lend under these circumstances, and seller financing may be absolutely necessary.

A seller may even use its willingness to provide financing as a way to market its business when it is difficult for buyers to obtain financing. By offering to finance a portion of the purchase price, the seller makes an implicit commitment to the buyer that shows confidence in the current and continuing financial viability of the business. It is this confidence that drives the willingness to take on a portion of the risk.

Exhibit 7-1 summarizes the alternative forms of security and sources of funds.

EXHIBIT 7-1 Financing Mergers and Acquisitions

Alternative Types	Debt	Equity
Asset-Based Lending (Collateralized by fixed assets, accounts receivable, and inventories) Cash-Flow-Based Lending (Based on projected cash flow)	Revolving Credit Lines Term Loans Sale/Lease Back	
Seller Financing	Deferred Payments Earnouts Installment Sales	Common Stock Preferred Stock
Public Offering and Private Placements	Senior Convertible Subordinated	Common Stock Preferred Stock
Alternative Sources	Commercial Banks Insurance Companies Pension Funds Investment/Merchant Banks Hedge Funds and Private Equity Partnerships	Hedge or Buyout Funds Private Equity Investors Venture Capital Strategic Investors Individual Investors ("Angels")

FINANCING STRATEGIES: SELLING DISCRETIONARY ASSETS

Discretionary assets are undervalued or redundant assets not required to operate the acquired business that can be used by the buyer to recover some portion of the purchase price. Such assets include land valued at its historical cost on the balance sheet or inventory and equipment whose resale value exceeds its fully depreciated value. Other examples include cash balances in excess of normal working capital needs and product lines or operating units considered nonstrategic by the buyer.

Target firm assets not considered critical to implementing the acquirer's business strategy could be sold to finance the purchase of the target firm.

Obviously, the best time to sell a business is when the owner does not need to sell, or when the demand for the business to be divested is greatest. The decision to sell should also reflect the broader financial environment. Selling when business confidence is high, stock prices are rising, and interest rates are low is likely to fetch a higher price. If the business to be sold is highly cyclical, the sale should be timed to coincide with the firm's peak year earnings. Businesses also can be timed to sell when they are considered most popular. In 1980, the oil exploration business was booming; by 1983, it was in the doldrums. It recovered again by the mid-1990s. What's hot today can fizzle tomorrow. A similar story could be told about many of the high-flying Internet-related companies of the late 1990s.

The selling process may be reactive or proactive. Reactive sales occur when a buyer unexpectedly approaches the parent with interest in either the entire firm or a portion of the firm, such as a product line or subsidiary. If the bid is sufficiently attractive, the parent firm may choose to reach a negotiated settlement with the bidder without investigating other options. This situation may occur if the parent is concerned about potential degradation of its business, or that of a subsidiary, if its interest in selling becomes public knowledge.

In contrast, proactive sales may be characterized as public or private solicitations. In a *public solicitation*, a firm can announce publicly that it is putting itself, a subsidiary, or a product line up for sale. Potential buyers then contact the seller. This is a way to identify interested parties relatively easily. Unfortunately, this approach can also attract unqualified bidders who lack the financial resources necessary to complete the deal. In a *private solicitation*, the parent firm may hire an investment banker or undertake on its own to identify potential buyers. When a list of perceived qualified buyers is compiled, contact is made.

In either a public or private solicitation, interested parties are asked to sign confidentiality agreements before given access to proprietary information. In a private solicitation, they may also be asked to sign a standstill agreement requiring them not to make an unsolicited bid. Parties willing to sign these agreements are then asked to submit preliminary, nonbinding "indications of interest" (i.e., a single number or a bid expressed as a range). Parties that submit preliminary bids are then ranked by the selling company in terms of bid size, form of payment (i.e., composition), the ability of the bidder to finance the transaction, form of acquisition (i.e., whether the bidder proposes to buy stock or assets), and ease of doing the deal. The latter factor involves an assessment of the difficulty in obtaining regulatory approval, if required, and of the integrity of the bidder. A small number of those submitting preliminary bids are then asked to submit a best and final offer (BAFO). Such offers must be binding on the bidder. At this point, the seller may choose to initiate an auction among the most attractive bids or go directly into negotiating a purchase agreement with a single party.

HIGHLY LEVERAGED TRANSACTIONS

Highly leveraged deals constitute some of the more complicated capital structures. A common example of a highly leveraged transaction (i.e., one in which a large portion of the purchase price is financed with debt) is the leveraged buyout, or LBO. An LBO investor is often called a *financial buyer* and may be inclined to use a large amount of debt to finance as much of the target's purchase price as possible. Financial buyers tend to concentrate on actions that enhance the target firm's ability to generate cash to satisfy their substantial debt service requirements. High leverage makes the potential returns to equity much more attractive than less-leveraged transactions with the 80 percent debt-financed purchase recording an after-tax return on common equity that is three times the return in an all-cash purchase (see Exhibit 7-2).

A *leveraged buyout* can be of an entire company or of a division of a company. LBO targets can be private or public firms. The funds borrowed

EXHIBIT 7-2 Impact of Leverage on Return to Shareholders*

	All-Cash Purchase	50% Cash/ 50% Debt	20% Cash/ 80% Debt
Purchase Price	$100	$100	$100
Equity (Cash Investment)	$100	$50	$20
Borrowings	0	$50	$80
Earnings Before Interest and Taxes	$20	$20	$20
Interest @ 10%	0	$5	$8
Income Before Taxes	$20	$15	$12
Less Income Taxes @ 40%	$8	$6	$4.8
Net Income	$12	$9	$7.2
After-Tax Return on Equity	12%	18%	36%

*Unless otherwise noted, all numbers are in millions of dollars.

are used to pay for most of the purchase price, with the remainder provided by a financial sponsor, such as a private equity investor group or hedge fund. Typically, the tangible assets of the firm to be acquired are used as collateral for the loans, with the most highly liquid assets—such as receivables and inventory—used for collateral to obtain bank financing and fixed assets used to secure a portion of long-term senior financing. Subordinated debt (often junk bond financing), either unrated or low-rated debt, is used to raise the balance of the purchase price.

When a public company is subject to an LBO, it is said to be *going private* in a public-to-private transaction because the equity of the firm has been purchased by a small group of investors and is no longer publicly traded. The buying group of the firm targeted to become a leveraged buyout often comprises incumbent managers from that very firm in what is called a *management buyout* (MBO).

LBO transactions surged in the 1980s, culminating in the $31.5 billion (including assumed debt) buyout in 1988 of RJR Nabisco by Kohlberg Kravis Roberts & Company. In the 1980s, companies that were targets of LBOs typically had substantial amounts of tangible assets and relatively low reinvestment requirements. Debt typically was reduced over time through asset sales and aggressive cost cutting rather than accelerating revenue growth. This boom period dissipated due to the 1991 recession and political backlash to such transactions. Following the tech boom in the late 1990s, the terrorist attacks of 9/11, and the 2001 recession, highly leveraged transactions once again surged upward, peaking in early 2007. The boom was largely fueled by a strong economy, low interest rates, and easy credit conditions.

Although private equity investors and hedge funds played an important role as financial sponsors (i.e., equity investors) in highly leveraged transactions throughout the three merger waves since the early 1980s, their role was largely a secondary one during the 1990s tech boom. The buyout binge came to a grinding halt when LBO financing dried up in late 2007 and throughout 2008.[9]

Exhibit 7-3 summarizes the types of securities and sources of funding often used to finance an LBO.

---

[9] When the boom came to a halt in late 2007 and early 2008, it forced private equity and hedge funds to retrench and—as a sign of the times—there were 91 defaults globally totaling $295 billion by private equity-backed companies during 2008 (according to Standard & Poor's). Reflecting the perceived risk associated with highly leveraged transactions, high yield spreads (i.e., the difference between high-risk corporate debt and U.S. Treasury bond rates) reached record levels in late 2008 of more than 17 percentage points, more than twice their historical average.

EXHIBIT 7-3 Leveraged Buyout Capital Structure

Type of Security		Debt	
	Backed By	Lenders Loan Up To	Lending Source
Secured Debt – Short-Term (<1 Year) Debt – Intermediate Term (1–10 Years) Debt	– Liens generally on receivables and inventories – Liens on land and equipment	– 50–80% depending on quality – Up to 80% of appraised value of equipment and 50% of real estate	– Banks and finance companies – Life insurance companies, private equity investors, pension and hedge funds
Unsecured or Mezzanine Debt (Subordinated and Junior Subordinated Debt, including Seller Financing) – First Layer – Second Layer – Etc. Bridge Financing Payment-in-Kind	Cash-generating capabilities of the borrower	Face value of securities	Life insurance companies, pension funds, private equity, and hedge funds
		Equity	
Preferred Stock – Payment-in-Kind	Cash-generating capabilities of the borrower		Life insurance companies, pension funds, hedge funds, private equity, and angel investors
Common Stock	Cash-generating capabilities of the borrower		Life insurance companies; pension, private equity, hedge, and venture capital funds; and angel investors

COMMON FORMS OF LEVERAGED BUYOUT DEAL STRUCTURES

The asset-based LBO has become the most common form of LBO today, thanks to the epidemic of bankruptcies of overleveraged cash-flow-based LBOs in the late 1980s. An asset-based LBO can be accomplished in one of two ways: the sale of assets by the target to the acquiring company, or a merger of the target into the acquiring company (direct merger) or a wholly owned subsidiary of the acquiring company (subsidiary merger). For small companies, a reverse stock split may be used to take the firm private. An important objective of "going private" transactions is to reduce the number of shareholders to below 300, which enables the public firm to delist from many public stock exchanges.

Lender Commitment Letters

The typical transaction begins with a term sheet or a letter of intent between the seller and buyer that stipulates basic terms such as price, terms of sale, assumption of liabilities, and closing deadlines. A *commitment letter* is secured by the acquirer (i.e., borrower) and represents a commitment by the lender to make a loan subject to the lender performing due diligence. The letter usually stipulates that the borrower pay the lender due diligence and other closing costs. Closing is conditioned on the acquirer's ability to obtain financing. The commitment letter gives the lender access to the target company's records for credit evaluation and to conduct asset appraisals. It outlines the maximum loan amounts, interest charges, repayment schedule, and ratio of advances to assets pledged (i.e., collateral). The commitment letter is conditioned on the lender having performed adequate due diligence and the execution of an agreement of purchase and sale between the buyer and seller.

Direct Merger

In a direct or cash merger, the company to be taken private is merged with a company controlled by the majority stockholder or a stockholder group. If the LBO is structured as a direct merger in which the seller receives cash for stock, the lender will make the loan to the buyer once the appropriate security agreements are in place and the target's stock has been pledged against the loan. The target then is merged into the acquiring company, which is the surviving corporation. Payment of the loan proceeds usually is made directly to the seller in accordance with a "letter of direction" drafted by the buyer.

Subsidiary Merger

LBOs may be consummated by establishing a new subsidiary that merges with the target. The subsidiary or affiliated entity then makes a tender offer for the outstanding public shares. This may be done to avoid any negative impact that the new company might have on existing customer or creditor relationships. If some portion of the parent's assets is to be used as collateral to support the ability of its operating subsidiary to fund the transaction, both the parent and the subsidiary may be viewed as having a security interest in the debt. As such, they may be held jointly and severally liable for the debt. To avoid this situation, the parent may make a capital contribution to the subsidiary rather than provide collateral or a loan guarantee.

Reverse Stock Splits

A reverse stock split is a process whereby a corporation reduces the number of shares outstanding. The total number of shares will have the same market value immediately after the reverse split as before, but each share will be worth more. Reverse splits may be used to take a firm private when a firm is short of cash. Therefore, the majority shareholder or shareholders retain their stock after the split, whereas the minority shareholders receive a cash payment.

How a reverse stock split works is illustrated by the case of MagStar Technologies, a Minnesota-based manufacturer of conveyor systems. Minnesota law allowed the firm to amend its articles of incorporation to conduct a reverse split without shareholder approval, and on January 9, 2008, MagStar announced a 1-for-2000 reverse split of the firm's common stock, which it intended to take private. Under the terms of the split, each of the 2,000 shares of the firm's common stock would be converted into one share of common stock; shareholders with fewer than 2,000 shares of common stock on the record date would receive cash of $0.425 per presplit share. The split would reduce the number of shareholders to fewer than 300, the minimum required to list on many public exchanges. After the split was executed, MagStar immediately ceased filing reports with the SEC.

Legal Pitfalls of Improperly Structured LBOs

Fraudulent conveyance laws are applicable whenever a company goes into bankruptcy following events such as a highly leveraged transaction, and are intended to preclude shareholders, secured creditors, and others from benefiting at the expense of unsecured creditors. These laws require that the new company created by the LBO be strong enough financially to meet its obligations to current and future creditors. If the new company is found by the court to have been inadequately capitalized, the lender could be stripped of its secured position in the company's assets, or its claims on the assets could be made subordinate to those of the general or unsecured creditors. Consequently, lenders, sellers, directors, or their agents (including auditors and investment bankers) may be required to compensate the general creditors.

Lender Due Diligence

The lender can be expected to make a careful evaluation of the quality of the assets to be used as collateral. Receivables will be analyzed to determine the proportion beyond normal collection terms. An assessment of how realistic it is that the receivables can be converted to cash also will be made. A physical inspection of the inventory will be made to establish both its quantitative and qualitative values. Professional appraisers will appraise fixed assets at their realistic "quick-sale" values. Values also should be placed on off-balance sheet assets, such as patents, trademarks, licenses, franchises, copyrights, and blueprints.

Leveraged Buyout Capital Structures

LBOs tend to have complicated capital structures comprising bank debt, high-yield debt, mezzanine debt, and private equity provided primarily by the LBO sponsor. As secured debt, the bank debt generally is the most senior in the capital structure in the event of liquidation. With such loans usually maturing within five to seven years, interest rates often vary at a fixed spread or difference over the London Interbank Offering Rate. Bank loans usually must be paid off before other types of debt.

Bank debt often consists of term loans in tranches or slices denoted as A, B, C, and D, with A the most senior and D the least senior of all bank financing. While bank debt in the A tranche usually must be amortized or paid off before other forms of debt can be paid, the remaining tranches generally involve little or no amortization. Whereas lenders in the A tranche often sell such loans to other commercial banks, loans in the B, C, and D tranches often are sold to hedge funds and mutual funds. In recent years, bank debt typically would comprise about 40 percent of the total capital structure.

The remainder of the LBO capital structure comprises unsecured subordinated debt, also referred to as junk bonds. Interest is fixed and represents a constant percentage or spread over the U.S. Treasury bond rate. The amount of the spread depends on the credit quality of the debt. Often callable at a premium, this debt usually has a 10-year maturity date when the debt is paid off in a single payment. Such loans often are referred to as "bullet" loans to reflect their repayment at a single time. Because it usually takes some time to sell such debt, LBO sponsors seek bridge loans from banks (repaid within one year with the proceeds of the junk bond issue) to finance the purchase price at closing.

As an alternative to high-yield publicly traded junk bonds, second mortgage or lien loans became popular between 2003 and mid-2007. Such loans, privately placed with hedge funds and collateralized loan obligation (CLO) investors, are secured by the firm's assets but are subordinated to the bank debt in liquidation. By pooling large numbers of first and second mortgage loans (so-called leveraged loans) and subdividing the pool into tranches, CLOs sell the tranches to institutional investors, such as pension funds and insurance companies.

ESTIMATING THE IMPACT OF ALTERNATIVE FINANCING STRUCTURES

To estimate the impact of alternative financing structures, the acquiring firm runs the target and its own financial statements—adjusted to reflect the net effects of synergy—through a series of scenarios to determine how they affect variables such as earnings, leverage, covenants, and borrowing costs. For example, each scenario could represent different amounts of leverage as measured by the firm's debt-to-equity ratio.

Selecting the Appropriate Capital or Financing Structure

Various sources of funding can be used to arrive at a capital structure targeted by an acquiring firm. For instance, in an effort to reduce the amount it would have had to borrow to finance its purchase of chemical company Rohm and Haas, Dow Chemical renegotiated the terms of its original July 2008 agreement in March 2009, before it was willing to close the deal. Having reneged on its earlier agreement, Dow was under considerable pressure from the threat of litigation from Rohm. Although Rohm shareholders received $78 per share in cash (consistent with the original terms), the way it would be financed was considerably different. In the original transaction, Dow would have had to borrow most of the $15.3 billion purchase price, but under the new deal, Rohm's largest shareholders—Rohm's founding Haas family and the hedge fund Paulson & Company—agreed to buy up to $2.5 billion in preferred stock in Dow in what effectively represented seller financing. Rohm also won an option to sell $500 million in common stock to these two shareholders. Dow would pay a 15 percent dividend on the preferred shares rather than taking on additional debt. Warren Buffett's Berkshire Hathaway conglomerate, along with the Kuwait Investment Authority, agreed to purchase jointly $4 billion in convertible preferred stock in Dow after the deal was closed. Dow also would sell noncore discretionary assets, including its Morton Salt division, to raise $4.1 billion in cash.

In theory, the optimal capital or financing structure is the one that maximizes the firm's share price or market value (i.e., the number of shares outstanding times the price per share). Reinvesting borrowed funds at a return above the firm's cost of capital (i.e., the minimum financial return required by investors and lenders) increases the firm's market value because demand for the firm's shares increases. However, higher debt levels also increase the minimum financial return investors require to invest in the increasingly leveraged firm as the potential for bankruptcy increases. Assuming the firm does not improve its expected financial returns, the increased leverage could lower the firm's share price as investors sell the firm's shares in anticipation of the firm's inability to make future interest and principal repayments. Because many factors affect share price, it is difficult to determine the exact capital structure that maximizes the firm's share price.

In practice, financial managers attempt to forecast how changes in debt will affect those credit ratios that affect a firm's creditworthiness. Factors include the interest coverage ratio (i.e., pretax and interest operating income/interest expense), debt-to-equity ratio, current ratio (i.e., current assets less current liabilities), and so on. Managers then discuss their projected *pro forma financial statements* (i.e., projected financial statements) with lenders and bond rating agencies, who may make adjustments to the firm's projected financial statements and who then compare the firm's credit ratios with those of other firms in the same industry to assess the likelihood that the borrower will be able to repay the borrowed funds (with interest) on schedule. Ultimately, this interaction among borrower, lenders, and rating agencies determines the amount and composition of the combined firms' capital structure (i.e., the acquirer's and target's combined amount of debt relative to equity).

Buyers often build financial models to determine the appropriate financing structure. The appropriate structure can be estimated by selecting that structure which satisfies certain predetermined selection criteria. These selection criteria should be determined as part of the process of developing the acquisition plan. For a public company, the appropriate capital structure could be that scenario whose debt-to-equity ratio results in the highest market value for the combined businesses, the least near-term earnings per share dilution, no violation of loan covenants, and no significant increase in borrowing costs. Excluding earnings per share (EPS) considerations, private companies could determine the appropriate capital structure in the same manner. In effect, the acquirer should select the financing structure that enables the following criteria to be satisfied:

- The acquirer is able to achieve its financial return objectives for the combined companies.
- The primary needs of the acquirer (e.g., retaining sufficient borrowing capacity to exploit future opportunities) and target firm's shareholders (e.g., the highest possible purchase price) are met.
- There is no significant increase in the cost of debt or violation of loan covenants.
- For public companies, earnings per share dilution, if any, is minimized and reductions in reported financial returns are temporary.

The financial return objectives of publicly traded companies are often couched in terms readily understood by investors, such as earnings per share. Acquiring companies must be able to convince investors that any EPS dilution is temporary and that the long-term EPS growth of the combined companies will exceed what the acquirer could have achieved without the acquisition. Financial returns for both public and private companies also may be described as the firm's estimated cost of capital, or in terms of the return on total capital (i.e., debt plus equity), assets, or equity. Moreover, the combined companies' cash flow must be sufficient to meet any incremental interest and principal repayments resulting from borrowing undertaken to finance all or some portion of the purchase price, without violating existing loan covenants or deviating from debt service ratios typical for the industry. If loan covenants are violated, lenders may require the combined companies to take immediate remedial action or be declared in technical default and forced to repay the outstanding loans promptly. Further, if the combined firms' interest coverage or debt-to-equity ratios deviate significantly from what is considered appropriate for similar firms in the same industry, borrowing costs may escalate sharply.

The Importance of Stating Assumptions

The credibility of any valuation ultimately depends on the validity of its underlying assumptions. Valuation-related assumptions tend to fall into five major categories. *Market assumptions* are generally those that relate to the growth rate of unit volume and product price per unit. *Income statement assumptions* include the projected growth in revenue, the implied market share (i.e., the firm's projected revenue as a percent of projected industry revenue), and the growth in the major components of cost in relation to sales. *Balance sheet assumptions* may include the growth in the primary components of working capital, and fixed assets in relation to the projected growth in sales. Note that implicit assumptions about cash flow already are included in assumptions about the income statement and changes in the balance sheet, which together drive changes in cash flow. *Synergy assumptions* relate to the amount and timing associated with each type of anticipated synergy, including cost savings from workforce reductions, productivity improvements as a result of the introduction of new technologies or processes, and revenue growth as a result of increased market penetration or cross-selling opportunities. Finally, examples of important *valuation assumptions* include the acquiring firm's target debt-to-equity ratio used in calculating the cost of capital, the discount rates used during the forecast and stable growth periods, and the growth assumptions used in determining the terminal value (i.e., cash flows the buyer anticipates the target firm will generate on a sustained basis).

★ ★ ★

Transactions may be financed using a wide range of debt and equity securities provided by various sources, from commercial banks to hedge and private equity funds. The use of leverage magnifies the return to shareholders, as providers of equity capital. Asset-based lending has emerged as an attractive alternative to the use of cash, stock, or public debt issues if the target has sufficient tangible assets to serve as collateral. Other forms of lending include unsecured debt, often referred to as mezzanine financing, which lies between senior debt and the equity layers. It includes senior subordinated debt, subordinated debt, bridge financing, and LBO partnership financing. It frequently consists of high-yield junk bonds that may also include zero coupon deferred interest debentures used to increase the postacquisition cash flow of the acquired entity.

Secured debt issues usually are called mortgage bonds or equipment trust certificates. Issues not secured by specific assets are called debentures. Common and preferred stock issues may also be used to finance transactions. So-called hybrid securities (i.e., those exhibiting both equity and debt characteristics) include convertible debt and preferred stock, which may be converted into a fixed number of common shares at some predetermined date.

Seller financing represents a highly important source of financing for buyers and involves the seller deferring the receipt of a portion of the purchase price until some future date. Typically, in a seller-financed transaction, the buyer contributes a large portion of the purchase price in cash, and then the buyer and seller negotiate a payback schedule and interest rate for the remaining balance. Selling target company assets not critical to implementing the acquirer's business strategy also represents a means of financing the purchase of the target firm.

Buyers often build financial models to determine the appropriate financing structure (i.e., mix of debt and equity). The appropriate structure can be estimated by selecting that structure which satisfies certain predetermined selection criteria. For a public company, the appropriate capital structure could be that scenario whose debt-to-equity ratio results in the highest market value for the combined businesses, the least near-term EPS dilution, no violation of loan covenants, and no significant increase in borrowing costs.

A Case in Point: Financing LBOs—The SunGard Transaction

With their cash hoards accumulating at an unprecedented rate, there was little that buyout firms could do but to invest in larger firms. Consequently, the average size of LBO transactions grew significantly during 2005. Late that year, seven private investment firms banded together as an investor group and acquired 100 percent of the outstanding stock of SunGard Data Systems Inc., a financial software firm known for providing application and transaction software services and creating backup data systems in the event of disaster. As a single buyer group, the firms—Silver Lake Partners, Bain Capital, The Blackstone Group, Goldman Sachs Capital Partners, Kohlberg Kravis Roberts & Co., Providence Equity Partners, and Texas Pacific Group—spread the risk of such a large deal and reduced the likelihood of a bidding war. It was a move reminiscent of the blockbuster buyouts of the late 1980s.

SunGard's software manages 70 percent of the transactions made on the NASDAQ stock exchange, but its biggest business is creating backup data systems in case a client's main systems are disabled by a natural disaster, blackout, or terrorist attack. Its large client base for disaster-recovery and backup systems provides a substantial and predictable cash flow. The software side of SunGard is believed to have significant growth potential, while the disaster-recovery side provides a large, stable cash flow.

Unlike many LBOs, the deal was announced as being all about growth of the financial services software side of the business. It was structured as a merger, because SunGard was to be merged into a shell corporation created by the buyer group. Going private would allow SunGard to invest heavily in software without being punished by investors because such investments are expensed and reduce reported earnings per share. Going private would also allow the firm to eliminate the burdensome reporting requirements of being a public company.

The buyout represented a potentially significant source of fee income for the investor group. In addition to the 2 percent management fees buyout firms collect from investors in the funds they manage, they receive substantial fee income from each investment they make on behalf of their funds. For example, the buyout firms receive a 1 percent deal completion fee, which was more than $100 million in the SunGard transaction. Buyout firms also receive fees for arranging financing, paid for by the target firm that is going private. Moreover, there are fees for conducting due diligence and for monitoring the ongoing performance of the firm taken private. Finally, when the buyout firms exit their investments in the target firm via a sale to a strategic buyer or a secondary IPO, they receive 20 percent (i.e., so-called carry fee) of any profits.

Under the terms of the agreement, SunGard shareholders received $36 per share, a 14 percent premium over the SunGard closing price as of the announcement date of March 28, 2005, and 40 percent more than when the news first leaked about the deal a week earlier. From the SunGard shareholders' perspective, the deal was valued at $11.4 billion dollars: $10.9 billion for outstanding shares and "in-the-money" options (i.e., options whose exercise price is less than the firm's market price per share), plus $500 million in debt on the balance sheet.

The seven equity investors provided $3.5 billion in capital, with the remainder of the purchase price financed by commitments from a lending consortium comprising Citigroup, JPMorgan Chase & Co., and Deutsche Bank. The loans financed the merger and were to be used to repay or refinance SunGard's existing debt, provide ongoing working capital, and pay fees and expenses incurred in connection with the merger. The total funds necessary to complete the merger, and related fees and expenses, were approximately $11.3 billion, consisting of approximately $10.9 billion to pay SunGard's stockholders and about $400.7 million to pay fees and expenses related to the merger and the financing arrangements (comprising nearly 4 percent of the purchase price). Ongoing working capital needs and capital expenditures required obtaining commitments from lenders well in excess of $11.3 billion.

The merger financing comprised several tiers of debt and "credit facilities" (i.e., arrangements for extending credit). The senior secured debt and senior subordinated debt were intended to provide "permanent" or long-term financing. Senior debt covenants included restrictions on new borrowing, investments, sales of assets, mergers and consolidations, prepayments of subordinated indebtedness, capital expenditures, liens and dividends and other distributions, as well as a minimum interest coverage ratio and a maximum total leverage ratio.

As part of the deal, the banks providing the financing committed to making up to $3 billion in loans under a senior subordinated bridge credit facility if the offering of notes was not completed on or prior to the closing. The bridge loans were intended as a form of temporary financing to satisfy immediate cash requirements until **permanent financing** could be arranged. A special-purpose SunGard subsidiary would purchase receivables from SunGard, with the purchases financed through the sale of the receivables to the lending consortium. The lenders subsequently financed the purchase of the receivables by issuing commercial paper, which is repaid as the receivables are collected. Based on the value of receivables at closing, the subsidiary could have provided up to $500 million. The obligation of the lending consortium to buy the receivables was negotiated to expire on the sixth anniversary of the closing of the merger.

Things to Think About:

1. SunGard is a software company with relatively few tangible assets. Yet, the ratio of debt to equity is almost 5 to 1. Why do you think lenders would be willing to engage in such a highly leveraged transaction for a firm of this type?

2. Under what circumstances would SunGard refinance the existing $500 million in outstanding senior debt after the merger? Be specific.

3. In what ways is this transaction similar to and different from those common in the 1980s? Be specific.

4. Why are payment-in-kind securities (e.g., debt or preferred stock) particularly well suited for financing LBOs? Under what circumstances might they be most attractive to lenders or investors?

5. Explain how the way in which the LBO is financed affects the way it is operated and the timing of when equity investors choose to exit the business. Be specific.

Answers can be found at:
www.elsevierdirect.com/companion.jsp?ISBN=9780123749499

CHAPTER 8

The Role of Takeover Tactics and Defenses in the Negotiation Process

Ownership of the beer giant Anheuser-Busch (AB), an American icon, changed hands on July 14, 2008, when the company agreed to be acquired by Belgian brewer InBev for $52 billion in an all-cash deal. The announcement marked a reversal from AB's publicly stated position only a week earlier that InBev's offer undervalued the firm. Subsequently, AB sued InBev for "misleading statements" it had allegedly made about the strength of its financing. To court public support, AB publicized its history as a major benefactor in its hometown area of St. Louis, Missouri. The firm argued that its own long-term business plan would create more shareholder value than the proposed deal. To make the transaction too expensive for InBev, AB contemplated acquiring the half of Grupo Modelo, the Mexican brewer of Corona, it did not already own.

While publicly professing to want a friendly transaction, InBev wasted no time turning up the heat. The firm launched a campaign to replace Anheuser-Busch's board with its own slate of candidates, including a Busch family member. Meanwhile, AB was under substantial pressure from major investors, including Warren Buffet, to agree to the deal, because the firm's stock had been lackluster for the past several years. In an effort to win additional shareholder support, InBev raised its initial $65 bid to $70. To eliminate concerns over its ability to finance the deal, InBev agreed to document its credit sources fully, rather than relying on more traditional but less certain credit commitment letters. In an effort to placate AB's board, management, and the myriad politicians who railed against the proposed transaction, InBev agreed to name the new firm Anheuser-Busch InBev, keep Budweiser as the new firm's flagship brand, and maintain the North American headquarters in St. Louis. In addition, AB would be given two seats on the board, including one for August A. Busch IV, AB's CEO and patriarch of the firm's founding family. InBev also announced that AB's 12 U.S. breweries would remain open.

Mergers and Acquisitions Basics
ISBN: 978-0-12-374949-9, DOI: 10.1016/B978-0-12-374949-9.00008-7

InBev's takeover tactics and Anheuser-Busch's defenses illustrate the types of takeover tactics and defenses that can characterize mergers and acquisitions—and that often capture newspaper headlines while negotiations unfold behind the scene. Buyers and sellers alike may use aggressive tactics to extract concessions from the other party.

Thus far, you have learned about the process of negotiation that typically goes unseen by the public. Here, in this final chapter, you will learn about the various takeover tactics and defenses and how they impact the negotiating process. Remember, whether a transaction is initially hostile or friendly, its resolution ultimately comes through negotiation.[1]

ALTERNATIVE TAKEOVER TACTICS IN THE CORPORATE TAKEOVER MARKET

Takeovers may be classified as friendly or hostile. In a friendly takeover, a negotiated settlement is possible without the acquirer resorting to aggressive tactics. These tactics may include a *bear hug*, in which the acquirer mails a letter that includes an acquisition proposal to a target company's board of directors, without prior warning and demanding a rapid decision; a *proxy contest*, which is an attempt by dissident shareholders to obtain representation on the board of directors or change a firm's bylaws by obtaining the right to vote on behalf of other shareholders; or a *hostile tender offer*, in which the acquirer bypasses the target's board and management and goes directly to the target's shareholders with an offer to purchase their shares. Unlike a merger in which the minority must agree to the terms of the agreement negotiated by the board after the majority of the firm's shareholders (i.e., 50.1 percent or more) approve the proposal, the tender offer specifically allows for minority shareholders to approve or deny the merger.

Following the tender offer, the target firm becomes a partially owned subsidiary of the acquiring company—under terms that may be imposed on the minority. This is achieved by the parent firm merging the partially owned subsidiary that resulted from the failure of the tender offer to obtain all of the target firm's shares into a new, wholly owned subsidiary. Alternatively, the acquirer may decide not to acquire 100 percent of the target's stock—and the minority becomes subject to a freeze-out or squeeze-out in which the remaining shareholders depend on the decisions made by the majority shareholders.

---

[1] See DePamphilis (2009), Chapter 3, for a more detailed discussion of alternative takeover strategies and defenses.

The Friendly Approach

In a friendly takeover, the potential acquirer initiates an informal dialogue with the target's top management, and the acquirer and target reach agreement on key issues early in the process. Typically, these issues include the long-term business strategy of the combined firms, how they will operate in the short term, and who will be in key management positions. Often, a *standstill agreement* is negotiated in which the acquirer agrees not to make any further investments in the target's stock for a stipulated period. This compels the acquirer to pursue the acquisition on friendly terms alone, at least for the period covered by the agreement. It also permits negotiations to proceed without the threat of more aggressive tactics, such as a tender offer or proxy contest.

Although the vast majority of transactions in recent years have been friendly, this was not always the case. The 1970s and early 1980s were characterized by blitzkrieg-style takeovers. Hostile takeovers of U.S. firms peaked at about 14 percent of all takeovers in the 1980s before dropping to a low of about 4 percent in the 1990s. The decline can be attributed in part to the soaring stock market in the 1990s—target shareholders are more willing to accept takeover bids when their shares are overvalued. In addition, federal prenotification regulations have slowed dramatically a process that used to be quicker. A number of states and public stock exchanges also require shareholder approval for certain types of offers. Moreover, most large companies have antitakeover defenses in place, such as poison pills. Hostile takeover battles now are more likely to last for months (as is discussed later in this chapter).[2]

Although hostile takeovers today are certainly more challenging than in the past, they have certain advantages over the friendly approach. One is that the friendly approach surrenders the element of surprise. Even a few days' warning gives the target's management time to take defensive action to impede the actions of the suitor. Negotiation also raises the likelihood of a leak and a spike in the price of the target's stock as arbitrageurs ("arbs") seek to profit from the spread between the offer price and the target's current stock price. The speculative increase in the target's share price can add dramatically to the cost of the transaction: the initial offer by the bidder generally includes a premium over the target's current share

---

[2] According to Thomson Reuters, 2008 saw the highest level of hostile or unsolicited deals since 1999, despite the inhospitable credit environment, as firms with cash on their balance sheets moved to exploit the decline in target company share prices. In contrast with the United States and the United Kingdom, the frequency of hostile takeovers in Continental Europe increased during the 1990s. In the 1980s, heavy ownership concentration made the success of hostile takeovers problematic. In the 1990s, ownership gradually became more dispersed and deregulation made unwanted takeovers easier.

price, and because that premium usually is expressed as a percentage of the target's share price, a speculative increase in the target firm's current share price will add to the overall purchase price paid by the acquiring firm. For these reasons, a bidder may opt for a more hostile approach.

The Aggressive Approach

Successful hostile takeovers depend on the premium offered to target shareholders, the board's composition, and the composition, sentiment, and investment horizon of the target's current shareholders. Other factors include the provisions of the target's bylaws and the potential for the target to implement additional takeover defenses.

The target's board will find it more difficult to reject offers exhibiting substantial premiums to the target's current stock price. Concern about its fiduciary responsibility and possible stockholder lawsuits put pressure on the target's board to accept the offer. Despite the pressure of an attractive premium, the composition of the target's board also greatly influences what the board does and the timing of its decisions. A board dominated by inde-pendent directors, nonemployees, or family members is more likely to resist offers in an effort to induce the bidder to raise the offer price or to gain time to solicit competing bids than to protect itself and current management.

Furthermore, the final outcome of a hostile takeover is heavily depen-dent on the composition of the target's stock ownership, how stockholders feel about management's performance, and how long they intend to hold the stock. Firms held predominantly by short-term investors (i.e., less than four months) are more likely to receive a bid and exhibit a lower average pre-mium of as much as 3 percent when acquired, and researchers speculate that firms held by short-term investors have a weaker bargaining position with the bidder.[3] To assess these factors, an acquirer compiles (to the extent pos-sible) lists of stock ownership by category: management, officers, employees, and institutions such as pension and mutual funds. This information can be used to estimate the target's *float*—the number of shares that are outstand-ing, not held by block shareholders, and available for trading by the public. The larger the share of stock held by corporate officers, family members, and employees, the smaller the float, because these types of shareholders are less likely to sell their shares. Float is likely to be largest for those companies in which shareholders are disappointed with the firm's financial performance.

Finally, an astute bidder will always analyze the target firm's bylaws (often easily accessible through a firm's website) for provisions potentially

---

[3] Gaspara and Matos (2005).

adding to the cost of a takeover. Such provisions could include a staggered board, the inability to remove directors without cause, or super-majority voting requirements for approval of mergers. These and other measures are detailed later in this chapter.

The Bear Hug: Limiting the Target's Options

If the friendly approach is considered inappropriate or is unsuccessful, the acquiring company may attempt to limit the options of the target's senior management by making a formal acquisition proposal, usually involving a public announcement, to the target's board of directors. The aim is to move the board to a negotiated settlement. The board may be motivated to do so because of its fiduciary responsibility to the target's shareholders. Directors who vote against the proposal may be subject to lawsuits from target stockholders. This is especially true if the offer is at a substantial premium to the target's current stock price. Institutional investors and arbitrageurs add to the pressure by lobbying the board to accept the offer. Arbs are likely to acquire the target's stock and to sell the bidder's stock short. The accumulation of stock by arbs makes it easier for the bidder to purchase blocks of stock.

Proxy Contests in Support of a Takeover

The primary forms of proxy contests are those for seats on the board of directors, those concerning management proposals (e.g., an acquisition), and those seeking to force management to take some particular action (e.g., dividend payments and share repurchases). Most commonly, dissidents initiate a proxy fight to remove management, due to poor corporate performance, or a desire to promote a specific type of restructuring of the firm (e.g., sell or spin off a business) or the outright sale of the business; or they do so to force a distribution of excess cash to shareholders.[4]

Proxy fights enable dissident shareholders to replace specific board members or management with those more willing to support their positions. By replacing board members, proxy contests can be an effective means of gaining control without owning 50.1 percent of the voting stock, or they can be used to eliminate takeover defenses, such as poison pills, as a precursor of a tender offer. For example, Weyerhauser succeeded in placing three directors on rival Willamette Industries' nine-member board in 2001, and the prospect of losing an additional three seats the following year ultimately brought Willamette to the bargaining table and ended Weyerhauser's 13-month takeover attempt.

---

[4] Faleye (2004).

In mid-2005, billionaire Carl Icahn and his two dissident nominees won seats on the board of Blockbuster and ousted Chairman John Antioco.

Initiating a proxy contest to replace a board is costly, which explains why there are so few contested board elections.[5] For the official slate of directors nominated by the board, campaigns can be paid out of corporate funds, but shareholders promoting their own slate of candidates must pay substantial fees to hire proxy solicitors, investment bankers, and attorneys. On top of this they face other expenses to print and mail the proxy statement and place advertisements. Litigation expenses may also be substantial and can easily become the largest single cost in a highly contentious proxy contest. Nonetheless, a successful proxy fight is a far less expensive way to gain control over a target than a tender offer, which may require purchasing a controlling interest in the target at a substantial premium.

Implementing a Proxy Contest

When the bidder is also a shareholder in the target firm, the proxy process may begin with the bidder attempting to call a special stockholders' meeting. Alternatively, the bidder may put a proposal to replace the board or management at a regularly scheduled stockholders' meeting. Before the meeting, the bidder may open an aggressive public relations campaign, with direct solicitations sent to shareholders and full-page advertisements in the press to convince shareholders to support the bidder's proposals. The target will respond with its own campaign and will have a distinct advantage in being able to deal directly with its own shareholders. The bidder may even have to sue the target corporation to get a list of its shareholders' names and addresses. Often, shares are held in the name of banks or brokerage houses under a "street name," and these depositories generally do not have the authority to vote such shares.

When shareholders receive the proxies, they may choose to sign and send them directly to a designated collection point such as a brokerage house or bank. Shareholders may change their votes until they are counted—which often takes place under the strict supervision of inspectors to ensure accuracy. Both the target firm and bidder generally have their own proxy solicitors present during the tabulation process.

The Impact of Proxy Contests on Shareholder Value

Despite their low success rate, there is some empirical evidence that proxy fights result in abnormal returns to shareholders of the target company

---

[5] Between 1996 and 2004, an average of 12 U.S. firms annually faced contested board elections (*Economist*: September 16, 2006).

regardless of the outcome. The gain in share prices occurs despite that only one-fifth to one-third of all proxy fights actually result in a change in board control. In studies covering proxy battles during the 1980s through the mid-1990s, abnormal returns ranged from 6 to 19 percent, even if the dissident shareholders were unsuccessful in the proxy contest.[6] The reasons for these gains may include the eventual change in management at firms embroiled in proxy fights, the tendency for new management to restructure the firm, investor expectations of a future change in control due to M&A activity, and possible special cash payouts for firms with excess cash holdings.

Pre-tender Offer Tactics: Purchasing Target Stock in the Open Market

Potential bidders often purchase stock in a target before a formal bid to accumulate stock at a price lower than the eventual offer price. Such purchases are normally kept secret to avoid driving up the price and increasing the average price paid for such shares. The primary advantage to the bidder of accumulating target stock before an offer is the potential leverage achieved with the voting rights associated with the stock it has purchased. This voting power is important in a proxy contest to remove takeover defenses, win shareholder approval under state antitakeover statutes, or elect members of the target's board. In addition, the bidder can sell this stock later if the takeover attempt is unsuccessful.

After the bidder has established a toehold ownership position in the voting stock of the target through open-market purchases, the bidder may attempt to call a special stockholders' meeting in an effort to replace the board of directors or remove takeover defenses. The conditions under which such a meeting can be called are determined by the firm's articles of incorporation governed by the laws of the state in which the firm is incorporated.[7]

Using a Hostile Tender Offer to Circumvent the Target's Board

The hostile tender offer is a deliberate effort to go around the target's board and management. Its early successes generated new, more effective defenses, and so takeover tactics had to adapt. For example, during the 1990s, hostile tender offers were used in combination with proxy contests to coerce the target's board into rescinding takeover defenses. Although target boards

---

[6] DeAngelo and DeAngelo (1989); Mulherin and Poulsen (1998).
[7] A copy of a firm's articles of incorporation can usually be obtained for a nominal fee from the Office of the Secretary of State of the state in which the firm is incorporated.

often discourage unwanted bids initially, they are more likely to relent when a hostile tender offer is initiated.[8] While they have become more common in recent years, hostile takeovers are also rare outside the United States.

Implementing a Tender Offer

Tender offers can be for cash, stock, debt, or some combination of the three. Unlike mergers, tender offers frequently use cash as the form of payment. Securities transactions involve a longer period to complete the takeover because new security issues must be registered with and approved by the SEC and because states have their own security registration requirements. During the approval period, target firms are able to prepare defenses and solicit other bids, resulting in a potentially higher purchase price for the target. If the tender offer involves a share-for-share exchange, it is referred to as an *exchange offer*. Whether cash or securities, the offer is made directly to target shareholders, is extended for a specific period, and may be unrestricted (any-or-all offer) or restricted to a certain percentage or number of the target's shares.

Tender offers restricted to purchasing less than 100 percent of the target's outstanding shares may be oversubscribed. Because the Williams Act of 1968 requires equal treatment of all shareholders tendering shares, the bidder may either purchase all of the target stock that is tendered or purchase only a portion of the tendered stock. For example, if the bidder has extended a tender offer for 70 percent of the target's outstanding shares and 90 percent of the target's stock actually is offered, the bidder may choose to prorate the purchase of stock by buying only 63 percent (i.e., 0.7×0.9) of the tendered stock from each shareholder.

Once initiated, tender offers for publicly traded firms are usually successful, although the success rate is lower if it is contested.[9]

Multitiered Offers

As noted, the form of the bid for the target firm can be presented to target shareholders either as a one- or two-tiered offer. In a *one-tier offer*, the acquirer announces the same offer to all target shareholders, which offers the potential to purchase control of the target quickly and thus discourages other potential bidders from attempting to disrupt the transaction.

---

[8] In a study of 1,018 tender offers in the United States between 1962 and 2001, Bhagat et al. (2005) found that target boards resisted tender offers about one-fifth of the time. In a study of 49 countries, Rossi and Volpin (2004) found that only about 1 percent of 45,686 M&A transactions considered between 1990 and 2002 were opposed by target firm boards.

[9] According to Mergerstat, the success rate of total attempted tender offers between 1980 and 2000 was more than 80 percent, with the success rate for uncontested offers more than 90 percent and for contested (i.e., by the target's board) offers slightly more than 50 percent.

In a *two-tiered offer*, the acquirer offers to buy a certain number of shares at one price and more shares at a lower price at a later date. The form of payment in the second tier may also be less attractive, consisting of securities rather than cash. The intent of the two-tiered approach is to give target shareholders an incentive to tender their shares early in the process to receive the higher price.

Once the bidding firm accumulates enough shares to gain control of the target (usually 50.1 percent), the bidder may initiate a so-called **back-end merger** by calling a special shareholders' meeting seeking approval for a merger in which minority shareholders are required to accede to the majority vote. Alternatively, the bidder may operate the target firm as a partially owned subsidiary, later merging it into a newly created wholly owned subsidiary.

An acquirer seeking a controlling interest in the target firm may initiate a *creeping takeover strategy*, which involves purchasing target voting stock in relatively small increments until the acquirer has gained effective control of the firm. This may occur at less than 50.1 percent if the target firm's ownership is widely dispersed. If about 60 percent of a firm's eligible shareholders vote in elections for directors, a minority owning as little as 35 percent can elect its own slate of directors. Acquirers generally will pay more for the initial voting shares than for shares acquired later because of the perceived value of gaining control.

There are a number of disadvantages to owning less than 100 percent of the target's voting stock. They include the potential for dissident minority shareholders to disrupt efforts to implement important management decisions, the cost incurred in providing financial statements to both majority and minority shareholders, and current accounting and tax rules. Owning less than 50.1 percent means that the target cannot be consolidated for purposes of financial reporting but instead must be accounted for using the equity method. Because the equity method will include the investor's share of the target's income, it will not change consolidated income; however, the target's assets, liabilities, revenues, and expenses are not shown on the investor's financial statements. Consequently, potential increases in borrowing capacity from showing a larger asset or sales base would not be realized. Furthermore, target losses cannot be used to offset bidder gains because consolidation for tax purposes requires owning 80.1 percent of the target.

DEVELOPING A BIDDING OR TAKEOVER STRATEGY

The tactics that may be used in developing a bidding strategy should be viewed as a series of decision points, with objectives and options usually well defined and understood before a takeover attempt is initiated. Pre-offer planning should involve a review of the target's current defenses, an assessment of the defenses that could be put in place by the target after an offer is made, and the size of the float associated with the target's stock. Poor planning can result in poor bidding, which can be costly to CEOs—they may lose their jobs.[10]

Common bidding strategy objectives include winning control of the target, minimizing the control premium, minimizing transaction costs, and facilitating postacquisition integration. If minimizing the cost of the purchase (i.e., the price paid to purchase the target firm) and transaction costs while maximizing cooperation between the two parties is considered critical, the bidder may choose the "friendly" approach, which has the advantage of generally being less costly than more aggressive tactics and minimizes the loss of key personnel, customers, and suppliers during the fight for control of the target. Friendly takeovers avoid an auction environment, which may raise the target's purchase price. Moreover, friendly acquisitions facilitate premerger integration planning and increase the likelihood that the combined businesses will be quickly integrated following closing.

The primary risk of the friendly approach is the loss of surprise. If the target is unwilling to reach a negotiated settlement, the acquirer is faced with the choice of abandoning the effort or resorting to more aggressive tactics. Such tactics are likely to be less effective because of the extra time they give the target's management to put additional takeover defenses in place. In reality, the risk of loss of surprise may not be very great because of the prenotification requirements of the Williams Act and the Hart–Scott–Rodino Act.

The bidder initiates contact casually through an intermediary (i.e., a casual pass) or through a more formal inquiry (see Exhibit 8-1, reading from left to right). If the target's management and board reject the bidder's initial offer, the bidder's options under the friendly approach are either to walk away or adopt more aggressive tactics. In the latter case, the bidder may undertake a simple bear hug, hoping that pressure from large institutional shareholders and arbs will nudge the target toward a negotiated settlement.

[10] Lehn and Zhao (2006), for a sample of 714 acquisitions between 1990 and 1998, found that 47 percent of acquiring firm CEOs were replaced within five years. Moreover, top executives are more likely to be replaced at firms that have made poor acquisitions sometime during the previous five years.

EXHIBIT 8-1 Alternative Takeover Tactics

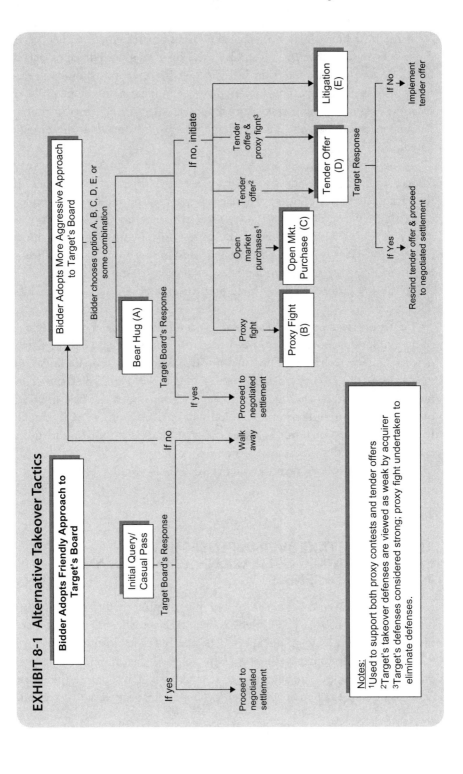

Notes:
[1]Used to support both proxy contests and tender offers
[2]Target's takeover defenses are viewed as weak by acquirer
[3]Target's defenses considered strong; proxy fight undertaken to eliminate defenses.

If the bear hug fails to convince the target's management to negotiate, the bidder may choose to buy stock in the open market. This approach is most effective when ownership in the target is concentrated among relatively few shareholders. The bidder may accumulate a sufficient number of voting rights to call a special stockholders' meeting if a proxy fight is deemed necessary to change board members or dismember the target's defenses.

If the target's defenses are viewed as relatively weak, the bidder may forgo a proxy contest and initiate a tender offer for the target's stock. If the target's defenses appear formidable, however, the bidder may implement a proxy contest and a tender offer concurrently. That, however, is a very expensive strategy. Tender offers are costly because they are offers to buy up to 100 percent of the target's outstanding stock at a significant premium. A proxy fight, although less expensive, is still costly, involving all the fees described earlier—including for extensive litigation, which is likely.

Litigation is a common tactic used to pressure the target board to relent to the bidder's proposal or remove defenses. It is most effective if the firm's defenses appear to be especially onerous. The bidder may initiate litigation that accuses the target's board of not giving the bidder's offer sufficient review or may argue that the target's defenses are not in the best interests of the target's shareholders and serve only to entrench senior management. In such a case, the acquirer will allege that the board is violating its fiduciary responsibility to the target shareholders.

Exhibit 8-2 relates takeover tactics to specific bidder objectives and strategies.[11]

ALTERNATIVE TAKEOVER DEFENSES IN THE CORPORATE TAKEOVER MARKET—PRE-OFFER AND POST-OFFER DEFENSES

Alternative takeover defenses are either put in place before receiving an offer or implemented after an offer has been received. Pre-offer defenses are used to prevent a sudden, unexpected hostile bid from gaining control of the company before management has time to assess their options properly. If the pre-offer defenses are sufficient to delay a change in control, the target firm has time to erect additional defenses after an unsolicited bid is received.

[11] For an illustration of how to develop alternative bidding strategies, see DePamphilis (2001).

EXHIBIT 8-2 Advantages and Disadvantages of Alternative Takeover Tactics

Common Bidder Strategy Objectives:
- Gain control of target firm
- Minimize the size of the control premium
- Minimize transaction costs
- Facilitate postacquisition integration

Tactics	Advantages	Disadvantages
Casual Pass (i.e., informal inquiry)	• May learn target is receptive to offer	• Gives advance warning
Bear Hug (i.e., letter to target board forcefully proposing takeover)	• Raises pressure on target to negotiate a deal	• Gives advance warning
Open-Market Purchases (i.e., acquirer buys target shares on public markets)	• May lower cost of transaction • Creates profit if target agrees to buy back bidder's toehold position • May discourage other bidders	• Can result in a less-than-controlling interest • Limits on amount can purchase without disclosure • Some shareholders could hold out for higher price • Could suffer losses if takeover attempt fails
Proxy Contest (i.e., effort to obtain target shareholder support to change target board)	• Less expensive than tender offer • May obviate need for tender offer	• Relatively low probability of success if target stock widely held • Adds to transaction costs
Tender Offer (i.e., direct offer to target shareholders to buy shares)	• Pressures target shareholders to sell stock • Bidder not bound to purchase tendered shares unless desired number of shares tendered	• Tends to be most expensive tactic • Disruptive to postclosing integration due to potential loss of key management, customers, and suppliers
Litigation (i.e., lawsuits accusing target board of improper conduct)	• Puts pressure on target board	• Expense

Exhibit 8–3 shows the most commonly used defenses; public companies use, on average, three of them when confronted with a takeover attempt.[12] These defenses are discussed in more detail later in this chapter.

Pre-offer Defenses

Pre-offer defenses generally fall into three categories: poison pills, shark repellents, and golden parachutes. The sophistication of such measures has increased dramatically since 1980, keeping tempo with the growing effectiveness of takeover tactics. The objective of these defensive measures is to slow the pace of the takeover attempt and to make it more costly for the bidder.

Poison Pills

The popular press uses the term *poison pill* to describe a range of protections against unsolicited tender offers. In practice, however, the **poison pill** is a very specific type of antitakeover defense.

Often referred to as shareholder rights plans, poison pills are a new class of securities issued by a company to its shareholders. Because pills are issued as a dividend and the board has the exclusive authority to issue dividends, a pill can often be adopted without a shareholder vote (unless the firm's bylaws limit such action). Consequently, poison pills can be adopted not only before but also after the onset of a hostile bid, which means that even a company that does not have a poison pill in place can be regarded as having a "shadow poison pill" that could be used in the event of a hostile bid.

Poison pill securities have no value unless an investor acquires a specific percentage (often as low as 10 percent) of the target firm's voting stock. If this threshold percentage is exceeded, the pill is triggered and has the effect of increasing the cost of the transaction for the acquirer by increasing the number of target shares that must be purchased for cash in a cash-for-share exchange or the number of new shares that must be issued by the acquirer in a share-for-share exchange. In a cash-for-share exchange, the change in the acquirer's cash outlay will depend on the number of target shareholders exercising their right to buy additional target shares. In a share-for-share exchange, the increased number of acquirer shares issued imposes a cost on acquirer shareholders by diluting their ownership position. News Corp. was using the poison pill when the firm announced on

---

[12] Field and Karpoff (2000).

EXHIBIT 8-3 Alternative Pre-offer and Post-offer Takeover Defenses

Pre-offer Defenses	Post-offer Defenses
Poison Pills*	Greenmail (Bidder's investment purchased at a premium to what it paid as inducement to refrain from any further activity)
Shark Repellants (Implemented by changing bylaws or charter): Strengthening the Board's Defenses Staggered or Classified Board Elections Cumulative Voting Rights "For Cause" Provisions Limiting Shareholder Actions Calling Special Meetings Consent Solicitations Advance Notice Provisions Super-Majority Rules Other Shark Repellents Antigreenmail Provisions (Discourages target's use of greenmail as a takeover tactic) Fair Price Provisions Supervoting Stock Reincorporation	Standstill Agreements (Often used in conjunction with an agreement to buy bidder's investment)
Golden Parachutes	Pac-Man Defense White Knights and White Squires Employee Stock Ownership Plans Leveraged Recapitalization Share Repurchase or Buy Back Plans Corporate Restructuring Litigation

*Although many different types of poison pills are used, only the most common forms are discussed in this text. Note also that the distinction between pre- and post-offer defenses is becoming murky as increasingly poison pill plans are put in place immediately following the announcement of a bid. Pills can be adopted without a shareholder vote because they are issued as a dividend and the board has the exclusive authority to issue dividends.

November 8, 2004, that it would give its shareholders the right to buy one share at half price for each share they own in the event any party seeks to buy a 15 percent stake in the firm. The pill would exclude the purchaser of the 15 percent stake.

Proponents of the pill defense argue that it prevents a raider from acquiring a substantial portion of the firm's stock without board permission. Because the board generally has the power to rescind the pill, bidders are compelled to negotiate with the target's board, which could result in a higher offer price. Pill defenses may be most effective when used with staggered board defenses in which a raider would be unable to remove the pill without winning two successive elections; this increases the likelihood of remaining independent.[13] Detractors argue that pill defenses simply serve to entrench management and encourage disaffected shareholders to litigate.

In recent years, boards have been under pressure to require shareholder approval of all rights plans and rescind existing pill defenses. Most pills are put in place with an *escape clause* that allows the board of the issuing company to redeem the pill through a nominal payment to the shareholders. This clause is necessary to avoid dilution of the bidder's ownership position in the event the acquiring company is considered friendly.

Shark Repellents

Shark repellents are specific types of takeover defenses achieved by amending either a *corporate charter* or the *corporation bylaws*. The corporate charter gives the corporation its legal existence and comprises the *articles of incorporation,* a document filed with a state government by the founders of a corporation, and a *certificate of incorporation,* a document received from the state after the articles have been approved. The charter identifies the corporation's name, purpose, number of authorized shares, and number and identity of directors. The corporation's powers thus derive from the laws of the state and from the provisions of the charter. Rules governing the internal management of the corporation are described in the corporation's bylaws, which are determined by the corporation's founders.

Shark repellents are put in place largely to reinforce the ability of a firm's board of directors to retain control. They predate poison pills as a defense, and their success in slowing down takeovers and making them

---

[13] According to Bebchuk et al. (2002), the likelihood of remaining independent rises from 34 to 61 percent with such a combination of defenses, and the probability that the first bidder will be successful drops from 34 to 14 percent.

more expensive has been mixed. Today, shark repellents have largely become supplements to poison pill defenses. Their primary role is to make it more difficult to gain control of the board through a proxy fight at an annual or special meeting. In practice, shark repellents as described here require amendments to the firm's charter, which necessitate a shareholder vote. Although there are many variations of shark repellents, the most typical are staggered board elections, restrictions on shareholder actions, anti-greenmail provisions, supervoting, and debt-based defenses.

Shark repellent defenses fall into three categories: those that strengthen the board's defenses, those limiting shareholder actions, and all others. Note that golden parachutes are generally not considered shark repellents because they are designed more to raise the cost of the buyout to the bidder and retain management rather than as a tool to gain time for the target board. They are discussed here because they are generally put in place prior to a takeover bid.

Strengthening the Board's Defenses

A *staggered board election* or *classified board election* involves dividing the firm's directors into a number of different classes. Only one class is up for reelection each year. For example, a 12-member board may have directors divided into four classes, with each director elected for a four-year period. In the first year, the three directors in what might be called "Class 1" are up for election; in the second year, "Class 2" directors are up for election; and so on. This means that an insurgent stockholder, even one who holds the majority of the stock, would have to wait for three election cycles to gain control of the board. Moreover, the size of the board is limited by the firm's bylaws to preclude the insurgent stockholder from adding board seats to take control of the board. The target may have to accede to the majority stockholder's demands because of litigation initiated by dissident shareholder groups. The likelihood of litigation is highest, and pressure on the board is greatest, whenever the offer price for the target is substantially above the target firm's current share price. Staggered boards can be effective in helping a target to ward off a hostile takeover attempt.[14]

Some firms have common stock carrying *cumulative voting rights* to maximize minority representation. Cumulative voting in the election of directors means each shareholder is entitled to as many votes as shall equal the number of shares the shareholder owns, multiplied by the number of

---

[14] Bebchuk, Coates, and Subramanian (2002, 2003).

directors to be elected. Furthermore, the shareholder may cast all of these votes for a single candidate or for any two or more candidates.

Again, using the example of a 12-member board, a shareholder who has 100 shares of stock has 300 votes for three open seats for Class 1 directors. The shareholder may cumulate votes and cast them for a specific candidate. A dissident stockholder may choose this approach to obtain a single seat on the board to gain access to useful information that is not otherwise readily available. *For cause provisions* specify the conditions for removing a member of the board of directors, narrowing the range of permissible reasons and limiting the flexibility of dissident shareholders in contesting board seats.

Limiting Shareholder Actions

The board can also reinforce its control by restricting the ability of shareholders to gain control of the firm by bypassing the board altogether. Limits can be set on shareholders' ability to call special meetings, engage in consent solicitations, and use super-majority rules.

Many states require that a firm call a special shareholders' meeting if requested by a certain percentage of its shareholders. Special meetings may be used as a forum for insurgent shareholders to take control by replacing current directors with more cooperative directors, or by increasing the number of board seats. To limit this type of action, firms frequently rely on the conditions under which directors can be removed (i.e., the "for cause" provision discussed previously) and a limitation on the number of board seats as defined in the firm's bylaws or charter.

In some states, shareholders may take action—without a special shareholders' meeting—to add to the number of seats on the board, remove specific board members, or elect new members. These states allow dissident shareholders to obtain shareholder support for their proposals simply by obtaining the written consent of shareholders under what is known as *consent solicitation*, a process that still must abide by the disclosure requirements applicable to proxy contests. The process circumvents delays inherent in setting up a meeting to conduct a stockholder vote.

There is an important difference between a consent solicitation and a proxy contest. Whereas the winning vote in a proxy fight is determined as a percentage of the number of votes actually cast (unless majority voting rules are in place, which require the counting of votes withheld), the winning vote in a consent solicitation is determined as a percentage of the number of shares outstanding. A dissident shareholder may, therefore, find it easier to win by initiating a proxy contest because many shareholders simply do not vote.

Corporate bylaws may include **advance notice provisions** that require shareholder proposals and board nominations be announced well in advance, sometimes as long as two months, of an actual vote. This buys time for the target's management. **Super-majority rules** require a higher level of approval than is standard to amend the charter or for certain types of transactions, such as a merger or acquisition. Such rules are triggered when an "interested party" acquires a specific percentage of the owner-ship shares (e.g., 5 to 10 percent). Super-majority rules may require that as much as 80 percent of the shareholders must approve a proposed merger or a simple majority of all shareholders except the "interested party."

Other Shark Repellents

The final category of pre-offer defenses includes antigreenmail and fair price provisions, as well as supervoting stock and reincorporation.

During the 1980s, many raiders profited by taking an equity posi-tion in a target firm, threatening takeover, and subsequently selling their ownership position back to the target firm at a premium over what they paid for the target's shares. In response, many corporations adopted charter amendments called **antigreenmail provisions** that restrict the firm's ability to repurchase shares at a premium. By removing the incentive for green-mail, companies believed they were making themselves less attractive as potential takeover targets.

Fair price provisions require that any acquirer pay minority sharehold-ers at least a fair market price for their stock. The fair market price may be expressed as some historical multiple of the company's earnings or as a specific price equal to the maximum price paid when the buyer acquired shares in the company. Fair price provisions are most effective when the target firm is subject to a two-tiered tender offer. The fair price provision forces the bidder to pay target shareholders who tender their stock in the second tier the same terms offered to those tendering their stock in the first tier.

A firm may create more than one class of stock for many reasons, including separating the performance of individual operating subsidiar-ies, compensating subsidiary operating management, maintaining control with the founders, and preventing hostile takeovers. As a takeover defense, a firm may undertake a **dual class recapitalization** with the objective of concentrating stock with the greatest voting rights in the hands of those who are most likely to support management. One class of stock may have 10 to 100 times the voting rights of another class of stock. Such stock is called *supervoting stock*.

Supervoting stock is issued to all shareholders along with the right to exchange it for ordinary stock. Most shareholders are likely to exchange it for ordinary stock because the stock with the multiple voting rights usually has a limited resale market and pays a lower dividend than other types of voting stock the corporation issues. Typically, management retains the special stock, which effectively increases the voting control of the corporation in the hands of management. For example, Ford's dual class or supervoting shares enable the Ford family to control 40 percent of the voting power while owning only 4 percent of the total equity of the company.

Under the voting rights policies of the SEC and major public exchanges, U.S. firms are allowed to list dual class shares. After such shares are listed, however, firms cannot reduce the voting rights of existing shares or issue a new class of superior voting shares. Although relatively limited among U.S. firms, dual class firms are very common in other countries.[15]

Reincorporation involves a potential target firm changing its state of incorporation to one in which the laws are more favorable for implementing takeover defenses. Several factors need to be considered in selecting a state for reincorporation, including how the state's courts have ruled in lawsuits alleging breach of corporate director fiduciary responsibility in takeover situations, as well as the state's laws pertaining to poison pills, staggered boards, and hostile tender offers. Reincorporation requires shareholder approval.

A *golden parachute* is an employee severance arrangement that is triggered whenever a change in control takes place, usually defined as any time an investor accumulates more than a fixed percentage of the corporation's voting stock. A golden parachute typically covers only a few dozen employees, who are terminated following the change in control and to whom the company is obligated to make a lump-sum payment. They are designed to raise the bidder's cost of the acquisition by creating a cost for retaining management, rather than to gain time for the target board.

---

[15] Research suggests that firms with dual class shares often underperform in the overall stock market. This may result from efforts to entrench controlling shareholders by erecting excessive takeover defenses and policies that are not in the best interests of noncontrolling shareholders, such as excessive compensation for key managers and board members. Moreover, such firms often have excessive leverage due to an unwillingness to raise additional funds by selling shares that could dilute the controlling shareholders. See Masulis et al. (2009) and Gompers et al. (2010).

Such severance packages may serve the interests of shareholders by making senior management more willing to accept an acquisition.

The Tax Reform Act of 1986 imposed stiff penalties on these types of plans if they create what is deemed an excessive payment—those that exceed three times the employee's average pay over the previous five years—and treats them as income and hence not tax deductible by the paying corporation. The employee receiving the parachute payment must pay a 20 percent surcharge in addition to the normal tax due on the parachute payment.

Post-offer Defenses

After an unwanted suitor has approached a firm, various additional defenses can be introduced. They include greenmail to dissuade the bidder from continuing the pursuit; defenses designed to make the target less attractive, such as restructuring and recapitalization strategies; and efforts to place an increasing share of the company's ownership in friendly hands by establishing employee stock ownership plans (ESOPs) and seeking white knights.

Greenmail

Greenmail is the practice of paying a potential acquirer to leave you alone. It consists of a payment to buy back shares at a premium price in exchange for the acquirer's agreement not to commence a hostile takeover. In exchange for the payment, the potential acquirer is required to sign a *standstill agreement*, which typically specifies the amount of stock, if any, the investor can own, the circumstances under which the raider can sell stock currently owned, and the term of the agreement.

Despite the discriminatory nature of greenmail, courts in some states (e.g., Delaware) have found it to be an appropriate response if done for valid business reasons. Courts in other states (e.g., California) have favored shareholder lawsuits contending that greenmail breaches fiduciary responsibility.[16]

White Knight

A target company seeking to avoid being taken over by a specific bidder may try to be acquired by a *white knight*—another firm viewed as a more appropriate suitor. To complete such a transaction, the white knight must be willing to acquire the target on terms more favorable than those of

[16] Wasserstein (1998), pp. 719–720.

other bidders. This does not necessarily mean at a higher price; the more favorable terms may be the willingness of the white knight to allow the target firm's management to remain in place to continue pursuing the firm's current strategy.

Fearing that a bidding war might ensue, the white knight often demands some protection in the form of a lock-up. This tactic may involve giving the white knight options to buy stock in the target that has not yet been issued at a fixed price or to acquire specific target assets at a favorable price. Such lock-ups usually make the target less attractive to other bidders. If a bidding war does ensue, the knight may exercise the stock options and sell the shares at a profit to the acquiring company. German drug and chemical firm Bayer AG's white knight bid for Schering AG in 2006 (which was recommended by the Schering board) was designed to trump a hostile offer from a German rival, Merck KGaS—and succeeded in repelling Merck.

Employee Stock Ownership Plans

ESOPs are trusts that hold a firm's stock as an investment for its employees' retirement program. They can be established quickly, with the company either issuing shares directly to the ESOP or having an ESOP purchase shares on the open market. The stock held by an ESOP is likely to be voted in support of management in the event of a hostile takeover attempt.

Leveraged Recapitalization

A company may recapitalize by assuming substantial amounts of new debt, which is used either to buy back stock or finance a dividend payment to shareholders. The additional debt reduces the company's borrowing capacity and leaves it in a highly leveraged position, which makes it a less attractive target to a bidder that may have wanted to use that capacity to help finance a takeover. Moreover, the payment of a dividend or a stock buyback may persuade shareholders to support the target's management in a proxy contest or hostile tender offer.

Whether the recapitalization actually weakens the target firm over the long term depends on its impact on shareholder value. Shareholders will benefit from the receipt of a dividend or from capital gains resulting from a stock repurchase. Furthermore, the increased debt service requirements of the additional debt will shelter a substantial amount of the firm's taxable income and may encourage management to be more conscientious about improving the firm's performance. Thus, the combination of these factors may result in current shareholders benefiting more from this takeover defense than from a hostile takeover of the firm. The primary differences between a **leveraged recapitalization** and a leveraged buyout are that the firm remains a public company and that management does not take a significant equity stake in the firm.

Recapitalization may require shareholder approval, depending on the company's charter and the laws of the state in which it is incorporated.

Share Repurchase or Buyback Plans

Firms repurchase shares to reward shareholders, signal undervaluation, fund ESOPs, adjust capital structure, and defend against unwanted takeovers.[17] These repurchases can be executed either through a tender offer or by direct purchases of shares in public markets.

When used as an antitakeover tactic, share repurchase or buyback plans aim to reduce the number of shares that could be purchased by the potential acquirer or by arbitrageurs who will sell to the highest bidder. This tactic reflects the belief that when a firm initiates a tender offer (i.e., a self-tender) for a portion of its own shares, the shareholders who offer their shares for sale are those most susceptible to a tender offer by a hostile bidder. This leaves the target firm's shares concentrated in the hands of shareholders who are less likely to sell, thereby reducing float. So, for a hostile tender offer to succeed in purchasing the remaining shares, the premium offered would have to be higher. The resulting higher premium might discourage some prospective bidders. A share buyback may work well in combination with a self-tender by allowing the firm to buy shares (perhaps at a somewhat higher price) in addition to those tendered to the firm. There is considerable evidence that buyback strategies are an effective deterrent.[18]

The repurchase tactic may, however, be subject to the "law of unintended consequences." Reducing the number of shares on the open market makes it easier for the buyer to gain control because fewer shares have to be purchased to achieve 50.1 percent of the target's voting shares. Moreover, self-tenders may actually attract potential bidders if they are seen as a harbinger of improving target company cash flows.

---

[17] According to Billett and Xue (2007), firms frequently increase their share repurchase activities when confronted with an imminent takeover threat.

[18] Potential acquirers are less likely to pursue firms with substantial excess cash, which could be used to adopt highly aggressive share repurchase programs (Faleye, 2004; Harford, 1999; Pinkowitz, 2002).

Corporate Restructuring

Restructuring may involve taking the company private, selling attractive assets, undertaking a major acquisition, or even liquidating the company. "Going private" typically involves the management team's purchase of the bulk of a firm's shares. This may create a win–win situation for shareholders, who receive a premium for their stock, and management, which retains control. To avoid lawsuits, the company must pay a price for the stock that represents a substantial premium to the current market price.

Alternatively, the target may make itself less attractive by divesting assets the bidder wants. The cash proceeds of such sales could fund other defenses, such as share buybacks or payment of a special stockholder dividend. A target company also may undertake a so-called *defensive acquisition* to draw down any excess cash balances and to exhaust its current borrowing capacity.

Litigation

Takeover litigation often includes antitrust concerns, alleged violations of federal securities laws, inadequate disclosure by the bidder as required by the Williams Act, and alleged fraudulent behavior. Targets often seek a court injunction to stop the takeover attempt, at least temporarily, until the court has decided the merits of the allegations. By preventing the potential acquirer from acquiring more stock, the target firm is buying time to erect additional takeover defenses.

Impact on Shareholder and Bondholder Value of Takeover Defenses

Most recent research suggests that takeover defenses may destroy shareholder value. For instance, the creation of a detailed "management entrenchment index" revealed that firms at which management's interests are more aligned with those of the shareholders have larger abnormal returns than firms with a high entrenchment index.[19] Another large study provides additional

---

[19] Bebchuk et al. (2009) created a management entrenchment index in an effort to assess which of 24 provisions tracked by the Investor Responsibility Research Center (IRRC) had the greatest impact on shareholder value. The index, which is negatively correlated with firm value between 1990 and 2004, comprises staggered boards, limits to shareholder bylaw amendments, super-majority requirements for mergers, super-majority requirements for charter amendments, poison pills, and golden parachutes. No correlation between firm value and 18 other IRRC provisions during the sample period was found. The researchers noted that the mere existence of correlation does not necessarily mean that these takeover defenses cause a reduction in the value of the firm. The correlation could reflect the tendency of underperforming firms that are likely to be takeover targets to adopt takeover defenses. These results supported the findings of an earlier study by Bebchuk, Cohen, and Ferrell (2004), which used a shorter time period.

evidence of the destructive effect of takeover defenses, finding that managers at firms protected by takeover defenses are less subject to the disciplinary power of the market for corporate control and are more likely to engage in "empire building" acquisitions that destroy shareholder value.[20]

When firms move immediately from staggered board elections to annual elections of directors, they experience a cumulative abnormal return of 1.82 percent, reflecting investor expectations that the firm is more likely to be subject to a takeover. Often, such firms come under considerable pressure from activist shareholders—and the presence of a greater proportion of independent directors means that these firms are often more willing to submit to the demands of those activists.[21]

Takeover defenses may add to firm value before a takeover attempt if they help the firm attract, retain, and motivate effective managers and employees. Furthermore, such defenses give the new firm time to implement its business plan fully and invest in upgrading the skills of employees.[22] There is also evidence that investors may prefer the adoption of takeover defenses during the early stages of a firm's development.[23]

★ ★ ★

Whether a takeover attempt is friendly or hostile, and regardless of which of the various tactics and defenses are employed, it is always the case that resolution comes through negotiation.

A Case in Point: Mittal Acquires Arcelor in a Battle of Global Titans

Ending five months of maneuvering, Arcelor—created in 2001 by a combination of steel companies in Spain, France, and Luxembourg—agreed on June 26, 2006, to be acquired by larger rival Mittal Steel Co. for $33.8 billion in cash and stock. Mittal is headquartered in the Netherlands and has plants outside Europe where labor costs are lower. Mittal acquired Arcelor to accelerate steel industry consolidation and reduce industry overcapacity. The combined firms could have more leverage in setting prices and negotiating contracts with major customers

---

[20] Masulis et al. (2007), a study of 3,333 completed acquisitions between 1990 and 2003.

[21] Guo et al. (2008).

[22] Stout (2002).

[23] This is suggested by the finding of Coates (2001) that the percentage of IPO firms with staggered boards in their charters at the time of the initial public offering rose from 34 percent in the early 1990s to 82 percent in 1999.

such as auto and appliance manufacturers and suppliers such as iron ore and coal vendors and eventually realize $1 billion annually in pretax cost savings.

The takeover battle was one of the most acrimonious in recent European Union history. It shows how far a firm can go in an attempt to halt an unwanted takeover.

Mittal first tried to consummate a friendly merger but was rebuffed by Arcelor's president. Then, in January 2006, Mittal launched a tender offer, mostly of stock and cash, for all of Arcelor's outstanding equity at a 27 percent premium over the share price at the time. Arcelor's management, European trade unions (fearing job losses), and government officials reacted swiftly and furiously.

Arcelor's president then undertook one of the most aggressive takeover defenses in recent corporate history. Early that February, Arcelor doubled its dividend and announced plans to buy back about $8.75 billion in stock at a price well above the then-current market price for Arcelor stock—aimed at motivating Arcelor shareholders not to tender their shares to Mittal. Arcelor also backed an unsuccessful move to change the law to require Mittal to pay in cash.

To counter these moves, Mittal Steel announced that if it received more than one-half of the Arcelor shares submitted in the initial tender offer it would hold a second tender offer for the remaining shares at a slightly lower price. Mittal pointed out that it could acquire the remaining shares through a merger or corporate reorganization. This rhetoric sought to encourage Arcelor shareholders to tender their shares during the first offer.

A host of other defensive steps were then taken. In April, Arcelor completed a deal initiated in 2005 to buy Canadian steelmaker Dofasco for $5 billion and then set up a special Dutch trust to prevent Mittal from getting access to the asset, which Mittal was proposing to sell to raise money and avoid North American antitrust concerns. Mittal immediately sued to test the legality of this tactic. Arcelor also cut a deal to exchange a 32 percent stake in Arcelor for the 90 percent stake held by a Mr. Alexei Mordashov in the Russian steelmaker OAO Severstahl, and then scheduled an unusual vote that created very tough conditions for Arcelor shareholders to prevent the deal from being completed. Some major Arcelor shareholders balked, and the Arcelor board was pressured at least to agree to talk to Mittal. When Arcelor first demanded and received an intricate business plan from Mittal, Arcelor still refused to talk.

In late May, Mittal raised its bid by 34 percent and said that if the bid succeeded, Mittal would eliminate its two-tiered share structure, which gave the Mittal family shares 10 times the voting rights of other shareholders. The Arcelor board rejected Mittal's sweetened bid and repeated its support of the Severstahl deal. Shareholder anger continued as many investors said they would reject the share buyback, some because it would increase Mordashov's ultimate stake in Arcelor to 38 percent by reducing the number of outstanding Arcelor shares—and thus give Mordashov "effective control" of the company under the law of most European countries.

Arcelor canceled a scheduled June 21 shareholder vote on the buyback and then—despite Mordashov's efforts to enhance his bid—the Arcelor board asked him and Mittal to submit final bids by June 25.

Finally, Arcelor agreed to Mittal's final bid. The new offer was $15.70 in cash and 1.0833 Mittal shares for each Arcelor share, valued at $50.54 per Arcelor share, up from Mittal's initial bid in January 2006 of $35.26. This final offer represented an unprecedented 93 percent premium over Arcelor's share price of $26.25 immediately before Mittal's initial bid. Lakshmi Mittal would control 43.5 percent of the combined firm's stock, and Mordashov would receive a $175 million breakup fee for Arcelor's failure to complete its agreement with him. Finally, Mittal agreed not to make any layoffs beyond what Arcelor already had planned.

Things to Think About:

1. Identify the takeover tactics employed by Mittal and explain why each was used.

2. Identify the takeover defenses employed by Arcelor and explain why each was used.

3. Using the Arcelor/Mittal example, discuss the arguments for and against encouraging hostile corporate takeovers.

4. Was Arcelor's board and management acting to protect their own positions (i.e., the management entrenchment hypothesis) or in the best interests of the shareholders (i.e., the shareholder interests hypothesis)? Explain your answer.

5. In an attempt to counter Mittal's hostile tender offer, Arcelor offered to increase its dividend and to buy back shares from current shareholders. In doing so, it hoped to discourage Arcelor shareholders from tendering their shares to Mittal. Explain how you, as an Arcelor shareholder, would decide whether to tender your shares to Mittal or support Arcelor's management.

Answers can be found at:
www.elsevierdirect.com/companion.jsp?ISBN=9780123749499

Accounting considerations The potential impact of financial reporting requirements on the earnings volatility of business combinations due to the need periodically to revalue acquired assets to their fair market value.

Acquirer; acquiring company A firm that attempts to acquire a controlling interest in another company.

Acquisition vehicle The legal structure used to acquire another company.

Advance ruling An IRS ruling sought by acquirers and targets planning to enter into a tax-free transaction. A favorable ruling is often a condition of closing.

Advance notice provisions Require shareholder proposals and board nominations be announced well in advance of the actual vote.

Affirmative covenant A portion of a loan agreement that specifies the actions the borrowing firm agrees to take during the term of the loan.

Antigreenmail provisions Amendments to corporate charters restricting the firm's ability to repurchase shares from specific shareholders at a premium.

Articles of incorporation A document filed with a state government by the founders of a corporation.

Asset impairment An asset is said to be impaired according to FASB Statement 142 if its fair value falls below its book or carrying value.

Asset purchase A transaction in which the acquirer buys all or a portion of the target company's assets and assumes all, some, or none of the target's liabilities.

Back-end merger The merger following either a single- or two-tier tender offer consisting of either a long form or short form merger, with the latter not requiring a target firm shareholder vote. Also known as a *squeeze-out merger*.

Balance sheet adjustment Increases or decreases made to shareholders' equity between the signing of an agreement and the closing of a transaction due to changes in the value of balance sheet components.

Balance sheet assumptions Assumptions related to growth in major balance sheet components.

Bear hug A takeover tactic involving the mailing of a letter containing an acquisition proposal to the board of directors of a target company without prior warning, and demanding a rapid decision.

Bidder See *acquirer*.

Boot The nonequity portion of the purchase price.

Breakup fee A fee that would be paid to the potential acquirer if the target firm decides to accept an alternative bid. Also called a *termination fee*.

Bridge financing Temporary, unsecured, short-term loans provided by investment banks to pay all or a portion of the purchase price and meet immediate working capital requirements until permanent or long-term financing is found.

Buyout Change in controlling interest in a corporation.

Cash-for-assets A purchase of assets in which the form of payment is cash.

Cash-for-stock A purchase of stock in which the form of payment is cash.

Cash-out statutory merger A merger in which the shareholders of the selling firm receive cash or some form of nonvoting investment (e.g., debt, or nonvoting preferred or common stock) for their shares.

Certificate of incorporation A document received from the state after the articles of incorporation have been approved.

Classified board election See *staggered board election.*

Closing conditions Stipulations that must be satisfied before closing can take place.

Collar agreement An arrangement providing for certain changes in the share exchange ratio contingent on the level of the acquirer's share price around the effective date of the merger.

Commitment letter A document obligating a lender to provide financing.

Confidentiality agreement A mutually binding accord defining how information exchanged among the parties may be used and the circumstances under which the discussions may be made public. Also known as a *nondisclosure agreement.*

Consent solicitation A process enabling dissident shareholders in certain states to obtain shareholder support for their proposals simply by obtaining their written consent.

Contingent value rights In M&A transactions, commitments by the acquirer to pay additional cash or securities to the seller if the share price of the issuing company falls below a specified level at some future date.

Control premium The excess over the target's current share price the acquirer is willing to pay to gain a controlling interest. A pure control premium would be one in which the anticipated synergies are small, and the perceived value of the purchase is in gaining control to direct the activities of the target firm.

Corporate charter A state license defining the powers of the firm and the rights and responsibilities of its shareholders, board of directors, and managers. The charter consists of articles of incorporation and a certificate of incorporation.

Corporation A legal entity separate from the individuals who formed it whose articles of incorporation have been approved in some state.

Corporation bylaws Rules governing the internal management of the corporation, which are determined by the corporation's founders.

Creeping takeover strategy A strategy involving purchasing target voting stock in relatively small amounts until the acquirer has gained effective control of the firm.

Cross-default provisions Clauses in loan agreements allowing a lender to collect its loan immediately if the borrower is in default on a loan to another lender.

Cumulative voting rights In an election for a board of directors, each shareholder is entitled to as many votes as shall equal the number of shares the shareholder owns multiplied by the number of directors to be elected. Furthermore, the shareholder may cast all these votes for a single candidate or for any two or more of them.

Data room The seller limits the acquirer's due diligence team to management presentations and selected data made available in a single room.

Deal-structuring process The process focused on satisfying as many of the primary objectives of the parties involved and determining how risk will be shared.

Debentures Debt issued that is secured primarily by the cash flow of the issuer.

Defensive acquisition An acquisition made to reduce a firm's cash position or borrowing capacity.

Dual class recapitalization A takeover defense in which a firm issues multiple classes of stock in which one class has voting rights that are 10 to 100 times those of another class. Such stock is also called *supervoting stock;* see also.

Earnout Payment to the seller based on the acquired business achieving certain profit or revenue targets.

Effective control Control achieved when one firm has purchased another firm's voting stock, it is not likely to be temporary, there are no legal restrictions on control such as from a bankruptcy court, and there are no powerful minority shareholders.

Employee stock ownership plan (ESOP) A trust fund or plan that invests in the securities of the firm sponsoring the plan on behalf of the firm's employees. Such plans are generally employee-defined contribution retirement plans.

Escape clause A feature common to poison pills enabling the board of the issuing company to redeem the pill through a nominal payment to the shareholders.

Escrow account An account established for the purpose of holding funds on behalf of the parties to a transaction until the consummation or termination of the transaction.

Exchange offer A tender offer involving a share-for-share exchange.

Fair price provisions A takeover defense requiring that all target shareholders of a successful tender offer receive the same price as those tendering their shares.

Financial buyer Acquirer who focuses on relatively short-to-intermediate financial returns.

Fixed or constant share exchange ratio An exchange ratio in which the number of acquirer shares exchanged for each target share is unchanged between the signing of the agreement of purchase and sale and closing.

Fixed payment collar value agreement A guarantee that the target firm's shareholders receive a certain dollar value in terms of acquirer stock as long as the acquirer's stock remains within a narrow range. Also called a *fixed value collar agreement*.

Fixed value collar agreement See *fixed payment collar agreement*.

Fixed value agreement The value of the price per share is fixed by allowing the number of acquirer shares issued to vary to offset fluctuations in the buyer's share price.

Float The amount of stock that can be most easily purchased by the acquirer.

Floating collar agreement An agreement that may involve a fixed exchange ratio as long as the acquirer's share price remains within a narrow range.

For cause provisions Specify the conditions for removing a board member.

Form of acquisition Acquisition that reflects what is being acquired (i.e., stock or assets).

Form of payment Payment that may consist of cash, common stock, debt, or some combination. Some portion of the payment may be deferred or dependent on the future performance of the acquired entity.

Forward triangular merger A type of merger that involves the acquisition subsidiary being merged with the target and the acquiring subsidiary surviving. The form of payment could involve stock or cash, although stock is the more common means of payment.

Fraudulent conveyance Laws governing the rights of shareholders if the new company created following an acquisition or LBO is inadequately capitalized to remain viable. In bankruptcy, the lender could be stripped of its secured position in the assets of the company or its claims on the assets could be made subordinate to those of the unsecured creditors.

General partnership A partnership formed with only general partners, in which each partner is involved in the day-to-day operations of the business and each partner bears personal responsibility for the liabilities of the partnership.

Going private The purchase of the publicly traded shares of a firm by a group of investors.

Golden parachute An employee severance arrangement triggered whenever a change in corporate control takes place.

Go-shop agreement A provision allowing a seller to continue to solicit other bidders for a specific time period after an agreement has been signed but before closing. However, if the seller accepts another bid, that seller must pay a breakup fee to the bidder with whom the seller had a signed agreement.

Greenmail The practice of a firm buying back its shares at a premium from an investor threatening a takeover.

Holding company A legal entity often having a controlling interest in one or more companies.

Hostile tender offer A tender offer that is unwanted by the target's board.

Income statement assumptions Assumptions related to projected growth in revenue, the implicit market share, and the major components of cost.

Indemnification A common contractual clause requiring the seller to indemnify or absolve the buyer of liability in the event of misrepresentations or breaches of warranties or covenants. Similarly, the buyer usually agrees to indemnify the seller. In effect, it is the reimbursement of the other party for a loss for which that party was not responsible.

Indenture A contract between the firm issuing the long-term debt securities and the lenders.

Jointly and severally liable A situation in which two or more persons are responsible for the same liability.

Junk bond A high-yield bond either rated by credit rating agencies as below investment grade or not rated at all.

Legal form of the selling entity A term that refers to whether the seller is a C or subchapter S Corporation, a limited liability company, or a partnership. These considerations can influence both the tax structure of the deal and form of payment.

Leveraged loans Unrated or noninvestment-grade bank loans whose interest rates are equal to or greater the London Interbank Rate plus 150 basis points.

Letter of intent A preliminary agreement between two companies intending to merge that stipulates major areas of agreement between the parties, as well as their rights and limitations.

Leveraged buyout (LBO) A transaction involving the purchase of a company financed primarily by debt.

Leveraged recapitalization A situation in which a firm assumes substantial amounts of new debt, often used to either buy back stock, finance a dividend to shareholders, or to make it less attractive to a potential bidder.

Loan agreement An agreement that stipulates the terms and conditions under which the lender will loan the firm funds.

Management buyout A leveraged buyout in which managers of the firm to be taken private are also equity investors in the transaction.

Market assumptions Anticipated growth rate of unit volume and product price per unit.

Marketing intangibles Factors that help a firm sell a product, such as a brand name.

Merger A combination of two or more firms in which all but one legally cease to exist.

Merger of equals A merger framework usually applied whenever the merger participants are comparable in size, competitive position, profitability, and market capitalization.

Mezzanine financing Capital that in liquidation has a repayment priority between senior debt and common stock.

Minority investment A less-than-controlling interest in another firm.

Negative covenant A restriction in a loan agreement on the actions of the borrower.

Net asset value The difference between the fair market value of total identifiable acquired assets and the value of acquired liabilities.

No-shop agreement An agreement that prohibits the takeover target from seeking other bids or making public information that is not currently readily available while in discussions with a potential acquirer.

One-tier offer A bidder announces the same offer to all target shareholders.

Operational intangibles Intangible factors, including management expertise and corporate culture, that help a business continue to function and generate income without interruption in the event of a change in ownership.

Partnership agreement An agreement among partners describing how business decisions are to be made and how profits and losses will be shared.

Payment-in-kind (PIK) securities Equity or debt that pays dividends or interest in the form of additional equity or debt.

Payment-in-kind (PIK) preferred stock Preferred stock for which the dividend obligation can be satisfied by issuing additional par amounts of the preferred security.

Permanent financing Financing usually consisting of long-term unsecured debt.

Poison pill A new class of securities issued as a dividend by a company to its shareholders, giving shareholders rights to acquire more shares at a discount. These securities have no value unless an investor acquires a specific percentage of the target firm's voting stock.

Postclosing organization The organizational and legal framework used to manage the combined businesses following the completion of the transaction.

Private solicitation The behavior of a firm seeking potential buyers on its own or hiring an investment banker to identify potential buyers.

Pro forma financial statements A form of accounting that presents financial statements in a way that purports to more accurately describe a firm's current or projected performance.

Production intangibles; product intangibles Values placed on the accumulated intellectual capital resulting from the production and product design experience of the combined entity.

Promissory note A legal document committing the borrower to repay a loan, even if the assets, when liquidated, do not fully cover the unpaid balance.

Proration clause Language in tender offers and merger agreements that allows an acquirer to fix—at the time the tender offer is initiated—the total amount of cash it will ultimately have to pay out.

Proxy contest An attempt by dissident shareholders to obtain representation on the board of directors or to change a firm's bylaws.

Public solicitation A firm announces publicly that it is putting itself, a subsidiary, or a product line up for sale.

Purchase method of accounting A form of accounting for financial reporting purposes in which the acquired assets and assumed liabilities are revalued to their fair market value on the date of acquisition and recorded on the books of the acquiring company.

Pure control premium The value the acquirer believes can be created by replacing incompetent management or by changing the strategic direction of the firm.

Reincorporation The act of a firm changing its state of incorporation to one in which the laws are more favorable for implementing takeover defenses.

Reverse breakup fee A fee paid to a target firm in the event the bidder wants to withdraw from a signed contract.

Reverse triangular merger The merger of the target with a subsidiary of the acquiring firm, with the target surviving. The form of payment could involve stock or cash, although stock is the more common means of payment.

Revolving credit line A credit line that allows borrowers to borrow on a daily basis to run their business. Under such arrangements, the bank agrees to make loans up to a specified maximum for a specified period, usually a year or more.

Secured debt Debt backed by the borrower's assets.

Security agreement A legal document stipulating which of the borrower's assets will be pledged to secure the loan.

Self-tender offer A tender offer used when a firm seeks to repurchase its stock from its shareholders.

Share exchange ratio The number of shares of the acquirer's stock to be exchanged for each share of the target's stock.

Shark repellents Specific types of takeover defenses that can be adopted by amending either a corporate charter or its bylaws.

Shell corporation A company that is incorporated but has no significant assets or operations.

Short form merger A merger not requiring the approval of the parent's shareholders if the parent's ownership in the acquiring subsidiary exceeds the minimum threshold set by the state in which the firm is incorporated.

Squeeze-out merger See *back-end merger*.

Staggered board election A takeover defense involving the division of the firm's directors into a number of different classes, with no two classes up for reelection at the same time. Also called a *classified board election*.

Standstill agreement A contractual arrangement in which the acquirer agrees not to make any further investments in the target's stock for a stipulated period.

Statutory consolidation The act of two or more companies joining to form a new company.

Statutory merger The combination of the acquiring and target firms, in which one firm ceases to exist, in accordance with the statutes of the state in which the combined businesses will be incorporated.

Step-up The increase in the value of an acquired asset to fair market value.

Stock-for-assets The purchase of assets in which the form of payment is acquirer stock.

Stock-for-stock See *stock swap merger*.

Stock purchase The exchange of the target's stock for either cash, debt, or the stock of the acquiring company.

Stock swap merger The acquisition of seller stock in which the form of payment is acquirer stock.

Subsidiary merger A transaction in which the target becomes a subsidiary of the parent.

Super-majority rules A takeover defense requiring a higher level of approval for amending the charter or for certain types of transactions such as a merger or acquisition.

Supervoting stock A class of voting stock having voting rights many times those of other classes of stock.

Synergy assumptions Suppositions that relate to the amount and timing of expected synergy.

Takeover Generic term referring to a change in the controlling ownership interest of a corporation.

Target; target company The firm that is being solicited by the acquiring company.

Tax considerations Structures and strategies determining whether a transaction is taxable or nontaxable to the seller's shareholders.

Tax-free reorganization Nontaxable transactions usually involving mergers, with the form of payment primarily acquirer stock exchanged for the target's stock or assets.

Term loan A loan typically having a maturity of 2 to 10 years and secured by the asset that is being financed, such as new capital equipment.

Term sheet A document outlining the primary areas of agreement between the buyer and seller that is often used as the basis for a more detailed letter of intent.

Transfer taxes State taxes paid whenever titles to assets are transferred as in an asset purchase.

Two-step acquisition An alternative to a traditional merger in which the acquirer first buys through a stock purchase the majority of the target's outstanding stock from the target's shareholders in a tender offer and then follows up with a back-end merger. See also *back-end merger*.

Two-tier offer An offer to acquire the shares of a target firm in which the acquirer offers to buy a certain number of shares at one price and more shares at a lower price at a later date.

Type A reorganization A tax-free merger or consolidation in which target shareholders receive cash, voting/nonvoting common or preferred stock, or debt for their shares. At least 40 percent of the purchase price must be in acquirer stock.

Type B stock-for-stock reorganization A tax-free transaction in which the acquirer uses its voting common stock to purchase at least 80 percent of the voting power of the target's outstanding voting stock and at least 80 percent of each class of nonvoting shares. Used as an alternative to a merger.

Type C stock-for-assets reorganization A tax-free transaction in which acquirer voting stock is used to purchase at least 80 percent of the fair market value of the target's net assets.

Valuation assumptions Key assumptions underlying the valuation of a firm, such as the acquiring firm's target debt-to-equity ratio used in calculating the cost of capital, the discount rates used during the forecast and stable growth periods, and the growth assumptions used in determining the terminal value.

Warrant A type of security—often issued with a bond or preferred stock—that entitles the holder to purchase an amount of common stock at a stipulated price.

White knight A potential acquirer that is viewed more favorably by a target firm's management and board than the initial bidder.

REFERENCES

Altman EI, Kishore VM: Almost everything you wanted to know about recoveries on defaulted bonds, *Financ Anal J* 57–64 (November/December 1996).

Angwin J, Drucker J: How News Corp. and Liberty Media can save $4.5 billion, *Wall St J* A3 (September 16), 2006.

Asquith P, Mullins D, Wolff E: Original issue high yield bonds: aging analysis of defaults, exchanges and calls, *J Financ* 44:923–952, September 1989.

Ayers BC, Lefanowicz CE, Robinson JR: Shareholder taxes in acquisition premiums: the effect of capital gains taxation, *J Financ* 58:2783–2801, December 2003.

Auerbach AJ, Reishus D: Taxes and the merger decision. In Coffee JC Jr., Lowenstein L, Ackerman SR, editors: *Knights, raiders, and targets*, New York, 1988, Oxford University Press, pp. 69–88.

Barclay MJ, Holderman CJ: Private benefits from control of public companies, *J Financ Econ* 25:371–395, 1989.

Bebchuk LJ, Coates JC, Subamaniam G: The powerful anti-takeover force of staggered boards: theory, evidence, and policy, *Stanford Law Rev* 54:887–951, 2002.

Bebchuk L, Cohen A, Ferrell A: What matters in corporate governance, review of financing studies, *Harv Univ Law Sch Discuss Pap* 22(49):783–827, 2009.

Bhagat S, Dong M, Hirshleifer D, Noah R: Do tender offers create value? New methods and evidence, *J Financ Econ* 76:3–60, 2005.

Billett MT, Xue H: The takeover deterrent effect of open market share repurchases, *J Financ* 62:1827–1851, 2007.

Carrington GR: *Tax accounting in mergers and acquisitions*, New York, 2007, CCH Inc.

CCH Tax Law Editors: U.S. master tax code, New York, 2005, Commerce Clearinghouse.

Chatterjee S, Yan A: Using innovative securities under asymmetric information: why do some firms pay with contingent value rights? *J Financ Quant Anal* 43:1001–1035, 2008.

Coates JC: Takeover defenses in the shadow of the pill: a critique of the scientific evidence, *Tex Law Rev* 79:271–382, 2001.

DeAngelo H, DeAngelo L: Proxy contests and the governance of publicly held corporations, *J Financ Econ* 23:29–60, 1989.

DePamphilis DM: *Mergers, acquisitions, and other corporate restructuring activities: an integrated approach to process, tools, cases, and solutions*, ed 5, San Diego, 2009, Academic Press.

DePamphilis DM: *Merger and acquisition basics: all you need to know*, San Diego, 2010, Academic Press.

DePamphilis DM: Managing growth through acquisition: time tested techniques for the entrepreneur, *Int J Entrep Innov* 2:195–207, October 2001.

Drucker J, Silver S: Alcatel stands to reap tax benefits on merger, *Wall St J* C3, 2006.

Dyck A, Zingales L: Control premiums and the effectiveness of corporate governance systems, *J Appl Financ* 16:51–72, 2004.

Economist, Battling for Corporate America, March 11, 2006, pp. 69–71.

Faccio M, Lang LHP: The ultimate ownership of Western European corporations, *J Financ Econ* 65:365–395, 2002.

Faccio M, Masulis R: The choice of payment method in European mergers and acquisitions, *J Financ* 60:1345–1388, 2005.

Faleye O: Cash and corporate control, *J Financ* 59:2041–2060, October 2004.

Field LC, Karpoff JM: Takeover defenses of IPO firms, *J Financ* 57:1629–1666, 2002.

Gale WJ, Morris JM: *Mergers and acquisition: business strategy for accountants*, ed 2, Cumulative Supplement, New York, 2006, Wiley & Sons.

Gaspara J-M, Matos P: Shareholder investment horizons and the market for corporate control, *J Financ Econ* 76:135–165, 2005.

Ginsburg MD, Levin JS: *Mergers, acquisitions and buyouts: a transactional analysis of governing tax, legal, and accounting considerations*, New York, 2004, Aspen Publishers.

Gompers PA, Ishii J, Metrick A: Extreme governance: an analysis of U.S. dual class companies in the United States, *Rev Financ Stud* 23:1051–1088, 2010.

Guo R-J, Kruse TA, Nohel T: Undoing the powerful anti-takeover force of staggered boards, *J Corp Financ* 14:274–288, June 2008.

Harford J: Corporate cash reserves and acquisitions, *J Financ* 54:1969–1997, 1999.

Hurter WH, Petersen JR, Thompson KE: *Mergers, acquisitions, and 1031 tax exchanges*, New York, 2005, Lorman Education Services.

Kohers N, Ang J: Earnouts in mergers: agreeing to disagree and agreeing to stay, *J Financ* 73:445–476, July 2000.

Lehn KM, Zhao M: CEO turnover after acquisitions: are bad bidders fired? *J Financ* 61:1383–1412, 2006.

Mallea J: A review of mergers of equals, FactSet mergermetrics.com, July 2008.

Massari M, Monge V, Zanetti L: Control premium in the presence of rules imposing mandatory tender offers: can it be measured? *J Manage Gov* 59:101–110, 2006.

Masulis RW, Wang C, Xie F: Corporate governance and acquirer returns, *J Financ* 62:1851–1890, 2007.

Maulis RW, Wang C, Xie F: Agency problems at dual class companies, *J Financ* 64:1697–1727, 2009.

Mergerstat Review, 2008. Factset Mergerstat.

Modigliani F, Miller M: The cost of capital, corporation finance and the theory of investment, *Am Econ Rev* 48(3):261–297, 1958.

Mulherin JH, Poulsen AB: Proxy contests and corporate change: implications for shareholder wealth, *J Financ Econ* 47:279–313, 1998.

Nenova T: The value of corporate voting rights and control: a cross-country analysis, *J Financ Econ* 68:325–352, 2003.

Officer MS: The price of corporate liquidity: acquisition discounts for unlisted targets, *J Financ Econ* 83:571–598, 2007.

Officer MS: Collars and renegotiation in mergers and acquisitions, *J Financ* 59:2719–2743, 2004.

Pinkowitz L: *The market for corporate control and corporate cash holdings. Working paper*, 2002, Georgetown University.

PriceWaterhouseCoopers: *Mergers and acquisitions: a global tax guide*, New York, 2006, Wiley & Sons.

Porter ME: *Competitive advantage*, New York, 1985, The Free Press.

Rossi S, Volpin PF: Cross-country determinants of mergers and acquisitions, ECGI- Finance Working Paper No. 25/2003, AFA 2004 San Diego Meetings, September 2004.

Sherman DH, Young DS: Tread lightly through these accounting minefields, *Harv Bus Rev* 129–137, 2001.

Srikant D, Frankel R, Wolfson M: Earnouts: the effects of adverse selection and agency costs on acquisition techniques, *J Law, Econ, Organ* 17:201–238, April 2001.

Stout LA: Do antitakeover defenses decrease shareholder wealth? The ex post/ex ante valuation problem, *Stanford Law Rev* 55:845–861, December 2002.

Stickney CP, Brown PR, Wahlen JM: *Financial reporting, financial statement analysis, and valuation*, ed 6, Cincinnati, 2007, South-Western College Publishing.

Truitt WB, *The Corporation*, Westport, CT, 2006, Greenwood Press.

Wasserstein B: *Big deal: the battle for control of america's leading corporations*, New York, 1998, Warner Books, pp. 601–644.

Wigmore B: The decline in credit quality of junk bond issues, 1980-1988. In Gaugahan PA, editor: *Readings in mergers and acquisitions*, Cambridge, UK, 1994, Basil Blackwell, pp. 171–184.

Wulf J: Do CEOs in mergers trade power for premium? Evidence from mergers of equals, *J Law Organ* 20:60, 2004.

Yago G: *Junk bonds: how high yield securities restructured corporate America*, New York, 1991, Oxford University Press.

INDEX